LIES OUR MOTHERS TOLD US

LIES OUR MOTHERS TOLD US

THE INDIAN WOMAN'S BURDEN

NILANJANA BHOWMICK

ALEPH

ALEPH BOOK COMPANY
An independent publishing firm
promoted by *Rupa Publications India*

First published in India in 2022
by Aleph Book Company
7/16 Ansari Road, Daryaganj
New Delhi 110 002

ISBN: 978-93-91047-73-3

1 3 5 7 9 10 8 6 4 2

To
all the women who are doing it all, and doing it alone:
I hear you; I see you

∽

CONTENTS

INTRODUCTION

My husband has a simple solution for most problems in life, a quality that comes from being a man in India. They do have all the answers. The cook didn't turn up? *Order takeout.* The domestic worker didn't show up? *Ignore the mess.* Unlike most Indian men, who, too, have solutions to these problems (*the wife will do it all, of course*) his solutions have always unconsciously centred around reducing my load by urging me to redistribute the work (very much along the lines of the International Labour Organization's Triple R framework that advocates recognizing, reducing, and redistributing unpaid care work shouldered by women worldwide). The days our domestic worker is on leave, he cleans the dishes. He was also a very hands-on father to our son when he was born. He changed more diapers than I ever did and kept him more engaged with stories and fun activities than I could, or would.

However, the mere fact that I'm calling attention to this and appreciating it is wrong. These actions shouldn't stand out as some kind of an achievement on his part and I shouldn't feel extraordinarily fortunate that he is doing his half of the work, because childcare—like household chores—should be a shared responsibility, no discussion, no adulation needed. In a country where a large percentage of men strongly believe that housework and caregiving are the woman's responsibility, this is a big ask. So, those of us who end up marrying men who are supportive of all that we are and all that we want to be, remain eternally grateful for this rare luck. But such men aren't created in a vacuum—these men grow up in households where their mothers are treated as equals. A friend once told me that she didn't cook, her husband did, and he did it as part of their daily routine and not as a favour or on a whim. Friends and acquaintances have always responded to her with something along the lines of *'how lucky!'* I, too, have been guilty of these exclamatory remarks more than once. On one of those occasions, she said to me, *'Nila, just imagine if it was the other way around, like the way it is generally—would people comment on how lucky my husband was because I cooked and cleaned?'* No, of course not. It was just what women did. Looking after the home is a non-negotiable part of being a woman in India, and it starts right from the moment we buy a doll's house for our daughters with the cute cooking and cleaning set while our sons are given a toy pistol or car.

I am in a much more privileged position than many of my middle-class compatriots. I have a full-time housekeeper to help me with housework and caregiving and yet I am the chief housekeeper, problem solver, menu maker, and caregiver. On the days I do not have this help, I struggle to get things done. But I rarely ask for help because I have grown up internalizing the fact that not only do I need to excel in my profession but I must also be a good homemaker. And to 'have it all', I had to become a superwoman. In my late twenties and early thirties, when I couldn't afford a live-in housekeeper or nanny, I tried to do it all, without asking for help from my husband or my extended family. I realize now that my attempt was, in part, payment to a society that allowed me some unexpected freedoms—education, employment, and the ability to choose my life partner—and for the 'luck' to have found a partner who tries to share my load and, most importantly, pushes me to prioritize my work, so that despite all the various obstacles that have been thrown in my path over the last two decades, I have still managed to have a career. The reason I end up shouldering a majority of household work and caregiving in our home is because I do not let my husband help. I am so grateful for his support that I want to pay him back by taking on the entire load myself.

I have also been trying to prove that I can wear all my hats effortlessly to an invisible jury throughout my life—if my mother could do it, why couldn't I? I am sure that I am not alone in this. I do not think there is even one woman in this country who wouldn't say she was physically and emotionally overworked. Yet, they wouldn't, or couldn't, ask for help because, like me, most had internalized the idea that being a good homemaker is our payment for a life lived on our own terms. Society has conditioned us to believe that the domestic is our primary realm, and everything else must come second. This toxic pattern keeps repeating itself in middle-class households across India. But we—middle-class women—rarely talk about this phenomenon, except in passing. It's easier to wear the cape of a superwoman and accept the accolades rather than exposing the reason for the dark circles under our eyes, the incessant anxiety, the suppressed anger. As a society, we do not know how to deal with people who can't cope, especially if those people are women. We expect women to manage, adjust, deal with everything. We bring up our daughters to fluidly fit into the myriad moulds that will be placed before them throughout their lives, including those of homemaker, mother, and caregiver. When I shared the first blurb of this book with my mother, she wasn't able to talk to me. Later, she sent me a voice message saying 'I thought women's overwork was invisible in this country—no one paid any attention to it. We just stewed in our own unhappiness. You wrote about us, our struggle, I didn't even think you ever noticed...I don't know what to say,' and her voice broke.

Indian women are among the most overworked in the world.[1] India conducted its first official time use survey, which helps in determining the distribution of paid and unpaid work among men and women in a country, in 1998–99. The second one was conducted two decades later in 2019. The 2019 survey found that women spent 299 minutes per day on housework and 134 minutes on caregiving duties per day. Men spent a mere ninety-seven minutes on housework, and seventy-six minutes a day on caregiving.[2] Women in our country shoulder over 82 per cent of the domestic work and almost 28 per cent of caregiving. Men shoulder a little over 26 per cent of domestic chores and 14 per cent of caregiving.[3] Modern Indian women are burdened with so much housework and caregiving that they are leaving their hard-won financial independence, dropping out of schools, and dropping off the labour force. Many women self-identify as housewives but work in low paid jobs in the informal sector,* and their struggle with the 'double shift'

---

*Of the forty million informal workers who registered on a national portal in 2021, over half were women. See PTI, 'Nearly 10 crore unorganised sector workers is largely invisible. These women soldier on, unhappy, stressed, and overworked; knowing they deserve better, that they deserve more, that they need help, but not knowing how, or whom, to ask.

∽

I am forty-five, and have finally been able to shake off two toxic personality traits—people-pleasing and trying to have it all. I learnt how to be a people-pleaser early in life. I adjusted so much that somewhere down the line, I forgot who I really was. I was who everyone else wanted me to be. Patient, kind, always smiling, super-efficient, a hands-on mother who fed her child only freshly cooked meals made from scratch, and a successful professional earning seven figures. *Superwoman*.

'*How do you do it all with so much elan?*' a friend once asked.

'*I hide the anxiety and nightmares well,*' I had replied, though I hadn't meant to. But in that moment, I realized how deeply I hated what it meant for me to have it all.

I learnt to be a superwoman from my mother and perfected it with years of practice; I have worn the epithet with secret pride for most of my life. Following the epiphany I had in the presence of my friend, my life unravelled in my mind. If 'having it all' means engaging in a constant battle to balance paid work with household management and caregiving without any institutional support (or familial support), participating in a never-ending fight not to be pushed out of workplaces or be discriminated against, going through life wary of sexual harassment on the streets and in the workplace, always worrying about 'losing it all', and not being able to realize my full potential because of all of these factors—then I guess I do 'have it all.'

Despite the various feminist movements worldwide that have helped women cross huge milestones, only a small percentage of women in this country have laid their claim to feminism and, hence, to equality. Maybe that explains why there's next to no discourse in India about the 'superwoman syndrome', a fallout of women's economic empowerment that has been called out in the West since the 1980s. Even though I was born in the United Nations Decade for Women, adopted by the UN to create equal rights and opportunities for women, I, too, remained unaware of much of the discourse surrounding the 'superwoman syndrome' for most of my young adult life. It was the same for most other women of my generation, too. My friend Pallavi Banerjee, a Canada-based sociologist and author, for example, only encountered the concept of the superwoman when she was doing her PhD in Sociology in the mid-2000s on work–family balance and gender theory. But the concept has been around in the US since the American feminist writer and activist Betty Friedan discussed the double shift of household chores that often await women who enter the workforce in her book *The Second Stage*.

After all these decades, American women are still struggling with the superwoman syndrome, while in India, and many other developing countries, we have internalized the double shift not as a fallout of but payment for women's empowerment. 'American women had thought that the work–life debate had been settled back [in the 80s] until it came back again in 2012–2013 with Sheryl Sandberg's and Debora Spar's books* and a rude awakening that women still need to grapple with the impossibility of superwomanhood because the larger institutions had failed them,' Banerjee told me.

In our country, this is pretty much an unacknowledged problem—there are few studies and no sustained debate on the double load that women carry. Women are trying to be both homemakers and breadwinners in the absence of any institutional or familial support. This has had a detrimental effect on their lives and especially their mental health.

When Banerjee was growing up in Kolkata, like most of us, she hadn't encountered the term at all. 'When I started working in

---

*In *Wonder Women: Sex, Power, and the Quest for Perfection*, Debora Spar discusses how the feminism of the 1960s contributed to an unattainable idea of feminist womanhood. In *Lean In: Women, Work, and the Will to Lead*, Sheryl Sandberg explores how working women can 'lean in' and secure themselves a seat at the corporate table. Both books were published in 2013.

2001, I had women co-workers who were married with kids. I was the youngest in my office at the time and was quite struck by the balancing act that many of the women had to do. They did not quite talk in the terms of being [superwomen] because most saw their jobs as supplementing the income of the family with the husbands as the main earners but they, for all purposes, were working full-time and taking care of their families full-time. That definitely left me wondering what that would mean for these women as they advanced in their careers,' she recalls.

The idea of having it all is at odds with the demands of male-dominated patriarchal societies where gender roles are rigid. We do not have it all because while women have become co-breadwinners, Indian men are yet to become co-carers. This is a global problem and the Covid-19 pandemic has spotlighted how caregiving and domestic duties are still considered 'women's work' around the world. But the magnitude of the problem is compounded manifold in our capitalist–patriarchal society, where the division between productive and reproductive labour, as stipulated by capitalism, finds unequivocal support in the skewed power dynamics between men and women that the patriarchy favours.

We often point out how far women have come in this country. I suppose this is true, for they are no longer forced to jump onto their husbands' funeral pyres, and sometimes they can even choose whom they marry, what they study, and the professions they will pursue. But child marriages are still rampant, taboos regarding widowhood continue, singledom is frowned upon, marriages are often forced or entered into with little to no information, and women have next to no sexual agency. When it comes to women from the so-called 'lower castes' or from lower socio-economic classes, they are doubly oppressed and exploited in their families, and outside of them. Those from among these groups who work as domestic or care workers lessen the double burden of privileged women, allowing them to continue in paid work, in an arrangement that is highly exploitative owing to its informal nature and also due to the largely unequal power dynamics (in terms of negotiating power) between the employers (mostly upper caste, upper class) and their employees. Women have come a long way in our country but have they all moved forward together?

Indian women have been accorded equal rights in the Constitution. Unfortunately, the Constitution of India could not change the mindset of the powers that be—men who control the majority of sociocultural and economic resources, and who have remained dismissive of women and their equal status in society. But these are the men who frame our laws and make policy decisions—they are the ones in various committees and panels—and so the policies they design are indifferent to women's different needs.

So, having these rights is akin to window shopping—what we see is technically within our grasp, but the attainment of it is not exactly a given. The Constitution grants women the same rights as men in terms of various freedoms such as the protection of life and personal liberty, and yet lakhs of girls die every year in the country owing to gender bias,[4] and more than 20,000 housewives die by suicide every year.[5] There's gender discrimination even in the way the pandemic has affected men and women in India—while the world over men have been found to be at a higher risk of dying from Covid-19, in India the exact opposite was witnessed. A recent study found that 3.3 per cent of infected women died of the disease as compared to 2.9 per cent of men.[6] During my research for an article for *Devex*, I found that women were lagging behind even in accessing Covid-19 vaccinations.[7] As of February 2022, India had vaccinated 38 million more men than women. What this underlines is that women have less access to healthcare and their well-being is not a priority in most Indian households. While reporting a story in February, I found out that women were lagging behind in receiving the Covid-19 vaccine because they simply did not have the time to queue up even for a life-saving measure.[8]

Article 14 of the Constitution promises equality before the law, while Article 15 prohibits any discrimination on the grounds of religion, race, caste, sex, or birthplace. Article 16 prohibits discrimination in the workplace on the basis of gender and yet we have not been able to provide women with enough opportunities or institutional support to work with dignity, which is perhaps why only a handful of

Indian women are part of the formal labour force—Indian women's participation in the labour force is the lowest among all major economies.[9] Then there are the marriage acts that are supposed to protect women's rights in a relationship. The Hindu code bills passed in the 1950s gave women equal access to divorce and maintenance. However, if a man decides to contest a divorce, the legal proceedings and maintenance battles can go on for years, a fact that likely pushes many Indian women to stay in bad marriages rather than end them. The Hindu Succession Act of 1956 and the Hindu Women's Rights to Property Act of 1937 gave women equal rights in family property. But many parents still prefer to make separate provisions for their daughters while ensuring that the majority of the family property is passed on to male heirs. Daughters who are not lucky enough to have such 'considerate' parents are just left out of the family property, unless they demand their share through legal channels. But our women are not the best at demanding things for themselves—things ranging from money, rest, time, respect, and so on. From childhood they are taught the virtue of sacrifice and compromise, of putting others ahead of themselves, and it is a hard habit to break.

Most Indian couples also continue to have children until they have a male heir.[10] Widows are thrown out of their marital homes despite the fact that the Property Act gives them the right to inherit their deceased husbands' property. The Dowry Prohibition Act of 1961 outlawed this regressive practice, yet, according to the National Crime Records Bureau (NCRB), in 2020, India recorded nineteen dowry deaths every day[11]—and these are only the reported deaths. Women rarely report violence by intimate partners or other family members because the one enduring middle-class mantra through the decades has been to not 'wash dirty linen in public'. The middle class' need for respectability and keeping up appearances is so strong that many would willingly send their daughters back to abusive marital homes just to keep the facade intact. Even today, the first advice most Indian parents give to their daughters would be to try and make it work, to not stir up trouble or involve the police. This is perhaps why, while one in every three Indian women is subjected to intimate partner violence, only one in ten is likely to formally report these incidents.[12]

When it comes to women who step out of their homes to work, the situation continues to be as dire as it is inside our homes. The Equal Remuneration Act of 1976 struck off wage discrimination between male and female workers. However, as of 2019, the gender pay gap stands at 19 per cent.[13] The right to education was made a fundamental right for all in 2010, and yet, of the 313 million illiterate people in India in 2018, an overwhelming 59 per cent were found to be women.[14]

Independent India granted universal suffrage to all adult citizens in 1950, and women have been exercising their right to vote since then. However, not many are allowed to vote as per their choice, instead being pushed to vote as per the diktats of the male members of their families. In rural areas, there's a 33 per cent reservation for women in village councils or panchayats. Women do contest for these seats but when they win these elections, most hand over the power of being the village head to their husbands or sons. In my travels across villages in India, I have rarely gotten to interact with or interview women village chiefs. Their husbands or sons have nearly always taken their place.

Perhaps all of this is not always forced. Buried under housework and caregiving, maybe they do not want to add more responsibilities to their never-ending list of chores. What this signals is the imminent need to devise ways to encourage an equal distribution of domestic duties and unpaid care work within households. Until this happens, no initiatives can bring women back into the public sphere and keep them there; after a while, when they can't balance the physical and mental load any more, they will retreat into the domestic space, as they have been doing over the last two decades. Sure, women's lives have changed since Independence, but not in a way that matters or that is sustainable. The laws and policies provide a backdrop of gender equality but our women are still not being equipped by their families or our institutions (including schools) to reap the benefits of these laws and policies to advance their status in society. They haven't been given the confidence to grab their place under the sun. We would pull up a chair to the table, but how to change the mindset of the people already in the room who believe that we would be better off cleaning the room than sitting at the table with them?

Middle-class women are uniquely challenged when it comes to empowerment, because middle-class families have mastered the art of simulating an environment of equality and empowerment in their homes that can confuse the best of us. Behind the facade lies the true challenge of women's empowerment. Middle-class women are aware of feminism, they are aware of the concepts of equality and empowerment, many of them have been educated by their parents and encouraged to work, and, at the same time, they mistakenly believe that giving in to the larger patriarchal value system is 'not a big deal', rather it is a show of respect and gratitude. Most begin to realize the folly of this thinking only later in their lives. The challenge, thus, is not to make them learn but to make them unlearn the biases they have internalized and accepted under the guise of traditional values.

I remember attending a small get-together some years back with a few women from upper middle-class families. They were all working women. They sipped cocktails and smoked slims, wore clothes that reflected the top trends in current fashion, and lived in nuclear family set-ups with their husbands and children. But one of them said something that day that stayed with me awhile: 'I feel there's too much feminism in our lives.' I could have explained to her how this was wrong, that she should instead thank the indefatigable work of our feminist activists for getting us what she called 'too much feminism', because it allows us the personal liberties we exercise today. But would there have been a point to such an outburst on my part? She would still remain a victim of the systemic patriarchy that defines the lives of women from middle-class families. She would have gone home that day and hastily tied her hair up in a high bun, maybe feeling guilty for having had fun without her family, and immediately set out to cook a sumptuous meal for her loved ones.

If education constitutes empowerment, then most middle-class women in India have willingly allowed themselves to be disempowered in exchange for what are essentially some frivolous freedoms. They have resignedly convinced themselves to abandon their own dreams and career aspirations to cater to the demands at home. This resignation is not just a setback for Indian society in general but comes with economic repercussions, too. A government labour survey in 2017–18 found that the number of (urban) women in higher education had increased from around 46 per cent in 2004–2005 to over 65 per cent in 2017–18, but—and here's the irony—only a little over 17 per cent of them were in paid work.[15] The United Nations Development Program's (UNDP) 'India Skills Report', in 2019, found that 68 per cent of women graduates in urban India were not working in paid jobs.[16]

This is a double blow to women's economic empowerment in our country. Due to the unavailability of quality, well-paid work for women, it is easy to convince them that if their spouses are earning well, they need not struggle in workplaces that are deeply unequal and hostile to women. It then becomes easy to make them buy into the idea of home first, and the roles of mother and wife first. They give up their jobs on the pretext of 'sacrifice' or 'duty'. Many also justify it as choice—but is it an informed choice? In subsequent chapters, you will have the chance to glimpse into the lives of many women who have learnt the hard way that having a job is not just about earning money, but about empowerment, self-respect, and being treated with respect.

During the writing of this book, I was in conversation with an academic and gender activist and when I explained to her what the subject of my book was, her instant reaction was, 'Thank God! Finally, someone is writing about this!' This has been, more or less, the response I have received from almost everyone that I have spoken to for this book. 'Everything is so hush-hush in middle class families—it's time we talked about what happens inside our homes.'

This is true. Rarely have we analysed the inside of our homes—middle-class Indian homes, where women's subjugation has been internalized to such an extent that it is now a way of life. The middle-class lifestyle thrives on the invisibilization of women's contributions and is symbolic of all that is wrong with a capitalist–patriarchal society.

In many homes in India women still eat last, are the last to sleep, and get up the earliest, constantly playing second fiddle to their male relatives; their marriages are arranged according to caste and class (a large majority of middle-class India is upper caste[17]), intimate partner violence is normalized, marital rape is not considered 'rape'.* This is an India where even when fathers encourage their daughters to fly, they prefer to keep their wives in cages.

Of late, there's been a murmur of dissent among young women on social media. I came across the following post on Twitter recently, and it is one among many that I have noticed in the past few years: 'There are too many girls and young women who feel the need to become financially independent asap just so they can escape their fathers and take their mothers with them'.[18] And while most mothers will not walk out of their marriages and run away with their daughters, they are increasingly willing to help their daughters flee.

∽

When feminist boomer mothers like mine stepped out to work, they found themselves in a difficult position. Sure, they were 'allowed' to work and earn money, but they were never allowed to forget that their first priority was their home. This, unfortunately, has not changed in the intervening four decades. They had to remember to be good daughters, daughters-in-law, mothers, and wives, as we do now. A majority of middle-class Indian families claim to be progressive, and bring up their daughters to have a voice, with a caveat—they may never raise that same voice inside their homes or against their family members. They send their daughters to the best schools but also ensure they know that rolling the perfect chapatti in the kitchen will be more useful than a 'fancy' degree. Middle-class India prides itself on being modern, while respecting traditional values. But inside their homes exists a patriarchal laboratory where misogyny and sexism are constantly reinvented and rebranded. So, while women are often expected to earn, they are not expected to be overly or overtly ambitious, and definitely not at the cost of their families. They need only go out to supplement their husband's earnings (for extra

---

*As of February 2022, the Delhi High Court is hearing petitions to criminalize marital rape. See Richa Banka, 'Delhi HC reserves verdict on marital rape criminalisation', *Hindustan Times*, 22 February 2022.

luxuries, better education for the children, paying off loans), never for their independence or personal growth. Often when the husbands are promoted and their financial situations improve, wives are asked to take it easy and look after the home and the children. They are also expected to remain strong in the face of all adversities but never publicly talk about their personal lives or the various indignities they are subjected to every day. Middle-class women have no choice but to do it all. When they don't, apart from the all-consuming guilt, for many there are serious consequences, including physical, verbal, and emotional abuse.

Overwhelmed with housework and care work, the additional burden of earning a living leaves most of these women with no time to think of their lives. Maybe this is why they have made their peace with the many forms of misogyny that exist in their homes because it is easier to ignore than confront what they know they cannot change. Their expectations and aspirations, dreams and desires for themselves are always flexible—the first to go, the last to be protected.

Women power through various forms of discrimination, domestic violence, violence on the streets, and bullying at work, surviving every day in battle mode. It is impossible to handle so much and expect that one's mental health would remain unaffected. Globally, women are nearly twice as likely as men to suffer from mental illness owing to stereotypical social roles based on gender inequalities, among other factors.[19] There also exists a direct correlation between mental disorders and gender inequality, including domestic violence, sexual abuse, unpaid care work, higher hours of work, low social status, lack of access to reproductive rights, and education.

In India's middle-class homes these inequalities loom large, which is why, quite unsurprisingly, large numbers of middle-class women battle depression (including post-partum depression[20] about which there is no awareness or acceptance) and anxiety disorders. They remain quiet because mental health is still a taboo topic in India and visible signs of it might be exploited by family members to disenfranchise them in many different ways.

These inequalities have survived the test of time, only growing stronger with passing years owing to scant efforts to address inequalities within our homes. Even when middle-class women gain economic empowerment, they remain largely immune to social and emotional empowerment because of the patriarchal nature of our homes and institutions, where even our children's textbooks consistently propagate the men–women=breadwinner–carer discourse. They prefer to toe the line because they have remained untouched by the true tenets of feminism, instead buying into the bra-burning, misandrist adaptation of the movement. As noted feminist Kamla Bhasin once said, 'Feminism is perhaps [the] world's most badnaam or defamed ism. There are all kinds of totally unfounded, unsubstantiated allegations against [feminism]. So many people are afraid of [feminism]. This is why even strong, independent, actually feminist women do not wish to call themselves a [feminist].'[21] On the other end of the spectrum are women who have no qualms attributing the term to themselves, while alienating others. I once heard an anecdote from a lawyer friend, who had attended a house party where she was told off by a young, upper-middle-class, upper-caste feminist for tying up her hair in a ponytail. 'It's unfeminist', she was told. The young woman, an educator, had also jumped to the conclusion (from my friend's simple appearance and gentle nature) that 'she was a housewife'. This lazy interpretation of feminism by a section of privileged young women is why we have managed to alienate a large chunk of our female population from feminism. But as Bhasin had noted, even 'a housewife and full-time mother who brings up her daughter with dignity, who teaches her sons equality and respect for women, is a [feminist]. You do not have to go and join protests and shout slogans to qualify as a feminist, although if you do that also, things would change faster.'[22] Middle-class women are largely characterized by a lack of confidence, awareness, and courage—they already think nothing of themselves. If we are going to burden them with more expectations that have nothing to do with the true spirit of feminism, of course, they will stay away. We have to stop telling women what to do, and focus on providing them with safe, non-judgemental spaces to learn and unlearn.

Women's empowerment comes in many different variations.

It could take the form of educational empowerment or economic empowerment, but rarely have any initiatives in our country systematically focused on the intellectual empowerment of women. Intellectual empowerment doesn't come from just education because our country's education system is focused on degrees and not learning. Intellectual empowerment for women, for example, would come from being exposed to the writings and teachings of feminist thinkers, not just when young adults decide to study gender in higher education but at the school level. Women's confidence, broken by the patriarchy, needs to be rebuilt from scratch. It needs to begin where it all begins—at homes and in schools. Intellectual empowerment is not a privilege most middle-class, first or second generation educated families enjoy.

Many middle-class women are also wary of calling themselves feminists because they have often been made to feel that feminism is more an affectation than a natural state of being. To explain this more, I need to draw on a recent experience that forced me to think of the way we (middle-aged, middle-class feminists) are perceived by our male peers. A progressive friend of mine made what I thought was an utterly thoughtless and loose comment on a social media platform recently. *Most middle-class women discover feminism in their middle-ages*, he had written (I could almost hear him sneering). He then added that the reason they come to feminism when they are middle-aged was to advance their careers. He was right and also very wrong, in the typical entitled man's blinkered fashion. Many middle-class women—working professionals as well as homemakers—do discover feminism in their late thirties and early forties. They discover it so late not because it will advance them in their careers (since many don't have a career to speak of) but because most of them grow up in patriarchal households, attend misogynist schools, and do not receive good quality higher education. They are not taught to rebel but to comply. They are not taught to fly but to ignore the shackles on their feet. They discover feminism in their middle-ages in an act of organic dissent, after having lived half their lives without any control over their own lives. It is only once they hit their forties that they find some amount of control over their lives, the time to educate themselves, and most importantly, it is then, after years of subjugation laced with humiliation and physical and mental exhaustion, that they begin to give a bloody damn.

မ

Being a middle-class Indian is more indicative of a certain state of mind than a social status based on income or consumption patterns. Within the scope of this book, middle-class women constitute a diverse group of women whose families might have been recently lifted out of poverty as well as women who are fairly well-off. If we consider income, according to most global organizations, people who live on under US$ 2 (around ₹148) a day are considered poor,[23] but in India, the middle classes comprise people who spend US$ 2 to 10 or ₹740 a day, as per economists from the University of Mumbai. By that definition, the middle classes now constitute approximately half of India's population.[24]

Even so, there have been scant sociological studies of the Indian middle class and even fewer on the women who are part of this class. This is perhaps because Indian 'sociology as a discipline has historically been identified with the concerns of the less privileged members of society, making its practitioners reluctant to turn the spotlight on a class that until recently consisted largely of the upper castes', as academic Jyothsna Belliappa argues.[25] Additionally, the overwhelming perception that this class is made up of the aam aadmi, the average joe, makes it appear harmless and unremarkable, which has kept it protected from rigorous sociological scrutiny.

I come from a middle-class family. In my family, my mother, a cop, was an anomaly. She was also the only woman in our large family who was a college graduate and who not only had a job, but worked in a male-dominated field. My sister and I were the first women in our upwardly mobile family who had master's degrees. All my uncles and aunts were well off and while they chose to educate their sons, their daughters were made to drop out of school and subsequently married off. These bright and intelligent women, with so much potential, became unrecognizable after a few years of marriage and some children. They were shadows of their former selves—dull and dour, unwilling or unable to talk of anything else but their homes and children. They laughed differently, spoke differently, and looked years older than their age. I remember one cousin in particular, whom I met around five years after her wedding. I found that her diction, pronunciations, and inflections had changed. When she spoke, it appeared as if she was out of practice—and yet she was the cousin that my mother always pointed to when she wanted us to act better. She was a good student with a bright future and her mother was a teacher and yet her many abilities were relegated to the background when her family found the perfect husband for her, a man ten years older but with a steady government job. It is a truth universally acknowledged in our homes that daughters are to be married off as soon as a good match is found. This, I think, is done due to a mix of deep insecurity arising from living a 'middle-class' life and an aspiration to move up higher in the class hierarchy. My cousin's days were spent in providing care to her family and taking care of the housework. I never forgot her transformation and have always wondered how a marriage could have the power to change the whole essence of a woman's existence. These girls thought marriage would free them of their patriarchal homes, of the constant parental surveillance and the curbs on personal freedom. Marriages, however, added a huge dollop of housework and caregiving to the mix.

My mother's dreams for us were average, too. She knew one thing for certain—she didn't want us to have her life. For her, jobs were important for financial empowerment, so one was not dependent on a husband for every need. But when it came down to it, she didn't want us to rock the boat too much either. That, in a nutshell, is an Indian middle-class family, where women are increasingly aspiring for independence and are working to substantiate the family income and support an aspirational lifestyle, but they are also the first to drop out of the workforce when they can't balance work and life, and especially if their husbands begin to earn enough to support said aspirational lifestyle. They are the ones who cannot afford full-time domestic help because they need to save for a better future. They exist in public spaces and use public facilities. They are among the many who stand in bus queues and jostle in local trains. They are ill-equipped to stand up against the patriarchy. And despite being vulnerable in so many different ways, they remain invisible mainly because they want to. Too much attention has never worked in their favour—it has only cut into their hard-won independence.

Our middle-class society never let my mother rest, not even for a minute, inducing guilt into every decision she made. I am five, I have fever; my mother, specifically her job, is to blame. I am twelve, my exam marks are not that great; my mother is to blame. My sister is twenty-seven, an eternal rebel. My mother, of course, is to blame for this as well. While she struggled to wear all her hats efficiently, society kept telling my mother she was not doing enough. Forty years later, women are still reporting suffering through the same experiences. During the writing of this book, one woman told me that while her husband was supportive of her decision to complete her PhD and start working, he would still blame her for neglecting her children and home when they argued. 'You are always working,' he would accuse her every time. 'You neglect your duties as a mother and a wife. That is why your children are out of control.'

Women can never get it right. You have to be the right amount of intelligent (so you don't upstage the men), you have to be the right kind of sociable (so you don't become more popular than your male partner), you have to earn the right amount (less than your husband), you have to be the right kind of ambitious (housewife first, career-oriented second—non-negotiable). You must be more maternal, more wifely, more daughterly, more subservient. Leave the complicated calculations, the leadership roles to men. Some women take this as a challenge, and a majority choose to diminish themselves so as not to upset the status quo.

Someone I interviewed for this book said that her mother told her that financial independence was important, but she added a caveat—family comes first, always. 'It's so damn confusing,' she said. 'I cannot be everything—I tried but it doesn't work. It shatters your mental health. And then of course you can't even talk about mental health because then you are just being hysterical or hormonal.'

'It's all in the middle-class mindset. On the one hand, you are educating your daughters, teaching them to be financially independent and then, in the same breath, asking them to compromise, not talk back,' another told me.

For this book, I spoke to women aged fifteen to sixty—homemakers, retired professionals, professors, therapists, marriage counsellors, teachers, scientists, small entrepreneurs, healthcare professionals. Some of them were highly educated, some barely, some were from metropolises, some from small towns, some from villages, but all of them identified as middle-class. Some were friends, most were friends of friends. Some were just random subjects I picked up from social media posts or contacts on the grounds. Some of the experts became stories themselves. I had suspected from my everyday conversations and observations that many women were feeling stuck, cornered, and overwhelmed in their lives, but I had no idea that the scale would be so huge. And the one thing I came away with from all these stories was that when it comes to Indian women, our experiences do not just shape who we are but also who we could not become.

India's middle-class women are reeling under the dual force of tradition and modernity. The two have dumped on them more expectations than they can handle, more fears than they can live with, and more sleepless nights than they care to admit—even to themselves.

That's how it plays out when you have to do it all, and do it alone. *That's the Indian woman's burden.*

I

FEMINIST MOTHERS AND THE LIE

When we see the world through the eyes of women, only then we get a perspective of the marginalized, the excluded, and the oppressed.

—Kamla Bhasin

In the mid-1970s, in the first flush of her job, my mother had gone out and bought herself a fancy purse. It was pristine white, with fake pearl detailing. Though not hugely expensive, it was the first non-essential purchase she had made with her own money—it was a big deal for her.

'A fancy purse,' one of her brothers-in-law had scoffed when she got home, the purse dangling from her shoulder. 'We will talk when your job destroys your family and your daughters turn out to be wasters.'

The idea that my mother worked outside the house was bad enough, but that she would flaunt her economic independence in this way was unacceptable. This offhand remark, however, had a much bigger and sustained impact on my mother. From that day on she was determined to prove him, and others like him, wrong. She wanted to make sure that she was seen not only as a professional woman earning a salary but also a good homemaker. From all outward appearances, my mother had it all. She had a government job—highly prized in India even today—with great benefits, including a good pension, and she raised two empowered daughters. However, this was far from the truth. Her life, as it appeared to many, was a lie. She was just an overworked, abused, depressed woman, who was struggling to balance her life and work through random means; it was sheer luck that everything came together for her to continue to work. At any moment, however, if a supporting piece had fallen off, she would have had no choice but to surrender the empowerment she fought so valiantly for throughout her life.

At work she kept her head down, always hoping and praying that she would not be needed for a night shift or an out-of-town assignment. She was ambitious and many times started preparing for the sub-inspector promotion exam, but would never actually appear for the test. A promotion would mean more responsibilities at work and that would come in the way of her fulfilling her responsibilities at home. Some days her only ambition would be to get through the day without getting into a fight with my father which would inevitably end with him stonewalling her for the rest of the week—making her life as difficult as he could. He never screamed or shouted at her, at least not in front of my elder sister and me, but he knew how to emotionally torment her until she apologized. Most of the time, she was just apologizing for being assertive. Their fights were almost always followed by him asking her to leave her 'stupid job'. And my mother always apologized because that's exactly what she did not want to do. Her job brought some much-needed peace and sanity to her life and she clung to it with all her might. She also knew it would be key in deciding her daughters' futures because the job and the money she handed over to her husband every month gave her some negotiating power in the home. When she stood her ground, as she always did when it came to her daughters, he backed down. In my mother's eyes, my father is an unreasonable, and, sometimes, outright unpleasant man. To the world, and to us (my sister and I), he is an affable and kind man who cares deeply about the people around him. But when I think back now, I see only an entitled man who believed he came first and that he owned not just my mother but also her dreams and aspirations. Even though he let us fly, he preferred to keep her in a cage. Maybe he knew no better. But even now when we know better, Indian men retain this same dynamic with the women in their lives. I have seen my mother's ambition erode over the years, the fight going out of her as she resigned herself to thinking of her work as just another task to get through each day.

Her resignation truly set in when we were older and she was in her late thirties, and living in a nuclear set-up. Earlier, when we lived in a joint family, she had some help from our family members.

My paternal grandmother was the de facto head of our family, as my grandfather chose to live in a secluded village a few hundred kilometres from Kolkata. While my grandmother handled our day-to-day affairs, she still deferred to my grandfather for major decisions—he was the karta, the patriarch. My grandfather rarely came to visit us; he didn't like the city. We visited him twice a year to celebrate two festivals of the utmost importance for us: Chandi Puja, in the summer months, and Durga Puja, in September–October. Our family Durga Puja was a grand affair and relatives from far and wide would descend upon the village every year to celebrate it. My grandfather ran a free homeopathic dispensary in the village and led a very frugal, Gandhian life. He was not particularly interested in being the family patriarch, but my grandmother deferred to him in even the smallest of matters.

My grandfather was an unusual man for the times—not only did he give his wife unlimited authority over the family, he also actively encouraged my mother to work. The other members of our family included my two uncles, one of whom was married with a son. My aunts, my father's sisters, lived nearby and were an integral part of our daily lives. Perhaps because my grandfather did not spend enough time with his family, and because my grandmother had very rigid ideas about the different roles of men and women in a household, she ran a household full of mostly misogynistic men. Of course, because of my grandfather's open support of my mother's career aspirations, my grandmother made peace with her job and, albeit grumpily, helped her manage the children and house as much as she could. My aunts did too. His was a strict diktat, not said in too many words but understood perfectly by his wife and daughters. 'Do not bother Rekha. Help her. I am proud of her. She is doing what none of you can even think of.' Kind as my grandfather's support was, it definitely did not put my mother in the good books of her sisters-in-law and mother-in-law. When we moved to a house nearby because it was getting too crowded in the two-room set-up where we lived before, my grandmother made sure that she continued to cook for the family. Though she was just fulfilling what she considered to be her responsibility as a woman, her decision worked in my mother's favour, who had no love for the kitchen or cooking (she still doesn't).

While we lived with my grandmother, and even when we moved to a nearby apartment, my mother never had to cook or worry about the well-being of either my sister or me. My grandmother's domestic worker came by every morning to clean the room in which we had just slept. We would have our breakfast at our apartment and our mother would give us packed lunches. My father dropped us off at school and then my parents left for their workplaces. My uncle would pick me up from school and we would go to our grandmother's house. My sister was already in senior school and would arrive later. In the evenings, my sister would take me to the neighbourhood park, after which we would go back to our tiny studio apartment where our father would be waiting. Sometimes he picked us up from the park, too. He kept us occupied until my mother came back from work at 7 p.m. and at 9 p.m., on the dot, a giant aluminium tiffin box, with my father's name engraved on the side, would arrive from my grandmother with our dinner. At least a few days each month that tiffin box would go flying out of our door—my father would have thrown out all the food in a fit of anger. He did it so frequently that the wall had a permanent mark of splattered dal. While he has mellowed as the years have passed, growing up around emotional and physical manifestations of violence has left me with a nervous energy that years of therapy haven't been able to heal. Emotional trauma, of course, is unavoidable as one negotiates life, but the systemic trauma that women in our country grow up with is neither justifiable nor humane.

My father's actions were focused on controlling my mother, not just physically but also emotionally. But my mother's mind was always out of his reach. He was always scared that if he couldn't control her mind, he wouldn't be able to control her movements either, so he clamped down as hard as he could on her. This is also perhaps a very unique form of domestic abuse, where otherwise reasonable and pleasant men, who are not physically abusive by nature, cross all boundaries to control their wives. This also indicates how patriarchy messes with men's lives, too, and why it is also in their interest to eradicate it.

For my mother, it was expected that her weekends or other days off were to be devoted to the family, especially to helping my grandmother in the kitchen. My mother hated this. She would much rather cook a simple meal and curl up with a book for the rest of the time, but instead my grandmother continued to try and make her into a 'good housewife'. That it didn't work was obvious when we first moved to our own house in the late 1980s and my mother began to cook for the family, with disastrous results. My mother was not bad at cooking, she just didn't want to do it, her biggest fear being that if she started dishing up delicious food, her life would get restricted to the kitchen. She might have learnt this from her mother, who was also not overly bothered about housework or cooking and didn't introduce her daughters to these skills either, instead pushing them to study. She did her work and performed her duties as expected, but her one true passion was reading, a quality she passed on to my mother. My earliest memories of my mother include her rushing through her chores so she could bury herself in her novels—she loved Bengali novels by Ashapurna Devi, which had strong, rebellious middle-class women as protagonists. My grandmother's efforts to teach her how to cook, among other things, were met with quiet resistance—she would show up in the kitchen with a book in her hand—which only increased the rancour between them. My father's family all agreed that my mother was 'uppity' and thought 'too much of herself'.

My mother hated living in a joint family and couldn't wait to move into her own house. But once she did, she realized that though she had escaped the unpleasantness of the other family members, the autocracy of her mother-in-law, and the lack of personal freedom, she no longer had a support system in place. Suddenly, she was the one who was handling it all—she was mother, teacher, wife, chef, housekeeper, and nanny, and had an inexperienced domestic worker who came once a day to clean. There was no dinner waiting for her when she got home from work exhausted. There was no one to take care of me and my sister in her absence. She had to wake up at ungodly hours, cook breakfast and lunch, prepare snack boxes, and get a head start on dinner. She did all this before 9 a.m. when she had to leave for work. The last two decades of her working life were a maze of despair and overwork. To her credit, though, she didn't let go. She was a quick learner and managed to hold on to her job despite not being able to invest enough time in it. She probably would have risen higher through the ranks if her housewifely duties didn't stand in her way. Talking of her experience, my mother told me, 'There was no love lost between your grandmother and me. We never even pretended to like each other. I maintained a formal relationship with her as well as with your aunts; I felt like they were always judging me. But I am immensely grateful to them, and will always be, for looking after you and your sister. If I didn't have that support, I would have had to leave my job. It would have been very hard to look after two young kids and hold on to a job.'

We were looked after not just by my grandmother and aunts, but also by neighbours. 'Without these related and unrelated women, I would have had to step down from my job.'

My childhood is replete with the love and care—sometimes unusual love and care—of women who became my surrogate mothers, bringing me up alongside their own children but never discriminating or differentiating between us. When my sister was young and we still lived in the same house with our grandmother, the two of them were inseparable. But I grew up mostly in our one room apartment, where I had the company of my family in instalments—grandmother, sister, father, mother, aunts. And my nicher ma.

When I first met my nicher ma, my mother from the ground floor, I was three years old. On some days, my grandmother would bring me to our apartment around 1 p.m., take a nap alongside me, then leave me in the room to go back and cook dinner. I stayed in the room alone for a few hours until my sister came back from grandma's after her evening snack. I was a lonely child, and nicher ma was the equally lonely, much younger, second wife to a man with two grown-up sons. Every day before my mother left for work, nicher ma would assure her that she would keep watch over me until my sister's return. Although our flat looked down into her pretty little house with a neat garden, given the winding roads and lanes in the old parts of Kolkata, her house was quite a distance away. So, we never met in person. And yet for years, she comforted me when I cried, and sang lullabies to me when I was unwell or needed to sleep. I would have called ours a virtual relationship had the internet been invented by then. When I look back, I wonder: how was she able to do this?

My mother's other source of strength was one of my aunts. After school, when I was at my grandmother's house, my aunt told me stories, fed me, bathed me, and sang to me. I sat rolling chapattis with my little hands, while she hummed songs. She was a trained classical singer and had a beautiful voice, and when she came home after her marriage, her family had lovingly sent her tanpura along with her. *There was such hope in that gesture.* My aunt never sang in the presence of my grandmother or her husband. They did not approve. My uncle, the same one who had taunted my mother about her purse, finally sent the tanpura back to her parent's house saying it was taking up too much space. She still sang to me and my cousin. Her voice—loud and confident in the high notes—still rings in my memories. I can still see her face flushed with happiness and elation as she meandered through a song of her choice.

When we moved to our own house, my aunt and uncle moved away to the family's ancestral home; my mother lost the support system she had depended on for so long. Until this point, her life had closely resembled the life of many working women at the time. Many women in the 1970s and 80s were able to have a career because of the support of other women in their circles, Naina Lal Kidwai, the first Indian woman to graduate from Harvard Business School in 1982, who went on to have a long and successful career in the male-dominated investment banking sector, wrote in her book *30 Women in Power*.[1] She maintained that the extended support of family members made it easier for women in India to succeed. But this doesn't explain why women's participation in the formal workforce dropped from 40 per cent in 1983 to 38 per cent in 1999 and since then has consistently been dropping.[2] Some of it could be ascribed to liberalization in the 1990s that brought millions of Indians out of poverty.[3] The middle-class was expanding but women's agency was shrinking because there was no need for a second income, and women were expected to return to their household duties.

The joint family system didn't aid women's empowerment—in certain cases it merely allowed them to work. Women who could continue to work and progress in their careers while living in joint families did so despite familial restrictions and emotional abuse. Though they received help with childcare, in return they were forced to sacrifice many personal freedoms. My mother, for example, rarely spent enough time outside the home to sustain lasting friendships because she was always rushing home so she could relieve her mother-in-law or sisters-in-law from caring for her daughters. There are various reasons why the joint family structure disintegrated, including economic migration, but one overwhelming reason, especially in urban areas, was that women had no agency at all in the joint family structure and most of them hoped that a nuclear set-up would give them more voice and choice in their daily lives.

In most of these nuclear set-ups, the husband's parents would form part of the family unit and their care would also become the woman's responsibility, in addition to caring for her children. Unfortunately, however, as the joint family structure disintegrated, and more women stepped out to work, our governments made no provisions for institutional care structures. Everything was left to the market, which means quality day care centres continue to be prohibitively expensive and out of reach for most middle-class families. Full-time nannies are also a privilege not many families can afford, and there's little to no provision for eldercare apart from hiring expensive private attendants. In such situations, the woman leaving her job is almost always the solution. The government urges women and girls to study and work. It launches initiative after initiative to ensure women's financial empowerment, and yet, building quality care centres that would cover the general population of children and the elderly has not been prioritized.

'I thought everything would have changed by the time you had your family,' my mother told me ruefully one day. 'But you are struggling, too, and struggling alone.'

She was right. I was living far away from my husband's parents and my own parents. Even when we were in the same city, we lived in separate houses. But I did receive a semblance of support from my mother and mother-in-law in the form of occasional childcare and babysitting. But once we moved out of Kolkata and settled in the Indian capital, I was suddenly pushed into the deep end.

'It's not like the joint family system is great or anything,' my mother hastily added. 'It comes with the same expectations, less agency and freedom in return for support in your home and caregiving duties. I don't think that's a fair swap. Either way you are just struggling with the pressure to prove yourself. At home to prove you are a good housewife, at work that you are a dependable worker who won't have to go on leave every time a child is sick.'

As we have advanced as a country and society, clocking enviable growth, and educating and empowering women, all kinds of gender inequalities have only deepened. In trying to cope, women are taking extreme measures that have ruined, and continue to ruin, the futures of an entire generation of women and girls. Girls are often taken out of schools to help their mothers with housework, or they are so burdened with caregiving and domestic work that they are unable to concentrate in school.[4]

I thought my mother had it all. It was a lie. She made me believe the world would be a fairer, more equal place for women when I grew up—she told me that I could have it all. That was a lie, too.

HER DOMESTIC BURDEN

*The overburden of unpaid household work begins in early childhood and…
[as] a result, girls sacrifice important opportunities to learn, grow, and just
enjoy their childhood. This unequal distribution of labour among children also
perpetuates gender stereotypes and the double–burden on women and girls
across generations.*

—Anju Malhotra, UNICEF's Principal Gender Adviser, 2016

Back in 2010, when India made education a fundamental right, I visited a local government school in western Uttar Pradesh, only a few hours drive from the Indian capital, to report on what this would mean for the country's girls for *TIME* magazine. Inside the rustic classroom, around twenty children sat on mats and stared at the blackboard, where a teacher was scribbling something so furiously that chalk dust caked her fingers. At the very back of the classroom, I spied a girl, nodding off. I watched her as she struggled to keep her eyes open.

Dimple was only ten years old but was already shouldering a lot of responsibilities at home. Her lassitude could have been an indication that she had been up too early, that she hadn't had enough sleep, or maybe that she was too bogged down with adult responsibilities at a young age. She woke up early to help her mother with housework and cooking and getting her brothers ready for school. At school she was tired and drowsy and missed most of the day's lessons. Returning home by noon, she would help her mother cook and clean and then work in the fields. At the time I met her, she was helping her mother with the cucumber harvest. Her days were so busy with housework, that apart from the cursory hours spent in school, dozing in the back, she couldn't find even a minute to look at her books. 'I have to help my mother, otherwise she can't manage,' she told me matter-of-factly.

'I like going to school but my mother needs me at home too. It's very tough sometimes. I am so tired. I do not understand anything that goes on in school.' Her attendance in school was low; she underperformed in class and was often too tired to concentrate on her studies or follow her teacher's instructions.

Dimple's parents worked various odd jobs, including as agricultural labourers. At night, her mother would tailor clothes for some extra money. Between the two of them, they earned enough to eke out a lower middle class existence that allowed them to send their three children to school instead of sending them out to work, and pay for other small luxuries like a television set, cycles for the children, a gas stove, and a sound system. Dimple's parents had migrated to Noida in search of a better life. Her mother didn't have any help with her domestic chores and so Dimple had to become her mother's little helper.

'There are girls in this school as young as seven or eight who work like slaves at home; looking after siblings, [doing] household chores, and during harvest time, crop cutting. They don't get enough sleep. I cannot blame them for falling asleep in the class. I see so many of them with so much promise, but it all ends with dropping out before finishing primary school. There is family pressure to drop out and they are really only children and they find it hard to cope with working such long hours and then attending school,' her class teacher had said, just as the bell rang signalling the start of the lunch break. The children at the school were provided free, hot meals as part of the government's popular mid-day meal scheme. The children lined up with plates in their hands and while the steaming dal-chawal was served to them, a young girl sulkily approached the teacher.

The girl, named Manju, had been absent from school for the past three days. 'Where have you been?' the teacher asked her, more with resignation than anger. 'My mother was busy with the cucumber harvest,' Manju mumbled, looking at the ground, her toes digging into the soft mud. It had rained the previous evening.

'It was going to rain so we had to get the harvest out otherwise it would have been spoilt,' she added.

'So, why couldn't you come to school?'

'There was no one to look after the home and the cattle.'

'I am going to strike off your name from the school if you keep skipping school,' the teacher said. 'Tell your mother that you need to be in school.'

'She will beat me, teacher.'

The teacher asked me a very pertinent question: 'The law can bring them to school, how do we keep them here, especially the girls, till there is a societal change? Till parents realize they cannot keep them at home for chores?'

A majority of Indian girls are expected to help their mothers with housework and caregiving across social classes and across the rural–urban divide. India made education a fundamental right for all children between the ages of six and fourteen in 2009. But the act doesn't consider housework or agricultural labour as child labour,[*] neither does the Indian government's legislation against child labour. In the late 1990s, a government Time Use Survey found that girls between the ages of six and fourteen spent almost eight hours a day caring for other younger children[1] which adds up to over forty hours a week, which is detrimental to a child's ability to attend school and learn.[†]

But things must surely have changed in the intervening decade since education was declared a fundamental right in our country? In my article for *TIME*, written in 2010, I had predicted that girls would not be able to reap the benefits of this Act.[2] I wanted to be proved wrong. So, when I went back to the story once again in 2018 and 2019, it was with a heart full of hope. I had travelled to Bundelkhand, a drought

---

[*]The International Labor Organization (ILO) defines child labour as 'work that deprives children of their childhood, their potential and their dignity, and that is harmful to physical and mental development.' See 'What is Child Labour', ILO, available at <www.ilo.org/ipec/lang--en/index.htm>.

[†]According to the ILO, household chores beyond twenty-one hours per week negatively affect a child's ability to attend school and benefit from it. See 'Global Estimates of Child Labour', International Labour Organization: Results and Trends, 2012–2016, Geneva, 2017, p. 12.

ravaged region in Uttar Pradesh; a particularly underdeveloped and patriarchal region where women are still expected to observe purdah.[3] There, I met Neha and her sister, Kalpana.

∽

When I arrived at Suman and Mannu's house in Deoria, it was late. I was exhausted after ten straight hours on the road. After spending the night in their house—attended to and fussed over by the women of the house—I left for Suman's mother's home in a village around 100 kilometres away, accompanied by Neha, their middle daughter. As we travelled the two hours to her grandparents' house, Neha didn't talk much, but she would turn around and smile at me from time to time. When we reached her grandparents', it was late evening; I had stopped in every village on my route to meet and talk to people. At night, I slept in the open courtyard under the stars, with Neha sharing a charpoy with her sister some distance from me. I don't know when I fell asleep listening to their shallow breathing and counting the stars.

The next day, I woke to the sounds of spices being ground on a flat grindstone. I opened my eyes to see Neha sitting near the kitchen manoeuvring a pounder twice her size. As I silently watched her, she wiped her eyes with the back of her hand carefully. The strong odour of the dried, brittle red chillies was making her eyes water as she ground them into a paste with onions, garlic, cumin, and coriander. Later, she expertly chopped okra and fried them in a large wok, gripping the ladle with both hands as she stirred. While it cooked, she measured out atta in a large bowl and poured water over it, her small hands struggling to tame the flour into a dough. But she had also kept one eye on me, and as soon as she saw me moving in my blanket, she was by my side with a cup of tea and biscuits. Her day had started early at 5 a.m., when she had swept the yard, eyes heavy with sleep.

Neha is almost the same age as the Right to Education (RTE) Act. She did enrol in a school but dropped out soon after because her mother needed help with the household duties, especially to look after her younger brother, undoubtedly the star of their home. During my visit, Sunny would sit in a chair next to me, fiddling with a mobile phone.

His sisters and mothers fussed around him. He was served food first and the sisters waited for him to finish before serving themselves. As I sat in the corner of their kitchen, my gaze suddenly fell on Sunny, all of seven, sitting alone in a plastic chair, trying to look all important in his starched shirt and trousers, and his father's mobile phone in his hand, while his sisters and mother fussed around him—and I wondered, how would he ever learn about equality from that perch?

Little Neha was taken out of school to help her mother because Suman's eldest daughter insisted that she wanted to not just finish school but also go to college.

'She is a good girl,' her grandmother told me when we reached their home and Neha immediately set herself up in the kitchen. 'Her sister, now....' She shook her head despondently. 'She doesn't know anything about housework. She is useless. She just wants to study. Is that going to help her when she is married?' she asked me with a conspiratorial air. 'I mean, I know you will not really understand this because I am sure you have a domestic helper at home who does the cooking and cleaning but tell me something—when she doesn't come, you are the one who has to cook and clean, right?'

In its 2018 report on gender inequality in India, the McKinsey Global Institute found that housework accounts for 85 per cent of the time women in India spend on unpaid care work.[4] When it comes to young girls, in 2018 the National Commission for Protection of Child Rights (NCPCR) said almost 40 per cent of girls were not attending schools and a vast majority—around 65 per cent—were 'either engaged in household activities, are dependents, or, are engaged in begging, etc'. The report also pointed out that adolescent girls were 'among the most economically vulnerable groups who typically lack access to financial capital and have more limited opportunities to gain the education, knowledge, and skills that can lead to economic advancement'.[5] Just a year earlier, in 2017, the non-profit Save the Children said that girls were lagging behind boys in India when it came to education because they were viewed as 'future housewives and family caretakers'.[6] Mothers justify pulling daughters into housework as preparing them for their future marital life. 'Abhi se seekh legi toh accha hai na, didi? Baad me sasural mein toh karna hi padega,' Suman had told me, pulling the end of her sari tightly around her face. It's better if she learns now; after marriage this is what she will have to do anyway.

These findings have remained pretty consistent over the years. In 2019, a Child Relief and You (CRY) study found that a high number of girls between eleven and fourteen years of age dropped out of schools and a majority who dropped out were engaged in household chores. The study also found that 'more than half of dropout girls (59 per cent) wanted to continue their education at the time of dropout and equal percentage (50 per cent) were willing to go back provided given an opportunity'.[7]

Yes, the RTE brought girls back to school—from 20 per cent in 2018, the number of out-of-school girls between the ages fifteen and sixteen fell to 13.5 per cent in 2018.[8] However, greater rates of enrolment have not meant that all these new students have actually finished school, with girls dropping out as and when their parents deem it necessary. In 2014, a study by Save the Children had found that 24.4 per cent of girls discontinued their education before completing Class V, while 41.3 per cent dropped out before they completed Class VIII.[9]

This is not something that happens only in poor families—Neha's family belongs to the rural upper middle class. They have a good amount of land and her father is aspiring to contest in the village council elections. In rural agricultural economies, of course, women play a very important (but unacknowledged) role. They are rarely called farmers but they put in as much labour in the farms as the men. The farm work they do is considered an extension of their household duties. Being middle class in rural India means girls must face added pressures that affect their education, like having to fetch water because a vast part of rural India has no access to piped water,[10] or perform agricultural and household labour.

In urban India, this works slightly differently. While girls are usually not taken out of schools, they still end up helping their mothers with housework and caregiving more than is advisable. The core idea behind their increased contribution to the household remains the same—the idea that it is perhaps good for them to learn these things to prepare for their final goal, which is marriage.

There is little doubt that there is an increased interest in sending girls to school in our country, but often that desire is not fulfilled owing to a lack of quality gender-responsive infrastructure that could support girls' continued attendance. Something as simple as a clean toilet can make a huge difference. Research has shown that in developing nations, poor sanitation, particularly a lack of toilets, keeps girls away from schools, especially when they are menstruating.[11] When young girls reach puberty and begin to menstruate, they often miss school during this time owing to an absence of hygienic toilets in their schools. This becomes yet another excuse for parents to keep their daughters at home.

Menstrual hygiene is one of the most important aspects of women's empowerment in developing nations, especially when it comes to the education of adolescent girls. But this has not received its due attention yet from the government, although many non-profits are working to address the gap. The non-profit WaterAid found in 2020 that 'a sizeable population of girls and women continue to grapple with challenges to access safe and hygienic menstrual hygiene products, information, and sanitation facilities required to manage periods hygienically and with dignity'.[12]

The fact that this is still not a priority from a policy perspective was witnessed during the pandemic when, first, the government did not include menstrual products in the list of essential items that were exempt from restrictions during the lockdown in March 2020,[13] and, then, when a shortage of sanitary pads was recorded across the country owing mostly to the fact that manufacturers had stopped the production of sanitary napkins and switched to making face masks[14].

Lack of access to basic rights such as menstrual hygiene, of course, affects poor and underprivileged women disproportionately. But the middle classes are not immune to this either. Maya Vishwakarma, a social activist—also known as the 'padwoman of India'—told me that during the pandemic, when many men lost their jobs and livelihoods and middle-class families had to reduce expenditure, women's sanitary products were the first items to be cut. Access and cost were the obvious reasons but the underlying reason is that women's requirements are often the lowest priority in our homes. The reason the men of the house think these are not essential items follows the same thinking that makes our government not include sanitary products in the essential items list during a national emergency.

We need to invest in quality education for girls and create quality job opportunities for them; build skills among girls to aspire for jobs across sectors, and, most importantly, create an atmosphere for them to study and work without any constraints. All of these will incentivize parents to keep their girls in school for longer. But women's needs have never been prioritized by any government in our country. We have various policies and programmes, including a gender budget that was introduced in 2005, and laws in accordance with global agenda, but very few of them are implemented in a gender-responsive manner or pay sustained attention to reforming normative behaviour. The RTE Act is a prime example—though it managed to bring girls back to schools, could it keep them there? According to UNICEF, education is one of the most critical areas of empowerment for women but also an area where they are discriminated against the most. Education 'enables them to make decisions for themselves and to influence their families', the global agency has underlined. 'It is this power that produces all other developmental and social benefits.'[15]

According to World Bank estimates in 2018, when countries do not invest in the education of girls and women, they stand to lose between US$ 15 trillion and US$ 30 trillion in lost lifetime productivity and earnings.[16] But these warnings come and go every year, just as the Sustainable Development Goals (SDGs) replaced the Millennium Development Goals and will be replaced with another set of goals after 2030. In 2020, the Global Gender Gap Report had said it would take the world almost a hundred years to achieve gender parity—thanks to Covid-19 we are now looking at 135.6 years.[17]

One educated and economically and socially empowered woman is enough to change her whole community. The government cannot wash its hands off women's current predicament, referring to social ills like dowry and son preference as historical and social challenges, as though society cannot be reformed.

We need our governments to be gender-responsive, not just to achieve the SDGs or other global agendas, but to truly include women in the country's progress. Let's start with mandatory gender studies in schools right from primary levels to strip children of the gender biases they inculcate from their surroundings, raise awareness among girls and women about their fundamental rights, provide basic amenities such as piped water to every home, build neighbourhood day care systems, focus on upskilling or reskilling women who have been out of the work force, create quality job opportunities for women, and, most importantly, provide them with an environment that enables them to study and work and also have a family, if they so choose. Such measures will allow girls to continue their education beyond enrolment. With these changes girls will be able to consider education a tool that can change their lives rather than just being a stopgap until marriage.

When girls drop out of schools, they are more likely to be married off early. Every hour nearly 150 minor girls are married off in India—which means every hour education is taken away from 150 girls in India.[18] According to UNICEF, nearly 1.5 million girls in this country are married off before they turn eighteen. As of 2019, one in three of the world's child-brides lived in India.[19] In 2021, the Indian government announced that they would raise women's legal marriage age to 21.[20] The most that this legislation can achieve is that a few parents would feel compelled to wait before marrying off their daughters, and perhaps some girls would get the opportunity to access higher education. However, a good education can only do so much to instil confidence in our daughters unless we stop telling them that marriage is non-negotiable.

∽

Women who work outside the home often find it a financially exhausting process. When my son was a toddler, I spent more than ₹40,000 per month to outsource my domestic and caregiving work.

I consider writing to be my business and I have been running a loss-making venture for years now. While I earn way more than any full-time job could offer me, I, individually, still have zero savings. I consider the money I earn an investment into my identity. And yes, even this is a privilege not available to a large majority of middle-class women, a privilege I earned through the luck of birth but also with my blood and sweat. I have worked ungodly hours throughout my life just to retain my financial independence. I have dropped out of vacation plans or plans with friends and family. I work through holidays, weekends, and even sick days. I still only sleep three or four hours a day and I have invested the time saved into my work. I also run on a steady prescription of anti-depressants and anti-anxiety medicines and copious amounts of strong black coffee. I do not have the luxury to stop and think of what all of this is doing to my body.

I was forced to become a freelancer after being pushed out or not allowed to grow in almost every company I have ever worked for. I pay as much, or perhaps more, tax as a man in my position does and yet I have to spend as much as I earn to keep working because the state will do nothing for me, neither in terms of ensuring my access to equal opportunities and wages, nor in terms of care support. Our country is a prime example for why the provisioning of care work cannot bet left only to the market. It has to be a collaborative effort between families, the market, and the government. Shahra Razavi, a senior United Nations official specializing in gender and social development, introduced the concept of the Care Diamond in 2007, where each of the four corners represented the family or household, markets, the public sector, and the not-for-profit sector.[21] In patriarchal societies like ours, when the triangle of the market, public sector, and not-for-profit sector fails to offer the required support, the burden of care gets passed on to wives and then, daughters, irrespective of how young they are, or if they are based in urban or rural India.

It is ironic how much we talk about putting the family first in India, considering everyone has just outsourced the responsibility of the family to the women or, more alarmingly, to young girls. The value of a family in India rides on the devaluation of women's work.

If we truly valued the family, we would value all of its components, including the women and children. We would have more affordable state-subsidized models of childcare and parental leave till children can attend childcare centres. A UNICEF report in 2021 had ranked Luxembourg, Iceland, and Sweden as countries that provide the most affordable and organized childcare to its citizens. These countries also record a high rate of women's formal labour force participation at over 54 per cent, over 71 per cent, and over 61 per cent respectively.[22]

In my conversations with American women, I have often been asked if the availability of low-wage domestic workers doesn't make the lives of working women in India easier than theirs. I'm sure that it does, but it comes at the cost of a major portion of their earnings, and also at the cost of the domestic worker's own family. When we outsource our care duties to poorer women in the informal sector, we are not just taking away the proper care and nurturing of their children, but often also the education of their daughters. Educating new generations is a sure shot way of reducing poverty significantly.[23] Taking this option away from them is a disservice to the cause of women's empowerment. I have always taken care of the education and care expenses of my domestic workers and I am not alone. I know many women who do this out of gratitude to the women who look after our children and our homes like their own while being forced to neglect theirs, but such individual munificence cannot bring about any lasting change. Unless the government devises policies to provide all women with the option of affordable and regulated childcare, we will continue to witness this toxic loop of exploitation.

The amazing fact is that we don't have to look too far for a solution. Our country has one of the world's oldest and largest child development schemes, the Integrated Child Development Services, under which it runs anganwadis or free childcare centres for low-income groups and the rural population. There are 13.77 lakh anganwadis operating in the country as of now, but there have been issues of quality.[24] In December 2019, Women and Child Development minister Smriti Irani told the upper house of the Indian parliament that 362,940 anganwadi centres do not have toilets facilities and 159,568 anganwadi centres do not have drinking water facilities.[25] In 2011, a team of researchers reported that most of these centres were either closed or if they were open 'food supplies are extremely sporadic, children sit in a single room choking with cooking fire smoke, and equipment like growth monitoring scales are often broken or missing. Anganwadi workers do not regularly receive supervision, support, supplies, or training'.[26] During my travels in Bundelkhand, I found the same—most of these centres were barely operational. The anganwadi's one principal aim was to tackle malnutrition among children and yet India continued to be the worst performer in that development indicator.[27] Owing to this, even mothers belonging to low-income groups often opt not to leave their children in these centres.

But some policy changes and incentivized quality control could not just improve but also expand this programme to include every working woman in this country. Those above the poverty level could be charged a higher fee for the centres—the money raised going towards the improvement of facilities—while keeping them free or subsidized for the low-income groups. The first step to ensuring this would be to start valuing the work of anganwadi workers by paying them decent salaries and not honorariums. Anganwadi workers earn between ₹4,500 and ₹10,000[28]—how can they be expected to provide quality service when that service is being devalued every month? Adequately paying and training community health workers to provide standardized care could change the face of care provision in our country and, by extension, women's labour force participation. Children have the right to quality care, irrespective of the socio-economic status of their families. When the state arranges for standardized care for all children it provides children a level playing field, irrespective of their socio-economic status. When it redistributes a woman's caregiving burden among trained and skilled childcare professionals, it is also encouraging women to take on more productive roles outside the home.

The desperation of our situation when it comes to unpaid care work, even in urban areas, cannot be stressed enough. In 2015, I came across a young couple in my apartment complex, with two daughters aged eleven and five. Both worked in India's vibrant tech industry; the woman spent months at a time working on offshore projects in the UK. For a while, the man's parents came and stayed with them to help with the children, but the visits stopped when his mother was diagnosed with cancer. The woman's mother suffered from Alzheimer's disease. I met and spoke to both husband and wife occasionally, mostly when we dropped our children off at the school bus stop. Then, for almost a year I didn't see her around. One morning, when I had walked down to buy some milk from the shop, I found her elder daughter standing there, looking upset. 'What happened?' I asked her.

'The shop has run out of milk and I don't know what to feed my sister for breakfast.'

I took her to a grocery store just outside the apartment complex to buy milk. While we were coming back home, she suddenly turned to me and asked, 'Have you ever left your son alone at home?'

I was taken aback. 'What do you mean? I have to when I go out to work.'

'No, I mean, totally alone for two days?'

'No, not totally alone, there's a woman who looks after him when I am not there. Why do you ask?'

'You know my mum is in the UK working and my father had to go away for two days. So, my sister and I were alone in the house. I had to manage. It was scary. But we didn't open the door to anybody.'

I didn't know what to say. I kept a watch on the sisters until the father returned. He must have been desperate to have left them on their own. But this two-day trip had already set a precedent and for months after, I saw her taking care of her little sister, including getting her ready for school, feeding her meals, and so on. This is not very different from what Neha was doing for her family in Bundelkhand. While their circumstances were very different, the fact that both of them were burdened with such care duties was a stark reminder for me of how far we still have to go to ensure an equal home and equal world for our girls.

THE LIE: EXPLAINED MORE

I am not free while any woman is unfree,
even when her shackles are very different from my own.

—Audre Lorde

Women are not just struggling to change gender roles at home and balance work and life, but also to reconcile their thoughts, dreams, and aspirations with societal diktats. Even feminist mothers, like mine, did not warn us of the 'double shift' or the fallout of the 'superwoman syndrome' because they so firmly believed that their problems existed because they were unique and that as more women stepped out to work, infrastructural support to balance home and work would follow. They also believed that our homes would have changed from the inside. With so many women taking on productive labour usually outside the home, our society should have ideally advanced in a way that men would look upon housework and caregiving not as a woman's duty but as labour to be shared equally. Unfortunately, cooking and housework are still considered women's work. Often men who split household chores with their spouses are either ridiculed (for engaging in feminine work) or exalted for this favour.

In 2019, the UN Women's report on the progress of the world's women had found that in developed countries 'even when women and men both work full-time and provide equal income, including instances when women earn more than their husbands, women tend to do more housework as if to "neutralize" their "deviance" from traditional gender roles. Social expectations of what women and men should do and how they should behave mediate the bargaining power that women may gain (or lose) as a result of their changing earning capacity. Social norms, which tend to be sticky, shape the impact of economic factors on gender power dynamics.'

It also noted that most of the changes 'that are heralded as "revolutionary" involve women moving into positions and activities previously limited to men, with few changes in the opposite direction.'[1] While women are often incentivized to take on paid work, men are not similarly incentivized to share unpaid care duties, which is not recognized as productive work but rather a duty or responsibility. This devaluation of care work and its categorization as a responsibility has meant women's unpaid work has remained largely unrecognized. The division of unpaid care work remains unequal in nearly all developed countries. As young girls become adults, they transition from being daughters to wives, graduating from being mommy's little helpers to head housekeepers in their marital homes. Their levels of education or their salaries (or lack thereof) don't matter, for most are just sucked back into the confines of domesticity.

A large majority of Indian women, many of them college graduates, are not available to work because of household duties. Though it is our patriarchal society that demands women's subservience, in many cases women impose this patriarchal bargaining on themselves. Like my mother did in the 1970s, and like I am doing now. As Bijayalaxmi Nanda, acting principal of Miranda House, told me, 'Somehow you felt you [were] a lesser woman if you didn't do everything at home. You would think that the narrative would have changed in the last fifteen years but no—it has remained the same.' Nanda is a women's rights activist who has been working with issues of domestic violence and son preference for many years now. 'If a man wants to cook, let him cook. I don't cook with my vagina, so it's alright.'

Ever since I turned forty, I have been waking up between 2 and 3 a.m. every day. This is followed by excruciating hours of trying to fall back to sleep accompanied by spiralling anxiety. If I don't start early, I won't be able to get through even half of my to-do list on any given day, and so, I don't sleep. I am not alone though—according to an ActionAid study, 80 per cent of the respondents consisting of women across categories expressed a desire for more sleep.[2]

They are not sleeping because they must provide unpaid labour in the form of housework, childcare, and eldercare within the home—work that forms the bedrock of our family structures. Stepping out to work brings with it different challenges. They must find someone to entrust their caregiving responsibilities to, strategically plan every commute to maximize safety and security, and then find the strength to ignore and sometimes stand up to sexism and bullying at work. This constant struggle to claim our 'half of the sky'[3] is traumatic, and may contribute to moderate to severe mental illness.

I think most women in India, especially married women, wake up between 4 and 6 a.m. every day. I have a vague memory of weekends long past when I would wake up at noon—grumpy because my mother had pulled open the curtains to force me awake. I can no longer remember what it felt like to sleep without a care in the world. But I do see now that I took my mother's love for granted. She allowed me to sleep in, and never let me know that it created even more work for her. Once I woke up, she would reheat my tea and breakfast, sometimes even cooking something fresh for me. She would wait to eat with me even though her day had started hours earlier. Those were the days when I could wake up at 2 p.m. on the weekends. Now, although there are no real compulsions forcing me to do this, I cannot even imagine sleeping past 6 a.m.

I could wake up at 12 p.m. because my mother woke up at 4 a.m.

And now, just like my mother, I am riddled with anxieties and a feeling that I am always running out of time. We try to control as much of our lives as we can because a large part of our lives are totally beyond our control. There is nothing praiseworthy about running from day to day, tired and frustrated. My late mother-in-law had once told me that as a younger woman she had endlessly feared leaving her son—my husband—behind on the bus, or forgetting to collect him from the school bus stop. She woke up in a sweat imagining these things. I had laughed at her then, not unkindly but a bit smugly; I was sure I would not have these same anxieties.

The first night I woke up in a sweat was when I thought I had forgotten to collect my son from day care. The nightmare continued until I was no longer in charge of taking him to and collecting him from school. When I stepped out, I would worry if I had locked our main door before leaving, if I turned off the gas, or the geyser. I would leave my home, only to return again to check if all was in order. These anxieties are random. Inexplicable. But they stem from the same place of deep insecurity, a result of trying to do it all, alone.

At 3 a.m., as I toss and turn in bed, I often wonder if we can ever be truly empowered and free in a society that does not support its women. There is no institutional backing for us, our homes are patriarchal, our public spaces are unsafe, and our workplaces are sexist. We live in a society where capitalism intertwines with patriarchy to deepen gender inequalities. We live in a society where housework has a gender, where women working within or outside the home are not considered key to the country's development. Can we call ourselves fully empowered until we have managed to bring in institutional change? But most importantly, can we really claim to have come a long way when we have been unable to bring about systemic change inside our homes?

A vast majority of modern Indian middle-class women suffer from the 'superwoman syndrome', a term coined in the 1980s. I see fellow sufferers all around me, but there is practically no awareness of the syndrome in India. The year 1976, when I was born and my mother started working, was a critical year for the discourse surrounding this term. It was when the superwoman complex was being identified and called out for what it was—a crisis that was creating overwhelming expectations for women and giving rise to what journalist Judith Serrin had called 'a new malady'.[4] When we say there's nothing that women can't do, what we actually mean is that women should do everything, which translates to paid and unpaid work and some emotional labour as a bonus. In *The Second Stage*, Betty Friedan defines superwomanhood as the double enslavement of women, both at home and at work. In the West, the superwoman syndrome is a by-product of feminism, while in India, and many other developing countries, the superwoman syndrome is a concomitant of patriarchy. When I discussed this with the sociologist Pallavi Banerjee, she confirmed that the basic premise of the superwoman syndrome is the same in the West and India in that it is 'the internalization of the impossible expectation by women, and by society, that if women work, they need to be perfect at home in the unpaid work they do and at the workplace in the paid work they do.' During her PhD research, she found that Indian-origin women in the US were expected to organize their work lives around their roles as wife, mother, and daughter-in-law. In other words, they are still 'working women/mothers/wives' instead of being people who work and have a family. Many of them told her that they chose to work, so the onus was on them to prove that they were also good mothers and wives, and that women were required to wear many hats and wear them all well. What this meant was that many of them were overworked and stressed. They did not see it as having it all, but rather as having to do it all.

For the Western middle-class woman, she says, the rhetoric is definitely 'having it all' because the idea of working and having a family are not at odds with each other in the same way as in India. Here, it's a given that most people will work and have a family. The idea of a woman having equal stakes in her career and her home life is at odds in our country, the problems that middle-class women face in their personal lives in India are way more severe than in any Western countries.

But in the 1970s, our mothers were flush with the promise of economic empowerment, and a different life from their own mothers. It was years after, possibly around the same time that the joint family system gave way to nuclear families, that they could fully grasp the realities of their lives—the double enslavement, the double shifts, and the mounting pressure to do it all. It surprises me that even after all these years, we have not begun to call out the myth of having it all for the capitalist–patriarchal ploy that it is to ensure women are relegated to the domestic sphere. Businesses and advertisements began targeting women who, in the face of rising aspirations, were encouraged to step out to work, to have career aspirations. But because patriarchy ensured that women remained shackled by reproductive labour, entry into the workforce simply burdened them with low-paying productive labour.* Have the many demands and inequalities of our society come together to define who we have failed to become? Because when I look into the mirror, I, for sure, never see the person I wanted to be. I see someone who is trying too hard to be someone she was never meant to be. My mother, and her generation, promised me a different world—one where I would be treated as an equal, where I would have all the rights that she had struggled for. This is the biggest lie my mother has ever told me.

∽

In the twenty-first century, technically, middle-class women have more of everything—freedom, access to education, economic opportunities—than ever before. But in reality, it is only the outside packaging of our lives that has changed. When we talk about 'New India', what are we referring to exactly? We are talking about increasing incomes and shrinking gender justice. New India has more money, more opportunities than before. In New India more and more women are stepping out to work, but it is not true that they are breaking free of their traditional roles. In New India, affluent couples fly abroad for sex-selective abortions[5] because prenatal gender determination and foeticide are prohibited as per the Pre-Conception and Pre-Natal Diagnostic Techniques (PCPNDT) Act of 1994. In this India, we have the rights on paper, but no support to exercise them. We can wear a short skirt to a club but we prefer to cover up when travelling alone or using public transport. We think twice before accepting a job that involves night shifts. We are constantly reminded to be on the phone with a friend or family member if in a cab alone in the evenings. We take these 'safety measures' for a reason: National Crime Records Bureau (NCRB) data shows that over 3 lakh cases of crimes against women were registered during 2020.[6]

---

*Labour that leads to the creation of material goods or assets for earning an income is productive labour, while reproductive labour includes cooking, cleaning, and caring for the elderly, the sick, and children.

Gendered violence came into sharp focus in India in the aftermath of the Nirbhaya rape case in 2012, a gruesome act that spurred protests across the country. There were some much-needed policy changes that included a stricter rape law in 2013 under which punishments for sex crimes were strengthened, including the death penalty for repeat offenders and the inclusion of stalking, voyeurism, and lewd expressions as a crime.[7] And yet, six years later, the country was again rattled by the brutal rape and murder of an eight-year-old girl in Kathua in Kashmir.[8] In 2011, India was fourth on a list of countries considered the most dangerous for women. In 2018, India had topped the list.[9] Our public spaces are hostile to women, and the same hostility can be found in our homes as well. In a majority of crimes against women recorded in 2018 in the country's capital, most of the perpetrators were known to the victim, and included friends, family members, and neighbours.[10] Out of the total number of crimes against women registered that year in Delhi, the most common were cruelty by husband or his relatives, followed by assault, abduction, and rape. It is important to note that domestic violence is not limited to intimate partner violence. It includes emotional abuse, controlling actions by a partner, and even neglect of children that can hamper their well-being and development.

This book happened over many years and many hours of conversations, interviews with women experts turned into confessions of their lives behind the doors of their homes. I remember speaking to a relationship therapist to understand the psychology of women in abusive relationships. After almost a year of conversation, she let me in on her own story—one of physical and emotional abuse over a period of thirty odd years.

What alarmed me the most was that even when I was getting in touch with women not for their stories, I ended up coming away with stories of emotional and physical abuse by partners, parental neglect, overwhelming caregiving expectations, lack of choice to walk out of abusive situations, lack of economic opportunities, and the internalization and acceptance of patriarchy. And while I saw in them the desire to break free, none of the women I interviewed told me anything different. They felt alone, overworked, and underappreciated, battling their constant state of anxiety and a feeling of not being enough.

Middle-class women rarely talk about violence or infidelity in their marriages or think of walking out on their partners. The women I spoke with wanted to move quickly past the violence in their marriages, almost as if they felt compelled to acknowledge that it was happening and yet not let it come up to the surface. One woman I spoke to only talked about the emotional and physical abuse when she was prodded by her daughter. Middle-class Indians thrive on social status and respectability and it dictates everything—from their emotions to their feelings to their relationships. In the face of this attitude, issues such as sexual abuse or spousal violence become things with which married women must learn to live.

Is that all our lives should be though—making the most of what we have, opting for the lesser evil?

Beginning with being given adult responsibilities even when they are young, then the pressure to get married and stay married, the subsequent pressure to prioritize the family over all other aspirations, and the general trauma of living a life where they can never feel safe—women in our country often find themselves caught between the deep sea and the devil. Owing to all of these, women like me, in their early forties to mid-fifties, are suddenly realizing what a lie their lives have been. We cannot have it all no matter how hard we try and the repercussions of this realization have been sending shockwaves through the population since the mid-nineties. Too many women in their thirties and forties have been succumbing to depression and suicides in our country every year.[11] It was in the mid-1990s that the National Crime Records bureau began to track 'housewife suicides' as a separate category because the numbers were growing at a steady pace every year. Researcher Peter Mayer told me that smaller family sizes, while an indicator of empowerment, led to higher rates of suicide in women, which points to overwork, lack of support, and, finally, an inability to cope with circumstances, often triggered by mental illnesses.

In 2018, the *Lancet* found that Indian women accounted for

36 per cent of global female suicide deaths in 2016, calling this a public health crisis. In India, as elsewhere in the world, the number of men who die by suicide is higher than the number of women but there are two factors to note here.[12] One was identified by the *Lancet* study: while the proportion of global suicide deaths in India since 1990 has increased for both sexes, the rate of increase was higher for women.[13] The other was identified by the National Crime Records Bureau in its annual accidental and suicide deaths reports. In 1997 and again in 2007, the NCRB noted that while the reason for men's suicide deaths were mostly owing to social and economic causes, women's suicide deaths were almost always attributable to emotional and personal causes.[14] The reports also consistently recorded a large number of deaths among married women—something that was corroborated by the *Lancet*—especially over dowry or physical violence. The *Lancet* report says: 'Marriage is known to be less protective against suicide for women because of arranged and early marriage, young motherhood, low social status, domestic violence, and economic dependence.'[15]

These striking figures are enough for us to deduce the crisis of our existence. In other nations, perhaps these would have led to solid data collection, studies, and reports, ultimately leading to a solution, but in our country they have just remained annual statistics on paper. When we talk about violence against women and girls, we rarely ever talk about these numbers, but these suicides are the end point of a life cycle peppered with indignities, inequalities, and oppression.

These suicides are a cry for help.

THE GRANDMOTHER I NEVER MET

Mental pain is less dramatic than physical pain, but it is more common and also more hard to bear. The frequent attempt to conceal mental pain increases the burden: it is easier to say, 'My tooth is aching' than to say 'My heart is broken.'

—C.S. Lewis, *The Problem of Pain*

She woke in the silence of the dawn, and walked out of the room, closing the door softly behind her. My grandmother walked along the narrow streets of the village, past the pond and the neighbour's house decorated with flowers and lights for a wedding, which is where everyone thought she was, helping with the wedding preparations, when she couldn't be found at home that morning. Had she hesitated even for a moment before she lay herself down on the train tracks? No one knows. What did she think as she lay there, waiting for the train to crush her, a slight, translucent visage in white, against the cold, hard tracks? She was only thirty-eight years old.

The neighbours had found her later that morning. Her children never saw the body, but they still live with the wound of a mother who would not—could not—carry on.

I imagine she lingered a while outside the room where her children lay asleep, small, dark bundles on the floor, sleeping as only children can—lost to the world, huddled in their own warmth. She must have wanted to touch them one last time, but she didn't. Instead, she stood over them until her eyes got used to the darkness. There was her eldest daughter, looking worried even in her sleep, there was her youngest, curled into her big sister, and a little distance away was her son, his face deeply embedded in the pillow. Her second child—my mother—had fallen asleep as usual with a book in her hand, near the oil lamp whose flame had died some hours back. She quietly walked up to her daughter, bent down, picked up the book, closed it, and held it in her hands for some time before putting it away amid her small stash of books. Many years later that was all my mother would remember—waking up to find the book she was reading neatly stacked among her other books. But she is still not sure if it was a dream or her imagination of her mother's last few hours.

The morning my grandmother killed herself was an uneventful one. In the days leading up to it, she had shown no signs of what was on her mind. The night before, she had cooked, fed her children, read for some time, and then gone to sleep. My mother, who was in the first year of college, had noticed nothing unusual. In later years, she would often try to mentally recreate her mother's last day—looking for answers, but never finding any.

'Why did she kill herself? I don't know. She was a young widow with four young children. She worked from dawn till dusk. She had no life. And although I was eighteen, we grew up in a different world, we didn't understand depression or anxiety or stress,' she told me. 'I wish I had paid more attention.'

My maternal grandmother was a woman who loved to read. She wanted her children to study and make a life for themselves. 'She used to fly into a temper if she felt we were slacking off in our studies,' my mother remembers. 'She once tore up my books because she thought I was not being serious enough. She knew education was the only thing that would ensure we didn't end up with her life.'

From my mother's account of her mother, I can glimpse signs of depression. She rarely smiled. She read a lot, she kept to herself, and flew into unexpected rages.

In her description, I see my mother. In my mother, I often see myself.

My grandmother came from a well-off family. Her brothers held high-ranking government jobs (they took good care of my mother and her siblings, ensured they finished their education after my grandmother's death; later, my mother joined the police force, and her siblings ended up in high-ranking government jobs, too) but she was not ready to live on their handouts forever. She was upset about having to depend on her brothers to bring up her children once the savings her husband left behind began to peter out. She was stuck—she had nowhere to go, no one to turn to, no hope of living her life with dignity.

Seven decades later, I, the granddaughter she never met, stared at a gaggle of pink, yellow, and blue pills. They were prescription pills, my psychiatrist had prescribed them for six months. I couldn't tear my eyes away from them. They were supposed to be happy pills but actually were quite useless. They didn't make me feel happy, they didn't lessen my exhaustion, a spiralling fear of never being enough, not doing enough, not being happy enough, grateful enough, talented enough, intelligent enough. They could surely end it all, end the constant streams of monologues in my head, putting me down, pulling me apart. My conflict with my father was at an all-time high—I could no longer ignore how he constantly mistreated my mother. I felt a helpless anger towards my mother because she wouldn't continue her treatment for depression, something that loomed over her, and our relationship, ominously. Every time we would speak on the phone, I would come away feeling absolutely wretched at her unhappiness. I couldn't make peace with the fact that she had become resigned to living this life and had to helplessly watch her suffer at an age when she should have been enjoying her retirement years. When she was younger, she had been confined to our home and her workplace. She was not allowed to have friends or meet her colleagues outside of work or invite them home. She wouldn't even give out our telephone number. And while my father was never physically abusive, at least not in our presence, there was a lot of emotional and verbal abuse. My father continued to control her until only recently when the combined forces of Parkinson's disease and dementia overpowered him. 'It's like being a prisoner,' my mother has often told me.

Years later, a friend in her early forties would tell me the same.

'He wants to know who I am texting, what I am talking to my friends about, we have to do everything together. I don't think I have ever taken a walk alone. If I want to listen to something, he would ask me to instead put it on the speaker so he could also hear. I know you think that these are very small things—but they choke you. You can't breathe. Tell your mother I understand how she feels. I feel like a prisoner, too,' she had told me. 'Sometimes I feel like I am choking.'

Two women, separated by four decades. Different times, same lives.

A casual acquaintance once said to me about her husband, 'There's this subtle annoyance when I hang out with my friends. When we plan a girls' trip, he wants to come. It's all very passive-aggressive. But it's suffocating.'

I have no such clouds hanging over me—my partner and I have allowed each other to grow in our own individual spaces. Despite various ups and downs, we have stayed with each other out of choice. But I live my mother's life vicariously. The mental baggage of my childhood and my mother's continuing unhappiness sit on me like a rock. Some days are very hard. And on days that are especially difficult, I wish I could run away to my childhood hiding place—the water tank on our terrace in my parents' home in Kolkata—and lie there staring at the stars. But that house is not there anymore, neither is the tank; sometimes in the search of a happier place, we end up somewhere darker.

In the emergency room that evening they pump my stomach. It's painful. The doctors tsk-tsk over the empty strips of the feel-good medicines that were inside me. Later, a doctor informs me that they have to report it to the police. But I suppose he finally must have put down the cause as 'accidental' because no one followed up with me. The doctor was kind and paternal; he did not think of me as a statistic. But maybe he should have. What gets reported and what doesn't, and the difference between the two, could mean that the reality is much more terrifying than we realize.

Later that evening, they moved me to the cool confines of the intensive care unit. My throat hurt from the tubes they had inserted to clean out my stomach. The white walls looked strangely unconcerned, distant and I felt the beginnings of a headache. Surrounded by deathly silence, save for the low murmur of the air conditioner, an overwhelming smell of medicines and pine floor cleaners, sombre doctors, and sympathetic, kind nurses, I looked up at the white expanse of the ceiling. It was oddly comfortable to lie in that room, surrounded by silence and the beeping of monitors. No rushing around to get things done. No ever-growing list of things to do on my mind, things to achieve, miles to travel. No anxiety about the little things of life. I felt relaxed.

And then, out of nowhere, I was assailed with the image of my mother. I realized with a sudden jolt that I had never seen my mother smile. She was the unhappiest person I knew. When I closed my eyes, I only saw her as harassed and anxious. Her depression was palpable and it hung over her like a dark cloud. I entreated my father many times that she needed to see a therapist. He was always dismissive. 'She will be okay. There's nothing wrong with her. You know how she loves a bit of drama!' And yet, there was so much that was wrong with her. When I finally managed to convince her to see a therapist, she went for just one session. 'I am fine,' she insisted. 'I don't need a therapist. I am not crazy.'

The social stigma surrounding mental illness in India has refused to shift in the last many decades. It is still a taboo topic across all strata of society, for men and women alike. In a country like India, if something is a taboo for men, then one need not imagine how bad things must be for women.

My maternal grandmother died by suicide because her life as a young widow was filled with unspeakable atrocities and the deprivation of the most basic of human rights—the right to life. She was worried about her future, the future of her children, and her own inability to look after them. But depression also takes away all rational thought. No one wakes up one morning deciding to kill themselves. They wake up one morning feeling such darkness that it clouds all judgment. One can then only think of putting a stop to that pain.

My grandmother's life was hard. In those days, being a young widow was not easy. The lives of widows are marginally better now—in 2009, the Indian government began a widow pension plan—widowhood still has a stigma attached to it, especially in rural areas.[1] Many widows are still abandoned by their families in religious towns and have to resort to singing for hours in temples in return for some grains or a cooked meal. The rest beg on the streets to survive. In the few stories I have written on widows in Vrindavan and Nabadwip (near Kolkata), I found many of them to be from middle-class families. Contrary to popular belief, it's not just the poor who abandon their old, widowed mothers. Back in the day, my grandmother knew there was no easy way out of her situation apart from the one solution that she ultimately chose. One can understand why she had to choose suicide to escape the realities of her life, but what is unfathomable is that women are still dying by suicide in this country. Mental health still remains a poorly understood, taboo topic, and the country still lacks the infrastructure to support its mentally ill citizens.[2]

When I talk about therapists, I am always reminded of when I had a nervous breakdown in university in the UK and was sent for counselling. When I entered Dr Vaughn's room, I found a man of average build, with an unassuming appearance, waiting for me. 'I don't know why I am here,' I told him. 'I have nothing to tell you.'

'That's okay; we don't need to talk,' he told me. 'You can sit there and tell me about yourself instead. We have forty-five minutes to kill.'

That session ended with me crying so much that I used up his entire tissue box. He said I was a people-pleaser and I needed to put myself first. But how? No one had ever taught me to put myself first. My sessions with Dr Vaughn taught me how. That year when I came home during Christmas break, my mother hugged me at the airport and then immediately said, 'There's something very different about you this time.' There was. I felt very different to how I normally was—pleasing everyone who came my way, perpetually worried that I was inconveniencing someone or that I was in somebody's way. Apologizing my way through life. But the change that Dr Vaughn brought to my life didn't last, unfortunately. Once I returned to India and began working here, all the toxicity that I had managed to escape for a few years re-entered my life, all at once. But this time, there was no Dr Vaughn. Instead, there were a string of psychiatrists who judged me, berated me, or plain ignored me—and all of them pumped me full of medication.

My first psychiatrist—one of the topmost in the city—never

made eye contact with me. He wouldn't talk to me, neither would he encourage me to talk. After five minutes of disinterested shifting in his chair, he would just write out prescriptions.

'How are you feeling?' he asked on my second visit.

'Same.'

He increased my dosage.

On my third visit, he asked again:

'How are you feeling? Any suicidal thoughts?'

'I am feeling the same.'

He sent me home with another prescription and a nagging thought in my head.

'Is he not taking me seriously because I do not have suicidal thoughts? Am I a fake? Am I just attaching too much importance to myself thinking I need the help of a shrink?'

'I think I need some counselling,' I said desperately on my last visit a few days before I ended up in the hospital.

'Uh...huh! Let's see how you do on this medicine first.'

'I have been on these medicines a while. I do not want to get used to them.'

More scribbling. New medicines.

After I was released from the hospital, I went back to see him. He heard me out. He didn't even flinch. No eye contact, still. He scribbled some new medicines for another three months.

I balled up the prescription in my hand and threw it into the bin. Good talk. Thanks for nothing.

I am a privileged woman. I have access to the best doctors and medical treatments. I am educated and aware. I still could not get my psychiatrist to take me seriously and diagnose me empathetically and correctly. That is how I ended up in a screaming ambulance the first time.

My second psychiatrist, another top doctor, took great pride in telling me that I would be 'fixed' in three months. It was his guarantee, or I'd get my money back. For the next three months he told me how good he was, wrote out generous prescriptions, and then went AWOL when he realized that I asked too many questions and his three months were up.

My third psychiatrist, a gentle woman, was so enamoured with her husband, a fellow psychiatrist, that she kept referring me to him. She kept expounding family values to me, asking me to adjust, and gave ample lectures on women's lives in India and how compromise was key to a happy life. I could see she had no interest in me. I was just forty-five minutes, a prescription, and ₹1000 to her.

There's more than one reason why women are killing themselves in this country, one important reason being that no one listens to them. And everything flows from there. The silent screams have gone unheard for decades now. Is there no hope that someone would sit up and take note? That someone would say 'I hear you'.

According to a paper published in 2019, more Indian women suffered from depressive or anxiety disorders than men. Depression was the highest among women who were forty-five or older.[3] If we take a look at the intimate partner violence rampant in the country alongside the severe lack of institutional and familial support for women, a correlation between depression and domestic violence can be drawn.

India ranked as the most dangerous country for women in 2018,[4] ahead of conflict-torn countries such as Afghanistan and Syria, in a Thomson Reuters perception poll of the world's most dangerous countries for women. The ranking was based on its performance when it came to the risk of sexual violence and harassment against women, the danger women face from cultural, tribal, and traditional practices, and the danger of human trafficking including forced labour, sex slavery, and domestic servitude. The survey was severely criticized in India for not being broad-based enough, but it was also criticized for being part of a larger conspiracy to defame the country. This is just one more indication of how no one wants to accept and address how women truly live in this country.

As mentioned earlier, the NCRB has been tracking housewife suicides since 1995. That year 16,028 of them had died by suicide.[5] Next year, it had jumped to 19,490.[6] Since then, every year it has progressively increased. In 2020, over 50 per cent of the 44,000 women who died by suicide in India were housewives.[7] Most of these women were between eighteen and forty-five years of age and the overwhelming reasons for their suicide were identified as marriage-related issues (including dowry deaths) and infertility. Since 1995, housewife suicides have been consistently the highest, second only to daily wage earners.

Marriage is a complex and deeply unequal institution in India. The skewed relationship between a husband and wife in the marital institution is a continuation of the daily injustices we endure in a patriarchal society. Depression and suicides are the end points of a lifetime of struggle and coming to terms with the death of their dreams. The reasons can vary from educational and career aspirations to familial issues, but they are almost always personal.

However, just like intimate partner violence, women rarely talk about depression. 'It's almost like a physical defect. And women will not talk about it because it will affect their marriage; they will be branded as crazy,' says Ashish Pakhre, a psychiatrist. 'The myths and misconceptions around mental health in our country need to be addressed imminently.' Depression among middle-aged women can sometimes also be the result of bodily changes such as perimenopause. In 2016, a study had found that 31 per cent of women who were experiencing perimenopause had a depressive disorder, 7 per cent had anxiety, while 5 per cent suffered from depressive disorders alongside anxiety. The study had concluded that perimenopause was a vulnerable time in a woman's life and 'attention to signs and symptoms of depression may be required' so women could lead a more productive life.[8] Perimenopause usually starts around five or six years before menopause, which can start any time between forty-six and fifty years of age, which means most women start experiencing symptoms of perimenopause when they are in their mid to late thirties or early forties. 'There are many different symptoms of perimenopause and onset of depression is one among them,' Noida-based gynaecologist Vandana Sharma told me. 'And it must be managed to allow women to lead a healthy and productive life.' She continued, 'For women with pre-existing depressive disorders, [their depression] deepens during this time.'

'Often, it's very hard to distinguish the boundary that demarcates depressive incidents. It's not like fever or other physical ailments. When you feel sad for more than a few hours, when it becomes a constant part of your life and begins to affect your daily functioning, you should know it might not be normal sadness and you should seek medical help,' Pakhre says. 'But most women either do not seek help or they discontinue treatment after a while.'

Maybe this happens because living with this feeling of sadness is like second nature to most women; depression often doesn't stand out. Even if they tried to address it with doctors or counsellors, as I did, they would confront a big blank. The dots are all there, waiting to be connected. The connection between depression and perimenopause or menopause, the connection between overwork and depression—one's mental health is directly connected with the quality of their life and yet there has been scant interest in connecting these dots. When I asked my interviewees about these various dots, there wasn't much response either from the doctors or the women I interviewed. When I asked about the link between overwork and depression, there was even less response. The mental health specialists I spoke to never really addressed it, preferring to talk around the subject.

Considered a taboo subject for some time, mental health issues are now filtering into the public discourse. However, there still remains a lack of clarity when it comes to data. For example, the NCRB data only started tracking housewife suicides in 1995. According to the NCRB, most women die from 'marriage-related' problems, but what are these problems? Does the category of housewife include women who work informally (tailors, domestic workers, etc.)? Such surveys need to have more detailed frameworks—if the problem is not known, then how can it be addressed?

I have never really questioned the cloud of gloom that has hung over me for much of my life. Instead, I have tried to cope with it and handle it, to co-exist with it and remain functional. There is no scope for women to be anything but 'functional'. They must learn to co-exist with the most debilitating physical or mental conditions. I remember reporting on the rise of breast cancer among women in India many years ago and during that time a doctor had told me that women were reluctant to consult a doctor until the pain became unbearable or they couldn't function. By that time it was often too late.[9]

Globally, more women than men are depressed—an educated guess would suggest this is true in India as well.[10] The World Health Organization says more research is needed to understand why depression ails more women than men.[11] Yet, women rarely talk about their mental health. Anecdotal evidence and my discussions with mental health specialists overwhelmingly indicate that this may be due to a fear of being branded 'crazy' or 'psycho'. For women, admitting to a mental health condition carries the risk of being abandoned by their partners. In India, mental illness is grounds for divorce, a clause exploited by many. Section 13 of the Hindu Marriage Act clarifies that divorce can be sought if the spouse is 'incurably of unsound mind' or has been suffering from a mental disorder intermittently or continuously to such an extent that it makes it impossible to live with them. It also makes mental disorders a valid ground for nullifying a marriage. A 2015 study recommended an amendment to these legal provisions pointing out that they are misused and many mental disorders such as 'recurrent depression, dysthymia, conversion disorders, and obsessive-compulsive disorders are frequently made the ground for divorce'.[12] These provisions are not just archaic, the study says, because very few mental disorders are now incurable, but also deepen the stigma surrounding mental illness, especially for women who are hesitant to seek help, fearing abandonment by their husbands or families. The women I spoke to all admitted to depression or depressive incidents; some wanted to remain anonymous, some were tentative, some spoke freely, but no one denied that they grappled with persistent sadness. 'I can't think of a time when I was not depressed or suicidal,' Suchi, a psychology professor, told me. 'It's a part of who I am now.'

I have battled with depression all my life but I was only diagnosed when I was in my late thirties. I grew up with the hope that education was my pass to a better life but the reality was very different. The fight for a place at the table was never-ending. No matter how much I achieve, I still feel strangely diminished in both my personal and professional lives. As a professional, I am so replaceable, so dispensable. In my personal life, I am more fortunate. But despite that my days seem unending, my nights are anxious, and no matter how much help I have, I still end up doing a lot more than I can cope with owing to the feeling of self-imposed guilt that suggests I'm not doing enough. I do not feel like I am doing any of it well—neither as a worker, nor as a homemaker, which is what all middle-class women are, after all. They could be flying a plane in a combat zone or saving lives or running a multibillion-dollar company or working as a clerk, they could be married, once-married, never-married, but they will always be housewives. I hit forty, and I had enough.

At this point if I had received the help I sorely needed for my depression and my childhood trauma, I would have been able to see through the darkness. 'It's not you, it's the depression,' my current, exceptionally empathetic psychiatrist told me during a session. 'When it takes over you, it's just a veil of darkness and you can't see clearly. It is at this time that you must reach out for help.' Identify someone who will help you when the darkness takes over, and reach out to them when the darkness falls. Believe me when I say that it is possible to dispel it.

My mother still doesn't know of my suicide attempt, which is just as well because until very recently I didn't know that my maternal grandmother had died by suicide. My mother kept it a secret from all of us, including my father. She never spoke about it because it was such a taboo topic for her; I only found out after years of probing. 'No one would understand,' she told me when I asked her why she kept this secret for so many years. 'I never talked about it, and slowly it was easier to pretend that it didn't happen.' The reason I have never told my mother about my suicide attempt is because I wanted her continue to believe that her struggles meant something, that what she did and suffered through changed the world for me. I honoured her lies because they came from a place of love and immense hope. But when has love and hope ever been enough to change the world?

THE FATHER WHO FORGOT TO PICK UP HIS DAUGHTER FROM SCHOOL

The poverty of being unwanted, unloved, and uncared for is the greatest poverty.

—Mother Teresa

Suchi was five years old. She patiently waited in her private tutor's living room that day for hours, with a slice of cake in her hand. Her father had forgotten to pick her up again. But she was used to this. She waited three hours every day for him to pick her up from school. Her father was a top doctor in the city of Kolkata, a busy man. He would pick her up only when it suited his schedule. So, she learnt to be patient. She learnt to wait and she learnt that she was not a priority. She learnt to adjust her expectations.

'My mother got married when she was nineteen. She lived in a joint family. My parents had two children and one of them was a son so they didn't want another child, but then I came along. I heard very often how I was an accident,' Suchi told me. Her young heart had interpreted it as being unwanted. Her parents hadn't needed another child after her mother had produced the male heir who would carry forward her dad's medical practice and the family name.

'I never had much of a relationship with my mother. My aunt looked after me. I forever hankered for their love, and it stayed with me throughout my life, making me the person I became, insecure, unsure, lonely.'

And always second best to her brother, for whom her father built an entire library of encyclopaedias and reference books so he could focus on becoming a doctor. No such elaborate futures were planned for the daughters.

Son preference or son 'meta' preference had led to the birth of 21 million 'unwanted' girls in India until the year 2017,[1] because Indian couples keep having children until they have a son. 'Families where a son is born are more likely to stop having children than families where a girl is born. This is suggestive of parents employing "stopping rules"—having children till a son is born and stopping thereafter.'[2] Girls are not people you grow attached to or invest in because they will ultimately marry and go to another's home. Boys, on the other hand, will stay with their parents and look after them in their old age—this is what most middle-class Indian parents believe and expect. At a practical level, parents also devote fewer resources to the development of their daughters (education and nutritious food). This means that if out of three siblings only two can go to school, the boys will go. This inherent belief is hard to shake because for Indian parents, children are investments for their future. Sons get the most support because the return on the investment is higher. Indian society as a whole must reflect on the reasons for son preference because 'it is a long-standing historical challenge, all stakeholders—civil society, communities, households—are collectively responsible for its existence and for its resolution'.[3]

While five-year-old Suchi was waiting alone at her teacher's house somewhere in eastern India, a young woman in her early twenties in Uttar Pradesh—an undeniably patriarchal part of the country—was already waging a full-on battle. Anima* had vowed to own the future her father had planned for her brothers. 'I wanted to do everything my brothers were doing or were expected to do,' Anima says. 'My father was keen for my brothers to study engineering but not for me—a girl—to do a professional course,' she told me.

He didn't change his mind even when Anima topped her district in science and mathematics, so she filled out an engineering admission form to study chemical engineering at the Punjab University on the sly. She was accepted into the course, but her father refused her permission to enrol. Anima was distraught and began fasting in protest. When she wouldn't relent, her father gave in. 'He took me to the college for all the formalities then brought me back and didn't allow me to go back for a month.'

She was allowed to go back only after her brother-in-law, at the

---

*Name changed to protect identity.

behest of her elder sister, intervened. 'He was a patriarchal man; he couldn't say no to his son-in-law.'

Anima is fifty-six, Suchi is forty-six, but Shiuli Vanaja is only in her early thirties. Vanaja—who is an economist—and her brother Iqbal Abhimanyu grew up in a progressive household. Their parents were social and political activists and there were continuous discussions in their household about various inequalities, including gender inequalities. But when they visited Vanaja's grandparents, they had to readjust their lenses.

'Our parents were activists and we didn't have a lot of money and we never went to fancy schools or camps with swimming and horse riding. My grandfather had wanted to send my brother to one such camp but my mother opposed it. She said you either send both the children, or none. Ultimately, nobody went,' the thirty-two-year-old remembers, adding, 'It's not like they don't love me. But it's just that sometimes you could just see the subtle preference for the male grandchild.' They are subtle acts, but they leave an indelible mark, which is why we remember them so vividly.

I clearly remember the day when my father had taken my sister and me out for a stroll and we met an acquaintance of his. My father introduced us to him. It was probably the look of pity on the acquaintance's face, the unsaid exclamation—*What a disaster! Two daughters!*—that prompted my father to say, 'They are like my sons.' He did the best he could but even so he unconsciously killed a little light in me. He always called me his son—I didn't want to be like a son. I wanted to be the daughter I was. It was a stark portent of what I would be fighting against throughout my life. 'One of the women in our communities shared a story that when you do something really impressive, like doing well in school or something, and parents would use the phrase "you are like a son to me". What was more interesting is that when the woman shared that story, it really resonated in the group. And I was so struck by that because we know biases start young, but to hear from your parents when you do something amazing that you are a son to them, it was a very interesting marker from a cultural standpoint as to how rigid gender roles were here,' Rachel Thomas, co-founder of the Lean In organization with Facebook COO

Sheryl Sandberg, told me. The Lean In organization runs circles in 174 countries across the world, including around 890 in India. These circles are support groups for working women and women who want to get back to work after having children. The stories in these circles had introduced Thomas to the startling gender biases in India.

But there are other kinds of biases in India, too. Biases of height, weight, complexion—too tall, too short, overweight, underweight, dark complexioned—affect a woman's prospects in life. A friend in college was married off when she was only nineteen because she was 'too tall' and her parents were anxious they wouldn't be able to find a suitable groom for her when she was older. She was a good student with a great academic future. She wanted to be a university professor. But for her family—upper caste, upper middle class, wealthy, and highly educated professionals—her future would begin and end with a good marriage. She did manage to continue her education after her marriage, but every time I met her or spoke to her after her marriage, I found her distracted and sometimes listless. The girl who had wanted to become a professor of English literature, ended up teaching in a private school. When I met her after many years, she told me, 'Teaching in a school suits me. It allows me to look after the home and my children.' By then she had two daughters.

Teaching, especially in private schools, is a popular profession among women in India because it seemingly does not place high demands on their time (events, late nights, night shifts) and allows them to balance home and work effectively. It is often equated with being a feminine job, a job that requires caring for children and, hence, something that many career-minded young women are nudged towards by their families. Additionally, it is not a high-growth job in this country and often does not require one to be highly skilled. While government schools do require applicants to have certain qualifications and to give entrance tests, low to mid-level private schools often circumvent such requirements. A 2018 study by the Azim Premji Foundation found that private schoolteachers had low academic qualifications, and scant or no professional training and experience as educators.[4] Interestingly, in public schools, where 90 per cent of the teachers were graduates,

98 per cent were professionally qualified and had taught over 160 months on average, most of the teachers were men. It should be noted that government school jobs are more secure and come with varied benefits as well as job security whereas private schools (as I have seen among my friends who are teachers) pay a much lower salary with less job security and longer working hours. Female teachers mostly taught in private schools where 76 per cent of the teachers were graduates, and 64 per cent were professionally qualified. In these schools, the average experience of teachers was seventy-four months.

But while teaching allows women more stable hours, it also kills any other ambitions they might have. Divya* was moving up in the corporate world when she had to hit pause to prioritize her two young boys and her husband's various job postings. When she stopped, she was working at a multinational company and earning more than her husband. She had deliberated staying behind in Delhi to keep her job but then she gave in to pressure from friends, neighbours, and family—how could she separate the family? She freelanced for a while before giving it up all together. When she eventually returned to full-time employment owing to an unforeseen misfortune, the only job available to her was that of a teacher. It was the only job that gave her the time to balance all her housework and caregiving duties with her professional commitments. She compromised, she adjusted, she reinvented herself. That's what women do constantly. She had learnt early on that true happiness was a mirage, that we have to work with what we have. And that's exactly what she did.

Overwork—or unpaid labour, if you prefer—is something every girl grows up negotiating right from her childhood. The constant devaluation of their capabilities and the constant over-evaluation of men's abilities manifests itself in all gender-related social ills in our country. The thinking that women and girls are only good for reproductive labour means that many are pushed into becoming wives and mothers before the time is right, before their bodies and minds have completed the transition into adulthood.

---

*Name changed.

6

WHEN THE KITCHEN REPLACES THE CLASSROOM

Let girls be girls, not brides.

—Ban Ki-Moon

In August 2006, I travelled to a village in West Bengal after receiving word that a public trial of parents was being held by child-brides, arranged by a local non-profit.* What I remember most from that afternoon are the faces of those child-women. Girls who were forced to turn into women too soon, much before they were ready. Girls who became wives and mothers while their bodies still needed nurturing care. Girls turned into childminders, domestic workers, and caregivers when they should have been running around in fields, playing hopscotch with their friends, their plaits flying in the air. Instead, they were condemned to a life of working in the fields and at home, pleasing their—often much older—husbands, and being abused or killed, or killing themselves when their bodies failed them.

On that day, the proceedings had centred around the death of a sixteen-year-old child-bride named Karabi Gharami, who had been studying in the fifth standard when she was married off. After her marriage, her life followed the same path as that of other child-brides. She was dumped with all the household responsibilities and caregiving duties. She was often beaten by her mother-in-law or her husband, sometimes by both, when she failed to work or cook according to their specifications. According to the testimonies at the hearing, the husband never spoke to Karabi. The only way he would interact with her would be to beat her for a shortcoming, whether imagined or real,

---

*The story I wrote after my visit can be found at www.boloji.com/articles/4841/tales-child-brides-tell.

often based on a complaint by his mother. She cooked fresh food for the family every day, but ate stale or leftover food herself. Soon, the young girl fell ill, unable to withstand the work and the torture. But an ill and inactive Karabi was of no use to her in-laws and so she was sent back to her parents' home. After a while, following negotiations between the two families, she was taken back to her husband's home. The very next day she was found dead. Her in-laws said she was mentally unstable and had committed suicide. Her parents alleged murder. Given the situation, both were possibilities.

That day I heard many, too many, similarly heartbreaking stories of child-brides like Karabi. There was Ameena, who was married off when she was only thirteen. There was Purnima, married at the age of fourteen, and Tumpa Halder who was married off at fifteen. These girls were put to work at home and in the agricultural fields soon after marriage. They all fell pregnant within a year and gave birth to three or four children even before reaching the legal age of marriage. Frequent childbirths at such tender ages had also broken them physically and mentally and left them with diseases that slowed down their productivity. Young Rupa Mondal went temporarily blind after the birth of her son. 'I break into a sweat throughout the day, and if I hurt myself or there is some tension, my head hurts so much that I feel like I am going mad,' she had told me at that time. Halder, who gave birth when she was fourteen years old, suffered from jaundice which affected her liver after the delivery. She was living on pills.

But broken girls and women are of no use, and so they must be returned to their parents. For the parents, this was a problem—the daughter they had thought to be a burden, and of whom they had rid themselves, was back in their homes, sometimes with the added burden of granddaughters.

'If I was a bit older when I was married, I could have coped with things better. But I just didn't know what was happening to me and how I was supposed to react. My husband often tried to strangle me and killed our six-month-old child in a rage,' Sujata, a child-bride at the public trial, had testified. Her mother told the judge they had married her off early because they could not to feed another mouth and also because 'the earlier we can marry them off the less dowry we have to pay'.

As the judges listened to the child-brides and made notes, and I scribbled in my notebook, suddenly there was a ruckus from among the audience. A man was trying to approach the bench, shaking his fist and shouting.

'My daughter has been staying with me for the last five years. I want compensation for that,' he shouted.

'Why did you marry her off so early?' one of the judges asked him.

'I had no other choice. There's no point in feeling sorry now. What's done is done. Now I want back all the dowry and maintenance to keep feeding her.'

His daughter, Torijaan, who sat nearby with downcast eyes, looked up for a moment, eyes filled with shame and despair. She looked like she wanted to disappear from the face of the earth. She was shrinking into the folds of her old and tattered sari, as though trying to become invisible.

A social worker at the hearing had explained to me how the villagers cannot afford to keep their daughters at home for more than just economic reasons. 'Girls in villages are not safe. If someone holds a girl's hand after 6 p.m. even by accident, her life is ruined forever. That is why they marry [off] their daughters as soon as they reach puberty.'

The thing that bothered me the most at the hearing were the girls and their total lack of interest in what was happening around them. It was like they were watching someone else's story. Now when I think back, they were indeed watching someone else's story unfold. In a rightful world they would be in school studying, they would be sneaking out with their friends, they would be gossiping, singing, laughing without a care in the world. But instead, here they were, their eyes large in their gaunt faces, their thin, malnourished bodies a reminder of how we have constantly failed our girls. Those child-women personified the unfinished story of Indian women for me.

This was in 2006. So, why am I talking about something that happened almost two decades ago? Surely things have changed since then? But it seems a decade is not long enough when it comes to improving the condition of women.

India still has the highest number of child-brides in the world.[1] Using census data from 2011, the NCPCR estimated that 27 per cent of girls in India are married before their eighteenth birthday. The rates of child marriage vary between states and can be as high as 69 per cent in Bihar and 65 per cent in Rajasthan.[2] In 2019, there were reports of child marriages being held in the Rajgarh district of Madhya Pradesh, on the occasion of Akshaya Tritiya, an annual springtime festival celebrated by Hindus and Jains.[3] Across India, young women and girls continue to be treated as economic burdens to be passed around between fathers and husbands and sons. They are still considered the property of male relatives and hence their destinies are controlled by them.

Marrying girls off early does not just mean saving on dowry. It is also aimed at subjugating their sexuality, to prevent them from having love affairs or marrying of their own choice, thereby bringing dishonour to the family. The National Plan of Action for Children (2005) had aimed to eliminate child marriages by 2010.[4] Twelve years later, the National Family Health Survey (2019–2021) estimates show women are still being married off before they turn eighteen, and there are still girls between the ages fifteen to nineteen who are mothers or pregnant.[5]

In 2015, Indian photojournalist Saumya Khandelwal had come across reports of an unusually high number of child marriages in Shravasti, around 200 kilometres from Lucknow, the capital of Uttar Pradesh. The state has over two million child-brides and Shravasti, according to media reports, was a hub of these early marriages. The reports had also pointed out that on average, a girl in the district gave birth to five or six children in her lifetime.

'I was intrigued by the reports because although there have been reports of child marriages from Bengal and Rajasthan and some other states, this area had never really come up as a hotspot,' she told me.

Towards the end of 2015, Khandelwal visited the village to check it out for herself; her iconic work on the child-brides of Shravasti was born out of this visit.[6] In 2017, she went back to the village to shoot the marriage of fourteen-year-old Aarti. Her marriage was fixed to Rajkumar, who was then in the first year of college, and her parents pulled her out of school. 'I asked her how she felt about her marriage and all she had to say was that what's there to feel, this happens to everyone. I am no different,' Khandelwal remembered.

During her interaction with the child-brides of Shravasti, Khandelwal was surprised at how much they were schooled to be housewives right from their childhood. 'There are no options for them. Marriage is such an integral part of their lives that they don't think beyond it. If you ask them, what do you want to do in your life, most times they wouldn't have an answer. If you push them further, they would say they want to be a teacher. Anything beyond that would be an anganwadi worker. Only one girl so far had told me she wanted to become a cop.'

So, while Aarti missed going to school, she also accepted that as a normal path for her life to take.

After the wedding, Aarti went back to living with her parents. In these parts, young brides begin their married life after a gap of around a year. 'This year is almost like a preschool of housework,' Khandelwal says, adding that now that Aarti was not going to school, she was in charge of every household duty in her parents' home. 'Right after her marriage Aarti could single-handedly cook all the meals, wash all utensils and clothes, and feed the cattle. She already helped her mother with housework, but now she was doing it full-time.' Aarti's family was not poor—her father was a former village council head and apart from owning land they also owned shops in the local market. Her husband Rajkumar finished his college education and began to teach in a school. His father and mother were also teachers. They were middle-class people.

A year later, following the gauna ceremony, a ritual associated with the consummation of marriage, Aarti left for her husband's home. It was late evening when Aarti reached her new home. Khandelwal had travelled with her too, documenting her journey to her in-laws' home. For the first night she slept in a separate room but was up at the crack of dawn, to have a bath and cook halwa—something that new brides in many Indian homes have to do. It is their official initiation into the kitchen of their new home, where they will cook for their new family. From that morning onwards, all chores from cooking to cleaning to caregiving were transferred to her from her mother-in-law. 'She doesn't help me at all,' Aarti had once complained to Khandelwal over the phone. 'But at least she doesn't grudge me any meals.' The husband was okay—he was not aggressive. Aarti was counting her blessings. There were families where they starved their daughters-in-law. And the husbands beat them.

Aarti's life followed the expected course. By sixteen, she was expecting her first child and before she turned seventeen, she had her first miscarriage. 'After the miscarriage, she became dull and quiet,' Khandelwal remembers. She complained of weakness. She was still waking up at 4 a.m. to take care of the household and its members. And then Khandelwal could not reach Aarti for months. When she finally managed to, in early 2020, Aarti was dead. The circumstances surrounding her death have remained shrouded in mystery. Her in-laws say she killed herself because of a quarrel over an expensive sari she wanted to buy. Her parents said they spoke to her a few hours before she allegedly committed suicide. They had wanted to pick her up to bring her home for a visit but she had declined. In the evening, they got a call from her in-laws informing them of her death. The deaths of Karabi and Aarti are separated by fourteen years, and yet the circumstances of their lives and deaths are uncomfortably similar.

Aarti's parents, like Karabi's, had suspected foul play but they didn't want to pursue the case or make a police complaint because their elder daughter—Aarti's sister—is married into the same family. The two sisters were married following a popular practice in many areas in India (and across South Asia), known as atta-satta, where parents simultaneously marry off their children to siblings. The rationale is to bind the two families together in such a way that if one of the girls is being abused, the parents will more often than not keep quiet for the sake of the other girl. If it's a brother and sister combination, it is expected to reduce domestic violence because of the fear of retaliation by the other side. Either way, the practice dehumanizes girls and women and strips them of autonomy over their own lives. The United Nations Population Fund (UNFPA) had documented the stories of such child-brides in 2015.

'I was sixteen and never missed a day of school. I liked studying so much, I would much rather spend time with my books than watch TV! I dreamt of going to college and then getting a good job so that I could take my parents away from the dingy house we lived in. Then one day, I was told that I had to leave it all, as my parents bartered me for a girl my elder brother was to marry. Such exchange marriages are called atta-satta in my community. I was sad and angry. I pleaded with my mother, but my father had made up his mind. My only hope was that my husband would let me complete my studies. But he got me pregnant even before I turned seventeen. Since then, I have hardly ever been allowed to step out of the house. Everyone goes out shopping and for movies and neighbourhood functions, but not me. Sometimes, when the others are not at home, I read my old school books, and hold my baby and cry. She is such an adorable little girl, but I am blamed for not having a son. But things are gradually changing. Hopefully, customs like atta-satta and child marriage will be totally gone by the time my daughter grows up, and she will get to complete her education and marry only when she wants to.'[7]

India has committed to eliminate child, early, and forced marriage by 2030, in line with target 5.3 of the SDGs outlined by the United Nations, which had replaced the Millennium Development Goals (MDGs).[8] However, the government did not present a progress report at the voluntary national review at the high level political forum in 2017. During that year's universal periodic review, India agreed to consider recommendations to improve enforcement of legal provisions against child marriage. In 2014, the CEDAW committee had said high rates of school dropouts among young girls in India made them vulnerable to child marriages.

According to an ActionAid report from 2016, nearly 103 million Indians, living as on 1 March 2011, had been married as minors; of this 85.2 million were girls.[9] Girl child marriages account for 30.2 per cent of the currently married female population of the country and the elimination of this alone could increase the number of literate women in the country by 5 per cent (or 27 million).[10] The World Economic Forum estimates that child marriages cost economies at least 1.7 per cent of their GDP.[11] In 2018, the first study on the economic costs of child marriages by the World Bank and International Centre for Research on Women (ICRW) looked at twenty-five countries where child marriages were prevalent and found that by eliminating the practice India could achieve over $10 billion in budget savings by 2030.[12]

The elimination of girl child marriages can avoid 27,000 neonatal deaths, 55,000 infant deaths, and 160,000 child deaths[13] and positively impact women's overall reproductive health. Nearly 16 per cent of adolescent girls between the ages of fifteen and nineteen are currently married in our country, so it is not a minor problem (excuse the unintended pun). But elimination of child marriages will only be possible when we eliminate the dowry system. For middle-class parents, marriage is often the be-all and end-all of a daughter's existence. This insistence on marriage means parents often use more energy looking for a groom and saving for dowry than seriously investing in their daughter's education or empowerment. When marriage is the aim, educational qualifications pale in front of domestic goddess credentials. When girls have their education paused, or when they attend schools and colleges with the knowledge that they will probably never get to use their degrees, that's when this cycle of inequalities begins. Our dreams die a thousand deaths throughout our lives but inside our homes is where it all begins.

Child marriage is a scourge not just of the poor or the rural middle classes—it is a scourge of all poor and middle-class homes across the country. Underage women are married off across the country and across social groups, including in urban areas. In 2017, media reports had cited census data that showed that child marriages were rising in cities.[14] In 2020, Child Relief and You (CRY) found in a report that between 2001–2011, while child marriages in rural areas decreased by a marginal 4 per cent, urban areas in India clocked a 41 per cent increase.[15]

During the pandemic, there was an overwhelming increase in child marriages (as well as domestic violence). In any situation of distress or conflict, it is the girls and women who are the most vulnerable. The World Bank–ICRW study on the economic costs of child marriages had found that the main reason girls were married off early in India was because families found more benefits in their reproductive labour than productive labour.[16] They preferred to push them into housework and caregiving, perceived to be the primary focus for women after marriage, than to study for jobs that do not exist or in which married women cannot invest their time. It's a vicious cycle that's devouring the future of girls which in turn makes it hard to empower women. To empower women, one has to convince their families to keep them in schools, to allow them to finish their education, and aspire for a career. The government has to create opportunities for women and girls, and not just in the low-paying, exploitative, informal sector. They also have to make care provisions to recognize, reduce, and redistribute women's unpaid care burden.[17] But the most important task must begin at home—parents must unlearn their biases and reimagine their daughters' futures beyond marriage.

In India, men are pressured to marry, too. But women are pressured, in myriad ways, to marry at the 'right age', an age wholly dependent on the whims of their parents and the dictates of society. This pressure affects most Indian women—as of 2019, the country had less than 1 per cent of women between the ages of forty-five and forty-nine who had never been married. In comparison, the world average stood at 4.3 per cent. In the US, this figure was 10.8 per cent.[18]

చ

'Let me show you something,' my friend's mother said to me. We were in twelfth standard and often stopped at her house for lunch. She took me to her bedroom where she lifted the bed frame to reveal a storage space crammed full. There were beautiful saris, cloth material, furnishings, crockery and cutlery, a variety of knick-knacks, even a toothpaste holder. It was a treasure chest.

'I have been collecting these things for the last eighteen years. I also get one piece of gold jewellery made every month. It's all for her wedding trousseau. We are middle-class people, no? We can only afford to build this up bit by bit.'

My friend was just eighteen and her mother had been preparing for her wedding ever since she was born!

A majority of Indian marriages are arranged by parents where family status—class and caste—is compared, but little attention is paid to emotional compatibility. This, more often than not, makes these marriages toxic and repositories of all kinds of social ills.

Avoiding an arranged marriage or even a semi-arranged marriage (where the couple is introduced by the parents and 'allowed' to date before getting married) in India is a herculean task. Yet, many educated young women from middle-class families are now questioning this practice. The younger generation of women is more vocal, more connected to global realities, and less likely to go along with their parents' wishes. However, the irony is that for most Indian women, even the ability to rebel is a privilege.

The idea of marriage as the be-all and end-all for women even among progressive people is our biggest challenge, and this challenge lies behind the closed doors of our homes.

ARRANGED AND APPROVED

As a woman, I have no country. As a woman, I want no country. As a woman,
my country is the whole world.

—Virginia Woolf

In 2011, I lived in a rented house in Noida. One night, there was furious knocking on my door. I rubbed the sleep from my eyes and hobbled to the door. A woman was standing there—I didn't know her. She looked scared and confused.

'Please come...he is going to kill us all.'

I ran after her, disoriented, to their house, at the other end of the floor, expecting murderers, robbers, rapists. I found a scene of utter chaos. I could see a woman crying, a man shouting, and an elderly couple looking anxious. I pieced the story together as I dialled the police. The shouting man and the woman who came to my door were my neighbours; the elderly couple were her parents—the woman had called them when her husband had started roughing her up to sign divorce papers.

My neighbour was a school dropout but a successful businessman. His wife held a business degree but did not get much use out of it. Her father met all their demands for dowry—the girl was 'overweight'—and gifted his son-in-law a luxury car and an expensive honeymoon abroad. He even fulfilled the man's periodic demands for cash. But alas! He couldn't arrange for a male heir. The day after she gave birth to their third daughter, she was served a divorce notice from her husband. His mother wanted a male heir, no matter what. So strong was her desire for a grandson and dislike for her three granddaughters that she had started calling her third granddaughter 'faltu', useless.

That night, the police came and advised them to settle it between themselves. My neighbour's wife was sent back to her parents with her three daughters and he got married again. All for a son.

When I think of this incident, I think of how arranged marriages continue to perpetuate the practice of dowry, son preference, and domestic abuse.

∽

In the last two decades, I have rarely come across a marriage which did not involve the exchange of high-value gifts or cash. Contradictory to the commonly-held belief that dowry is only prevalent in rural areas or among poorer communities, it very much remains an all-India scourge. The system of dowry, now practised clandestinely, forms a large part of arranged marriages and is the bedrock of the transactional nature of such marriages. This ultimately leads to the understanding that when a woman gets married there are certain things she needs to provide to her family in return for maintaining her status as 'wife'—at the top of the list is producing male heirs.

The late Mitu Khurana, a Delhi-based doctor and anti-foeticide activist, had taken India by storm when she had sued her husband and a hospital alleging that they had pressured her to abort her twin daughters; this was the first case of its kind in the country. My last conversation with her was in October 2018, when she had been unwell and we had promised to catch up once she was well enough to talk. 'I have fractures in both my hands,' she had written to me in an email. 'It's painful to write but let's talk soon.' However, she passed away before we could have that conversation.

Mitu's decade-long fight for justice is possibly one of the most well-known dowry cases in India.[1] Her struggle exposed the hypocrisy of the educated middle classes. It had lifted the veil of secrecy from son preference, the menace of dowry, and resulting domestic abuse, all intrinsically connected. It had also exposed how the system is stacked against a woman seeking justice as well as the patriarchy inherent in our justice system.

Mitu was born and brought up in Delhi. Her parents found her a match through a newspaper matrimonial—a well-established surgeon. Her mother-in-law was a retired school headmistress. She felt fortunate to be marrying into such a progressive, forward-looking family. The nightmare started soon after her marriage, as demands for dowry kept escalating. She also alleged that her in-laws pressured her to determine the sex of her twins when she was pregnant and later pressured her to abort her daughters. But Mitu gave birth to her daughters and stayed with her parents, who were supportive. Throughout her ordeal, Mitu said what shocked her the most was the apathy of the institutions from whom she sought justice. Every official she met advised her to settle with her husband, she had told me. 'The police, the judiciary...they all feel the law is for woman victims who are dead—not for survivors. If a woman has survived, she was misusing the law. So, they felt I was misusing the law.

'The mindset from top to bottom is that a woman's place is in her husband's house with her husband and if she is trying to step out of an abusive marriage or she is trying to do anything of the sort that I am doing then she is basically misusing the law.

'My parents encouraged me to study and be a professional woman. But today I realize education is no safeguard for women in this country. I am a doctor and if this can happen to me, what hope is there really? Our homes will have to change and that's what I am fighting for. But during my fight I have realized that I am not just fighting against my husband or in-laws but the whole system.'

∽

Around twenty-one women die in India every day owing to dowry harassment. They are either murdered or compelled to kill themselves. According to the latest NCRB report, there were 6,966 dowry deaths registered in 2020, while over 10,366 cases* were registered under the anti-dowry law.[2] While the numbers have come down from 2019 when 7,141 deaths and 13,307 cases were registered, this drop is not significant because under-reporting of crimes against

---

*In 1983, Sections 304B and 498A of the Indian Penal Code (IPC) were enacted to allow women to seek redressal for harassment by the husband's family. Section 304B relates to deaths within seven years of marriage as a result of dowry demands, by the husband or his family.

women in our country is a major issue.[3] Families and women rarely report atrocities, hoping to sort it through family mediations, fearing a that a scandal would destroy their family honour.

The NCRB's 2020 figures show that the conviction rate for dowry deaths was just 37.3 per cent, while the conviction rate in cases of cruelty by husbands/in-laws was a mere 13.5 per cent. Nationwide, around 93 per cent of the accused in dowry deaths are charged, but only about 34 per cent result in convictions. There were around 27 million pending cases.[4]

This is not for want of an Act though. The Dowry Prohibition Act outlawed the practice in 1961 with a penalty of five years, jail time and either a fine of ₹15,000 or the value of the dowry given, whichever is more. Section 498A of the IPC, known as the anti-dowry law, prohibits cruelty by the husband or his relatives towards a woman that might emotionally and physically harm her or push her to take her own life. This amendment had allowed for the immediate arrest and jailing of the husband and her relatives. But can any law dig out a practice that has such deep roots in our culture?

The practice of dowry is not a simple problem. As noted in the UN Women's report on the progress of women, 'Dowry remains widespread in Southern Asia despite longstanding feminist campaigns and legislation prohibiting the practice in, for example, both Bangladesh and India. Dowry practices can fuel violence against women when the bride's family fails to pay the dowry in full or the gifts are deemed unsatisfactory.'[5] The birth of a girl in a family sets her parents on a path where their final goal is to have enough dowry to marry off their child.

There is an irrefutable link between the dowry system, child marriages, and domestic violence. Poor and middle-class parents prefer to marry off their girls young because the older they are, the higher the dowry amount will be. According to a study by the International Center for Research on Women (ICRW), child-brides are often more likely to experience intimate partner violence and domestic violence and 'are also more likely to believe that a man is justified in beating his wife'. The study was carried out among girls in Bihar and Jharkhand and found girls who married early were also 'three times as likely to report being forced to have sex without their consent in the previous six months'.[6]

For a country that loves the institution of marriage as much as ours does, we haven't done much to reform or democratize it. Marriages have come to mean greater oppression, more unpaid labour, and less agency for a large majority of women in our country. Arranged marriages have added the extra burden of dowry and domestic abuse of all forms. Yet, despite the ills that it brings in its wake, a majority of people in our country still prefer arranged marriages. In 2009, a working paper with the Nobel Prize-winning economist Abhijit Banerjee as one of the authors was presented at a seminar. It examined the role played by caste, education, and other social and economic attributes in arranged marriages among middle-class Indians. They interviewed a random sample of 783 individuals who placed matrimonial ads in a major Bengali newspaper with a circulation of 1.2 million at the time. The authors found that most people who placed the ads were educated, relatively well-off, urban middle-class parents. A majority of the children they were advertising for had a college degree. While the sample group was niche and did not represent preferences of the representative Indian, it was a population with a 'reputation to be more liberal than average; the preference for respecting caste rules we see within this group is thus probably a lower bound for what we would find in the general population'.[7] The most interesting result the authors found was that the preference for finding a mate within one's own caste was so strong that parents were willing to 'trade off the difference between no education and a master's degree to avoid marrying outside their caste'.[8]

They found a 'relatively frictionless marriage market'[9] due to the strong preference for within-caste marriage by both sides. This lack of friction and unanimous acceptance of marrying within the same caste is what has allowed 'caste to remain a persistent feature of the Indian marriage market'.[10] The study also found that economic growth by itself was not enough to 'undermine caste-based preferences in marriage', and that 'caste-based preferences in marriage are unlikely to be a major constraint on growth'.[11]

The authors of the paper finally arrived at a hopeful conclusion. According to them, 30 per cent of people in their sample did not marry within their caste and since there was nothing to be gained from marrying out of caste, it means they were marrying for love. 'About 40 per cent of the sons and daughters of our respondents eventually marry through a channel other than the ads, and 20 per cent enter into a "love marriage". So, the institution that economic forces are not able to destroy may be endangered by love.'[12]

While that is something to ponder, I do wonder if 'love marriages' in India are always only about love?

A classic example of this would be a former young neighbour in Kolkata. Hers was a love marriage. She grew up in the same neighbourhood as her husband and the two were childhood sweethearts. Her husband did not continue with his education, although my neighbour completed her master's degree. When the two were married, she came to live with her husband and his parents. The family appeared progressive on the surface and there was no cause for me to think otherwise. Over the months, I grew closer to the young woman, who was so glad to have a sympathetic, non-judgmental ear that she would tell me all her troubles. 'Do you know my mother-in-law doesn't allow us to close the door to our bedroom in the night?' she had once told me, to my utter shock and surprise. 'If she found the door closed, she would beat down the door. There have been times when she has plonked herself on our bed so we wouldn't sleep together.' Her husband was nice enough but had no say in the household and definitely no say against his parents. His wife cooked and cleaned and worked from dawn to dusk catering to all their needs. She never mentioned any physical abuse, but the mental abuse and lack of support from her husband broke her. What I remember to this day is the impassivity with which she had just accepted her life as it was. 'I can't tell my parents any of this,' she had once told me. 'This marriage was my choice; I can't expect them to support me.' Many women have told me they prefer arranged marriages to love marriages because, in the former, the failure of the marriage can be blamed on the parents. When you have a love marriage and it fails, you are alone. Having gone against tradition, you can no longer demand support from your parents or from society at large. This means that even when people marry the person of their choice, emotional and social conditioning ensures that they opt for socially acceptable partners (same caste/same class/same religion).

Why is it that despite being a multicultural society, only 5.8 per cent of Indian marriages are inter-caste? During the India Human Development Survey-II (IHDS), 2011–12, around 73 per cent had said their marriages were arranged; of those who had chosen their partners, 34 per cent still only met their future spouse for the first time on their wedding day.[13]

Many have researched the apparent success of arranged marriages in India. Many have also hailed the success of the institution itself. But in a country that is deeply polarized along lines of caste, class, and religion, love marriages can sometimes turn lethal—in 2020, a study on honour killings in India and Pakistan found that out of the 100 people killed in India, seventy-nine of the victims were women.[14]

There is a subtle connection between arranged marriages and honour killings. At the bottom of both lies a clan mentality that has decided that women carry the community's honour in their bodies and must be controlled by their male guardians. When their sexual behaviour or public acts deviate from the strictures of the community, honour must be restored by 'destroying the body of the woman who caused the dishonour'.[15] Ultimately, it comes down to just one thing— women have no right to their own bodies or control over their own lives and, sometimes, even their deaths.

WHY WOMEN STAY IN BAD MARRIAGES

I think about it and yet I know
I'll never be able to leave this cage
Even if the warden should let me go
I've lost the strength to fly away

—Forough Farrokhzad

The feeling of being unwanted and unloved is the biggest of all burdens. Being unwanted leaves you with a debilitating sense of loneliness and 'can then feed into a pattern of being an outsider in adulthood'.[1] If the family you are born into makes you feel unwanted, you grow up believing that you will be unwanted your whole life. Then, you diminish yourself—you measure your words or self-censor, you feel compelled to make every moment of your existence productive to make it count, you work hard to be more likeable and, loveable. Then when a semblance of something akin to love or respect comes your way—you are hooked. This is how most women end up in bad marriages and this is why they stay.

'I have never felt good enough. When I met my husband, suddenly I was important to someone, someone cared about me. It brought me so much confidence. My grades in college improved. I cleared competitive exams with flying colours. For the first time, I began to like myself. For the first time I didn't stand in front of the mirror and cry. I knew he was aggressive by nature but the fact that he liked me for what I am and that he gave me attention was like a feel-good drug that I couldn't let go of. I was in absolute denial about the red flags in his personality because my need to be appreciated was so much stronger,' Suchi told me.

'And then he went against his family to marry me, I was so grateful that he chose me over his family.'

She was so grateful that she normalized his abusive behaviour, which began right after they got married. Suchi now teaches psychology in a reputed institution in eastern India. But the little girl who wanted to be no trouble, and who waited for hours every day for her father to pick her up from school, is still trapped inside her somewhere.

Meanwhile, Anima, who had fought with her father to continue her education, found out that the patriarchy she fought at home extended to institutions too. When she began her engineering degree at the university, she was shocked at the hostility of her male classmates.

'They openly told the girls in the class that we were wasting the seats that could have gone to a deserving male candidate because we were going to do nothing with our degrees. We would get married and ultimately leave everything and be a homemaker.'

Anima, who had bet on her education to change her life, found that her classmates had shown great prescience—she worked as a chemical engineer for a while after marriage but was forced to quit.

'Women get married for all the wrong reasons in this country,' she tells me. 'I was determined not to marry because I grew up seeing my mother being abused and humiliated by my father and his family. And yes, I fell in love, but mostly I married because my parents had died by then, I had no guardian and everyone, including my elder sister, thought marriage would bring me some security.'

In India, however, many men take on the role of the 'master' soon after marriage, falling back on established power dynamics to make sure that their wives fall in line.

Soon, both Suchi and Anima realized the mistake they had made. Suchi told me, 'He would ask me to massage his feet every day and that went against everything that I thought I was—the educated, empowered woman who was not less than her husband. And then he wanted me to become pregnant immediately. I didn't but I gave in because I, too, wanted a child, though maybe not so soon in our marriage. But he did, and that was the end of the discussion. He started hitting me when I was pregnant. I was a bad homemaker, I couldn't cook properly—he complained endlessly.'

While for Suchi the abuse was a gradual progression from the emotional to the physical, for Anima, the physical abuse started right after her marriage. 'He would fly off the handle at the smallest thing. And then my mother-in-law would ask me to apologize. She would tell me this is how women have to be,' Anima recalls. 'I was made to understand the verbal abuses and a slap here and there were okay. It went against everything that I believed in, the person I had wanted to be. He began to clip my wings and I let him because I wanted the security of a family. I put up with the abuse because I wanted my children to live in a happy family. It was also then that I truly began to understand my mother, her desperation, her silences.'

Almost a decade later, Suchi was also soldiering on, teaching herself ways to deal with her husband. Throughout our conversation, she spoke about the abuses she suffered but would try to tone them down with platitudes and justifications. She was still justifying her choices, choices that she had been forced to make because of the way women are brought up in this country.

'I left my career in its prime and moved cities with my husband. My daughter was young and I thought this would be a new beginning for us.' But this was not to be. 'The first few months were fine. I was pregnant a second time. After the second child was born, my husband became more aggressive. There was a point when I began to forget things, silly things, and he wouldn't understand why, and instead shout abuses at me, which would make me even more nervous,' Suchi remembered.

'He would ask me to get out of the room when he was shouting and shaking our daughter. I felt so helpless, I would just beat my head against the wall out of frustration. My daughter would just stand there in front of him—staring at him vacantly, not a single tear in her eyes. He would slap me when I had my son in my lap. One day, I forgot to buy medicines and when he asked for them, I told him that with all the childcare and housework I had forgotten to stock the medicines. He just hit me, cussed, and ordered me to serve him his food as if that was all I was worthy of,' she said, adding that this was her breaking point.

'At that point of time I felt horrible—who had I become?'

Saira,* too, had ignored similar questions, as she stood shivering in the biting cold of a Lucknow winter in a flimsy nightgown, tears streaming down her face, as her two-month-old daughter cried her lungs out inside the house. It was her first marriage anniversary.

'The area was lonely and deserted.... I wanted to shout and scream but I was so scared some other men would take advantage of my condition that all I could manage was a whimper. Finally, when they couldn't quieten the cries of my daughter, they let me in,' she told me.

Earlier that evening she had cooked a feast for her family and friends to mark the occasion of their anniversary. She had spent the day and much of the evening in the kitchen, while laughter and voices floated out from the living room where guests were beginning to gather, among them her parents and siblings. She longed to be out there, laughing and talking with her friends and family, but as the daughter-in-law it was Saira's duty to cook and serve food to the guests. When she left her marketing job in a leading media house to get married, an unwritten clause of the agreement was that she would be relieving her mother-in-law of household duties.

After the guests left for the evening, her mother-in-law accused her of bad-mouthing the family to her relatives. Her husband was riled up and started beating her. Finally, they threw her out of the house and locked the door in her face.

'Do you know my husband would start beating me a week before my birthday, and that would continue until a week after?'

'Why?'

'I was a pampered child. My parents and siblings doted on me. My birthdays at home were always very special. I looked forward to them throughout the year. He started beating me to kill any expectations I might have of him for my birthdays,' she says.

If Saira visited her parental home, her in-laws would often refuse to let her into their home on her return. She would sit outside with her mother for hours. Sometimes they would let her in. On other days, she would have go back to her mother's home to try again the next day.

---

*Name changed.

'Why did you leave your job?' I ask her.

'They had money—he was doing well for himself. I used to work in marketing and it involved long hours and evenings. He told me it was not safe and that I should think of moving to a less demanding job. I agreed to leave because I wanted to make him happy because I felt safe with him.'

This was the beginning of numerous compromises Saira would have to make in her marriage, in addition to dealing with an enormous amount of physical and mental violence.

Her husband began pressuring her to get money from her parents immediately after their marriage. Her father had died in 2002, the year she got married. Her mother had taken ill and Saira was taking care of her. It was during this time that Saira found herself a teaching job, although she was pregnant and had been advised bed rest by her doctor. 'He kept pushing me to get a job, saying he needed help as his business was not doing well,' Saira told me.

'While I was pregnant, I had to take long leaves. During this time, my mother-in-law would feed me stale food,' she told me.

And during the night, her husband would rape her.

'Sometimes sex is compassionate, sometimes it is to teach you a lesson,' she says. 'Every time it happened, I felt bruised, violated. I hated myself. Is this what I am meant for? And then I carried on.'

She stayed put through the beatings, the overwork, and the emotional torment. She carried on until she couldn't any more.

Anima was also put through as much emotional abuse as physical violence.

'I used to have very long hair that reached my knees and at the slightest thing he would pull my hair,' Anima had told me. 'I went to get it cut and the hairdresser asked me you have such beautiful hair, why are you cutting it off? I remember I told him, at least now no one would be able to drag me around by my hair.

'The emotional abuse was worse than the physical abuse actually. They would constantly tell me that I was mad. And after a while you start thinking maybe they are right and I am indeed crazy. These words that are being used now—gaslighting, stonewalling—they make sense now. Now I understand. Privately, he would constantly tell me to go and die, over and over again. And I would look at him wordlessly and wonder why is he asking me to die. He would constantly call me crazy.'

The torture that she put up with for thirty years had led Anima to the brink of suicide thrice. The last time she ended up in hospital, she overheard her mother-in-law tell the doctor that she had been undergoing treatment for mental illness for thirty years. Once she was back home, she heard her mother-in-law and her husband talking about proving that she was mentally unstable and committing her to a mental asylum. As discussed earlier, in India, mental illness is grounds for divorce and anecdotal evidence points to its wide usage. 'Despite becoming the best cook, the best homemaker, you are belittled in front of guests and your children and your relatives,' Anima told me. 'And after a while you start believing that you are useless. That you are a nobody and that you will never amount to anything on your own.'

Saira had learnt to cook fifty different chicken recipes just to keep her husband happy and ensure he would not abandon her. It was only much later that she would realize that her children did not even like chicken. 'My entire focus was on keeping him happy,' she told me. 'I wouldn't have left him if he hadn't left me first, because I just wouldn't have been able to survive financially. But once I was pushed into it, ways opened up for me.' For a while Saira was living separately from her in-laws with her husband and children. She worked in a school and earned around ₹12,000 per month. Her husband would make sure she spent that on household expenses so she couldn't spend it on herself or even save it for a rainy day. 'It's all about power.'

Emotional torture is like slow poisoning; it kills you a little bit every day. Today, my mother is a shadow of her earlier strong self, an anxious wreck. But she was not always like that. She was a tall, strapping woman who was fiercely independent, well-read, and who stood her ground and refused to give in to unjust expectations. But now I see her diminished in herself—always nervous, always expecting things to go wrong, things to fall apart. The light that has died in her has little do with her age. The amount of emotional abuse my mother has put up with throughout her marriage is unimaginable, and now all I see is the exhaustion that has set in after years of conflict.

My parents' ugliest rows would be over my mother's out-of-station assignments. She was among the second batch of women police officers in India and often needed to travel within the state when dignitaries came to visit, especially when they were women. Once she needed to be away for three days to provide security for the then prime minister Indira Gandhi, who was visiting West Bengal. This led to the most horrific argument in our household, which went on for days. My father never directly refused her but made it immensely difficult for her to go. He kept telling her to quit her job. 'I earn enough,' he would say. In the course of my childhood, I had often heard him say these words to my mother, and I had seen her stand up to him. She knew saying no to the assignment wouldn't bode well for her. This time she came to an agreement with my father. The next week, all of us (including my father) got into a car with my mother and we went with her to Santiniketan, where Mrs Gandhi was visiting. I still remember the embarrassment on my mother's face. The discomfort. She was walking on eggshells all three days. And yet, she knew it was a small price to pay to continue to work.

For as long as she worked, at the start of each month my mother would hand over her salary to my father. He would then distribute the money for various household expenses, including a monthly expense for my mother. My father earned enough and was an extremely generous man who rarely refused my mother money for anything. But he wouldn't let her handle her own money or spend it as she saw fit. For my mother, handing over her salary to him was another small compromise she made so she could continue working. For my father, keeping my mother's salary was about controlling her as an individual. The image of her handing over her money to him has haunted me throughout my life. There was something so disempowering about that image, something so sad, and so telling of the cages we live in, that it bothered me for years. Women are still doing that—handing over their salaries to male relatives to manage.

It is more rampant than we would like to believe or admit. Suchi's husband, too, doesn't allow her to spend her money.

'It's a control thing...a power thing. He likes to manage my money. He doesn't use or misuse it but he doesn't like me spending it either. He wants to provide for me, us. If I want to buy a laptop, he will say I will buy it for you. I have never cared about money or anything materialistic—I grew up with enough of it. But the fact that he doesn't allow me to spend my own money troubles me,' she said.

In 2017, I came across a first-person account article by a young Indian woman. 'I was a 26-year-old woman working in a small company when I got married. When I became a wife, I also became a permanent employee at home and in my office. Only one of those places paid. Every salary, along with the salary slip, was handed over to my brother-in-law who handled the family's finances and also skimmed off the top of it for himself,' she wrote.[2]

What she writes is supported by the last National Family Health Survey (NFHS-4), which found that women in our country rarely made decisions about how to use their earnings by themselves. 'It is most common for women to make these decisions jointly with their husband; only 21 per cent make these decisions alone. For 17 per cent of the women, the husband is the sole decision maker regarding the use of women's earnings.'[3] The survey also found that women's control over their earnings increased only marginally with education and wealth and that their 'participation in decisions about their own earnings has remained more or less unchanged' in the ten years since the last survey.[4]

The anonymous young woman then talks about the abuse she faced from her husband and his family and says her house was 'like an alternate universe, where I had to make the active choice between violence and slavery every single day'. Finally, she says, she had only two options—to kill herself or run away. Running away would bring disrepute to her parents, whom she refers to as 'middle-class Indians with middle-class courage'.[5]

I know my mother thought of running away constantly. My father always suspected her of having an affair. A woman stepping out of her home has always been suspected of having too much sexual freedom in our society.

Anu,* a friend of mine, is a single mother of one and a high-flying techie. She married an NRI when she was only twenty-two—an arranged marriage—and flew to Singapore, dreaming of a better life. She had thought marrying a man who lived abroad would ensure her personal freedom as well as better opportunities to build a career for herself. She started working soon after her move, but began feeling like her marriage had been a mistake. 'He always suspected me of having an affair. I just got tired of defending myself,' she said. 'For the first few years, I was struggling to come to terms with this but hadn't really thought of leaving him.'

She fell pregnant with her first child in the first year of her marriage. She moved back home to her parents to see through the pregnancy. 'It was a full-term pregnancy but I had a stillborn daughter. I was depressed and decided to go back to work within three to four months. And life went on, and I fell pregnant again after a few years.'

This time around, she had decided not to work during her pregnancy. 'I am not sure if that was a turning point in my mind, while staying at home, but I realized my marriage was not going to last long. We were just not compatible, something he refused to acknowledge or work on.

'It was a struggle to live with a person who had a very different world view. He was very conservative. I was expected to work, manage the home, raise children, and at the most have family friends or common friends. ...I had my own friends, from work or our general social circle, and he thought it was totally unnecessary.

'I trained in classical dance since I was in school—he and his family did not allow me to continue. I am a voracious reader, even that was frowned upon. He accused me of reading books on infidelity. I couldn't breathe in that house.'

Anu grew up in a middle-class home where she was taught from childhood to 'adjust and manage differences' and that financial security comes from the man of the house. 'The women might step out to work for some extra money, but the home remains her primary responsibility.

---

*Name changed.

I am still surprised when I meet women much younger than me, and they say they want to marry someone who earns more than them,' she told me.

'My parents were not supportive of my decision to end my marriage. It took me years to convince them that I tried my best to make the marriage work and failed. My mother came around finally but my father is still uncomfortable saying I am divorced.'

The fear of bringing disrepute to their parents or, worse, not being supported by them is one of the major reasons why middle-class women don't walk out of bad marriages.

'Why didn't you ever leave?' I have asked my mother often. Her answer has always been the same. 'When a mother of two daughters leaves her marriage, questions are raised about her character, which would not have been good for the two of you. I also did not have the courage—I didn't know how to manage on my own because I was never allowed to.'

'If only I had somewhere to run away, I would, and no one would be able to find me,' was a constant refrain I heard while I was growing up. My poor mother, an orphan, had nowhere to go. She knew life as a single, divorced woman would be harder than her life was then. So, she did what we are taught to do every second of our lives. *Compromise. Adjust. Keep the peace.*

A large majority of women would love to walk out of their marriages—this much was clear to me during the writing of this book. So, why do they stay? They stay because they are all struggling with these basic questions: Where will I go? How will I manage my finances? And, the ubiquitous, what will people say?

'I had stayed in my marriage because I knew I wouldn't be able to manage my finances, I won't be able to earn enough to provide a good life for my children and I would have never left if my husband had not abandoned me,' Saira told me. 'But once I was left to fend for myself, after the initial struggle I managed. Friends helped, family helped. I would just buy a load of Maggi noodles for us to eat when we ran out of rice and dal. Friends would order pizza for us. It was surreal—we would be enjoying pizza when there were no groceries at home. But those days passed and I remained afloat and emerged stronger.'

By the time her daughter was born, Anu had already decided to end her marriage but she knew she couldn't rush that decision. She decided to wait until she was earning enough to sustain herself and her daughter. 'It took me six years to reach there,' she told me.

Most women stay in bad marriages because there's no support for single women in this country. Family support is often not available in such situations—they are more likely to send women right back into the den of abuse. So, where would you go to avoid the abuse at home? The streets are hostile and unsafe, as are public shelter homes. Even if you have the means, single women often have difficulty finding a house to rent.

'My daughter keeps asking me why I don't leave her father,' Suchi says. 'I guess he is not all bad. Maybe I am normalizing his behaviour. Maybe I have decided to work with what I have. But I also wonder how I would manage on my own. My children go to the best of schools. They have everything they want. I don't think I would be able to provide them this life on my own.'

As Saira says, the first thing that comes to a woman's mind in this country when her husband dies or leaves her is 'what will happen to me now?' If the marriage fails, they are expected to live their lives as sexless, joyless beings. Our society constantly propagates the idea that 'good girls suffer in silence', and too many of them do.

There is no doubt that there is wide acceptance in our society of emotional and physical, even sexual, violence within marriages—even by women themselves.

In 1995, at the UN's Fourth World Conference on Women, India, along with 186 other member states, had adopted the Beijing Platform of Action to eliminate all forms of violence against women. Nevertheless, intimate partner violence remains widespread and often accepted and normalized in middle-class families as necessary tools to 'keep women under control'. In 2016, a research project on domestic violence led by the ICRW found that that 40 per cent of all Indian wives, across region, religion, or age, had reported 'being slapped, hit, kicked, or beaten by their husbands'.[6] The NFHS-4 had found that 52 per cent of women and 42 per cent of men believed it was okay to beat the wife if she goes out without informing the husband, neglects the house or children, argues, refuses to have sex, doesn't cook properly, is suspected of infidelity, or shows disrespect towards her in-laws.[7] These are the seven societal expectations to which women must conform if they wish to avoid being 'punished'. Additionally, many Indian women strongly believe in the division of labour on gender lines and 'think it is their duty to do household work once they are married into another family'.[8] The high rate of approval of wife-beating by the surveyed women should come as no surprise—it is an acceptance of a reality they can do little to change. I am guilty of advising women to leave, to not put up with violence, until I realized—where will they go? How will they support themselves?

The ICRW study found that while these women had access to legal counsel and women's police stations, there were 'significant gaps' in how these institutions responded to their complaints and the project put it to the 'widespread acceptance of domestic violence as a normal part of marriage'.[9] When it came to the men, the report found a majority had engaged in some form of violence against their wives, including emotional abuse, control, and sexual and physical violence.[10] One of the most common control behaviours among men was refusing to allow the wife to go out and talk to others. The most common form of emotional violence was shouting and screaming to instil the fear of violence in their wives. The report found the most common form of sexual violence was having sex with an unwilling wife. Slapping and hitting were the most commonly reported acts of physical violence, along with choking and smothering. Interestingly, the report points out that while physical violence decreased with increase in education, employment, and socio-economic status, sexual violence does not. A majority of the men agreed that violence was justified if the wife was sexually unfaithful, or if she was disrespectful to the husband or family elders. 'Violence within marriage or intimate relationship encompasses a range of forms beyond "wife beating",' the report said. 'The high level of sexual violence among the educated and high-socioeconomic status men is disturbing.'[11]

I remember one of my domestic workers once told me, 'Sometimes if the food is not to his liking or maybe the house is a bit dirty, my husband might get a bit angry. But honestly a couple of slaps here and there also keeps me on my toes.' She echoed a sentiment I have since heard from many women, no matter their socio-economic status. Let me here remind you of how Anima's mother-in-law—educated, upper middle class—repeatedly told her that it was okay to be slapped around.

The problem with domestic violence is that it continues in a loop until someone breaks the chain. Boys who grow up watching their father physically abuse their mother, might repeat the pattern later in life with a woman who may have grown up watching her mother take the abuse in her stride.

Anima managed to break the chain. 'My daughter doesn't want to get married. She has grown up seeing me being battered but she has also seen me fight back and my hope is that if she marries, she will be strong in her marriage. I was able to teach my son to treat women with dignity and respect and not as boxing bags.'

'Why don't we teach these things in schools?' she wonders.

Feminism has failed us, Saira says. 'Feminists do not show you the way ahead. In India, feminism doesn't empower. Just like our parents, feminists, too, have no plan B. At the end of the day, when nothing works, they also try and settle it between the couple. And it is all because there are no institutional backups to support us, our so-called empowerment.'

Why was Saira turned out of her home on that cold night on the evening of her anniversary? To instil fear in her. To make her understand that her husband was not just giving her food to eat and clothes to wear but also providing her 'safe' shelter—safe from strangers, but not from him.

'We put up with so much because outside of our homes it is a jungle. When I counsel women, I, too, often ask them to adjust a little, especially if they are economically dependent on their husbands. I can ask them to leave their husbands, but where would they go? Are shelter homes safe for women?' asks Saira.

They are not. Horror stories from shelter homes abound. Women and young girls in these homes are often repeatedly abused. In mid-August in 2018, cases of abuse against women and children had surfaced in the Indian media. At the time, there had been no national audit of around 10,000 shelter homes in the country and about 33 per cent of such facilities in the country were not even registered.[12] In August 2018, a surprise raid on a women's home run by an NGO in Uttar Pradesh had found that at least twenty-six women had gone missing.[13] The raid was planned after twenty-four girls were rescued from a shelter in the state, when one of the girls escaped and alerted the police about the alleged sexual exploitation at the facility. This what women fear; this is what keeps them at home.

What about initiatives like women's police stations? These police stations were established in 2005 under the federal Protection of Women from Domestic Violence Act 2005 to make it easier for women to report crimes against them. Many states, such as West Bengal and Kerala (which had a women-only police station as far back as in the 1970s), had experimented with such stations before, but those experiments had largely failed.

In 2017, I found out exactly how these police stations functioned. I walked into a women's police station near the Indian capital with a young woman who worked as a cleaner in my house. Earlier that day, Seema had arrived at our house in a state of great disarray and emotional distress. She had rolled up the sleeves of her kurti to reveal white scratch marks all over her arms. Three men her husband drank with and borrowed money from had barged into her room in the morning. Her husband had disappeared after borrowing a substantial amount of money from these men and they had threatened to rape her. She fought them and ran the two kilometres to my home. I took a picture of her scratch marks, her dishevelled appearance, and took her to the police station.

I was bolstered by my experience of my mother as the head of a similar women's police station in West Bengal. I walked in, along with Seema, only to face a wall of disinterested looking policemen. Five of them.

'Do you have no policewomen?'

'No, they will come in late.'

'Okay, so whom do we talk to?'

'There's no one to talk to right now. You will have to wait. We will call the officer in charge,' was the reply. The policeman then looked at Seema and said 'Oi! What's wrong?'

'Why are you talking to her like this? She has already been harassed by three men,' I intervened.

'Madam, you don't know these women. They lie. Must have had a fight with her husband. Oi, go home and make up with him, don't bother us.'

I was enraged but I had learnt from previous experience that you cannot by-pass patriarchy in this country by kicking it in its face. I fished out my phone.

'I am actually going to record this conversation,' I told him. 'And then send the video to the chief minister's office so they know exactly how you run a women-only police station. This is supposed to be a safe space for her, you are intimidating her.'

He was not to be deterred.

'Are you threatening me?'

'Yes, I am,' I said, holding his gaze. 'Where's your officer?'

'He is on his way. You will have to write a report of what happened to her. Make sure you write it in Hindi.'

I hadn't written in Hindi for years. But I channelled what I learnt a decade back and wrote up a detailed report. By the time I was done, the officer in charge arrived with all his derision and dismissiveness. Another battle ensued, after which we successfully registered our complaint. At this point, we had already spent two hours at the police station. Seema couldn't go to two of the houses she cleaned and I was late to work.

What came of the complaint?

Seema's husband surrendered at the police station. The policemen called the two of them to the station, 'counselled' them on the sanctity of marriage as an institution, then forced her to withdraw her complaint. A happy ending scripted by the patriarchy. That's how it always ends, even today.

How did it end for Anima after she left her job to focus on her family? In 2014, when she was fifty-two, she had dialled the emergency police helpline during a violent episode at home.

'My friends kept telling me to call the police,' Anima told me. 'So, I did. The police came and told me you are fifty-two years old, why are you making a spectacle of yourself. Get it sorted amongst yourselves inside the house.'

The police force is still dominated by male officers who have received no cultural or sensitivity training for the handling of cases of violence against women. Hence, initiatives such as women-only police stations remain mere symbolic gestures.

When Suchi had sought help from a female psychiatrist, she was not counselled on how to deal with the abuse, but rather on how to deal with her husband.

'My intellectualization of our relationship has helped me deal with it,' she tells me. 'It has helped me deal with a lot of things. He has stopped hitting me now because my daughter stops him. I have gained some power in the relationship, too. How? When I see him getting violent, I just see a man who can't handle his own weaknesses and insecurities. I can't connect with him anymore. We are just cohabiting. Someday I will have the courage to leave.'

The courage she is talking about is not just the courage to leave her marriage but the courage to step out of her home and into a world that is inhospitable to women. We have come such a long way and yet we remain anomalies on our own streets. We negotiate these streets gingerly because we are a visible minority in public spaces. If women cannot step out into the streets confidently, how do we expect them to work or have a truly free life? If the streets remain unsafe, how can we expect women to leave bad marriages? If the outside of our homes is so hazardous, is it any wonder that women prefer to stay in bad marriages, or with oppressive parents, instead of leaving? Women's relationship with public spaces is so fraught that they gladly accept all the overwork and invisible oppression at home because they know what lies outside their homes—more violence, fear of sexual assault and harassment, and lack of opportunities to become economically independent.

WHY ARE WOMEN MISSING FROM PUBLIC SPACES?

Feminism is the radical notion that women are human beings.

—Marie Meiselman Shear

In early 2019, I had gone to register my car papers at the motor vehicles office in Noida. As I stood waiting for a man to photocopy my documents, I became aware of the stares of people around me. This was, of course, nothing I was not used to, but these stares were slightly different, more uncomfortable, more in my face. I looked up and looked around slowly—all I could see were men, men, and more men. On that courtyard of easily a few hundred men, I was the only woman, or at least the only one unaccompanied by a man. I took a picture of the courtyard and when I looked at it later, I was amazed. We often talk about women missing from our public spaces but to see it captured was a different feeling all together.

Often, when I am in a car driven by a female friend, male drivers honk, try to corner the car—for them it's a sport, to see us flustered and scared, to push us back into our homes. Ask any woman who drives, especially in North India, she will have a similar story to tell. I have never wandered through the streets like I often see men doing. My relationship with the streets is strictly functional, as I believe is the case with most other women. We try to go from point A to point B, getting our work done without grabbing too much attention.

ఌ

In early February in 2018, in a small room in Madanpur Khadar, a resettlement colony in the Indian capital, a group of young girls were discussing their participation in a year-long project by the non-profit organization Jagori called Aana-Jaana (Comings and Goings) with a study group from abroad. As part of the project, the girls had recorded their daily struggles of negotiating a hostile public space on a closed WhatsApp group.

'Sheher (city) where no one listens to you', an entry read; a freestyle hip-hop song with over 40,000 views on YouTube followed the entry. That morning, they performed it for the study group.

'*Girls in this city have a tough life…but you cannot scare us away any more,*' sang the diminutive Khadar ki Ladkiyan (Girls of Khadar), in their knock-off jeans and long synthetic tops. Their anger was quiet but palpable.

'*More power to you sister,*' they spat out as they punched and slashed the air, swaying to the beats of finger snaps and knuckle raps.

But staking a claim to the city in real time has not been easy.

A Save the Children report in 2018 on safety in public spaces for Indian girls found that one in three adolescent girls was scared of traversing the narrow by-lanes of their localities, as well as the road to go to school or the local market. Nearly three in five girls reported feeling unsafe in overcrowded public spaces. Over one in every four adolescent girls perceived the threat of being physically assaulted, including getting raped, while venturing into public spaces, while one in three expected to be inappropriately touched or even stalked.[1]

'Khadar ki Ladkiyan' was part of a wider project titled 'Gendering the Smart City' funded by the Arts and Humanities Research Council, UK, and headed by Ayona Datta, a professor of Human Geography at University College London. The project aimed to understand how women used technology and how that technology impacted the ways in which they negotiated their homes and cities on a daily basis. The participants were from Madanpur Khadar, a resettlement colony in Delhi. Jagori, a feminist NGO in Delhi, and Safetipin, a well-known ICT social enterprise, partnered with Datta on this project.

Datta describes the Khadar girls as 'urban millennials, who are living the paradox of India's digital revolution in an urban age…. They are avid users of the mobile phone, and active on social media through which they create solidarities, friendships, and support networks… within these paradoxes they emerge as young, millennial, gendered citizens straddling the "new" and "old" India, eager to speak, but held back.' Their song, she continues, 'brings to light the opportunities and challenges of navigating the city as these women leave home to pursue paid work and education, and are simultaneously constrained by the boundaries of traditional gender roles.'[2]

A very important aspect of the everyday lives of the Khadar girls is violence—not just sexual, but also structural. In their song the girls reiterate that the state knows *we need better roads, they know we need public transport. They know we need water and toilets. They know we need safe streets. It's not a lack of knowledge that is the problem, rather a lack of attention.'*

'The song was really about using technology and not necessarily in the way that the smart city expects you to.... Like, you know, clicking on Facebook likes and Twitter likes and doing the surveys circulated by the government, but using technology in a way to draw attention and mobilize and advocate about continuing intergenerational problems around lack of infrastructure, gender-based violence, and so on,' Datta told me in 2020.

The impact of the song had left Datta amazed. 'We had not even thought of shooting a video initially but the idea came from the girls,' Datta remembered.

The girls had kept it a secret from their parents during the shoot, for the fear that they would not be allowed to take part in the project because dancing and singing were not considered appropriate. However, after the video went live, to everyone's surprise, many parents sent it to their extended families back home.

'It made us feel free—we were able to put into words the anger we feel at the fear we feel in a city where we were born,' said Ritu, one of the Khadar girls. 'Why do we have to run back home after school or work? Why can't we hang out like the boys or men do in public squares?'

Because when the public space is hostile, we have no choice but to accept this misogynistic definition of a woman's rightful place in society.

In 2012, a young student, Jyoti Singh, was raped inside a moving bus by six men and then thrown on the streets to die. Her parents had migrated to New Delhi from a small village in Uttar Pradesh in search of a better life for their children. Her father worked as a loader at the Delhi airport and sold his ancestral land to fund her education. The tragedy that befell her brought focus to the struggles of this new generation of underprivileged girls and women, empowered by education, having to step out to work to substantiate the family income. Her gruesome rape and murder had underlined the imminent need for making public spaces safer for women. Singh was the same age as the Khadar girls when she was murdered and came from a similar socio-economic background.

'When we talk about safety, we are not just talking about violence. It is to remove fear,' Kalpana Vishwanath, a sociologist and urban safety and gender rights activist said in an address to the International Association of Women in Radio and Television in September 2015. Citing the example of Delhi, she had added that 'there is a huge amount of fear, probably higher than the actual expression of violence. And our effort is to remove that fear.'[3]

Vishwanath, co-founder and CEO of Safetipin, a social enterprise that uses data and technology to build safer, more inclusive smart cities, held that safety was not just the experience of violence, it's the fear of violence that makes women more dependent on men for protection, or makes them restrict their mobility. She had also rightly pointed out that when women are perceived as victims, the narrative then becomes that of protection rather than rights. 'And we are saying safety is a right, without fear of violence.'

'Cities are not well planned; they are not gender inclusive. We have to ask whether we are planning cities for gender inclusion? Are we planning more transport facilities? Are the places well-lit? We need to address a lot of stakeholders, not only the police. We need to talk to urban planners, municipality, and local governments to build safer cities,' she said. 'Instead of a top-down model where city planners decide. We should build cities that local people want, women want. A safe city, where one can live without fear.'[4]

Urban planning in our cities continues to disregard gender as a factor precisely because of this idea that women must be protected and so, surveilled. According to Ayona Datta, who researches the politics of urban transformations in the global south, smart cities, in our current scenario, would merely result in increased surveillance.

'We know that surveillance can actually be highly unequal and highly debilitating for women because the first violence they face is from their families, from their kinship networks, from the neighbourhoods, from the neighbours. And this surveillance can be loaded with cultural perceptions about women's rightful place and women's rightful body, the attire and behaviour and demeanour,' Datta told me in an interview.[5]

In 2017, the Indian government approved a budget of ₹98,000 crore to turn eight major cities, including Delhi, perhaps one of the most unsafe cities for women in India, into smart cities.[6] But, as Datta says, the concept of smart cities as a policy is based on a corporate and technologically driven understanding of cities. Through her Gendering the Smart City project, Datta wanted to explore what such a concept could mean for women and what stakes they have in this sort of technology.

'Gendering the Smart City is a critique of smart city that has been conceptualized and driven from a very top-down policy through use of digital kinds of technologies, particularly making use of big data and real-time analytics, to efficiently manage and govern cities. And then to think, how can women use technology to support their everyday struggles or to, you know, circumvent different kinds of challenges in everyday life, whether it's about violence, whether it's about livelihoods, and so on and so forth.'[7]

In our country, the way men and women look at safety is very different. Policy makers, who are largely men, approach safety from the perspective of protecting women, rather than as a basic human right that needs to be guaranteed. The smart cities project comes from a belief that technology is the solution to all sorts of social problems. But technology cannot resolve discriminations that are internalized and embedded in our daily lives. 'If you read some of the reports by PricewaterhouseCoopers and Cisco, which are some of the main players in the smart cities sector globally, they generally treat smart safety as a question of surveillance by increasing CCTV cameras [and] by increasing police presence. Also, smart cities are a business model. So, the moment it becomes a question of surveillance, then you can sell CCTV cameras, then you can sell records and algorithms for command and control centres from where you can observe the streets and so on. But it doesn't really resolve the issue of patriarchy or misogynist patriarchy.'[8]

Datta says we should fear surveillance because 'it is a kind of masculinist patriarchal approach. It's more about really changing ways that we view women, or, you know, alternative sexualities in our society. And unless that change [occurs], really technology can't do much, it can do some, but it can really never resolve the problem. The idea of surveillance not just works well with patriarchy, there's a real fear that it will be turned into a technology tool.'[9]

Datta worked on a different project in Kerala, along with Safetipin, where the city authorities created a safety corridor for women as their initiative for gendering the smart city. 'It was literally a few miles between two government colleges. And when we mapped the city, we told them there were reports of gender violence from all across the city and a small narrow road between two government colleges is really not going to resolve the safety issue.'[10] India is spending billions to make cities safer for women and yet gender budgeting was only around 1 per cent of its GDP during the 2019 budget.[11]

Datta says changing mindsets requires far more in-depth measures, far more sensitive policymaking, far more consultations with feminist activists and groups that cater to these sorts of issues—it's a much more long-term, time intensive problem that cannot be just subcontracted out to a corporation. 'There's no quick fix. This is one problem you cannot outsource to technology for a quick fix and then say, well, we need to have smart people because we created all these safety apps. But look, women are not using them. So, they don't really want to be safe. Blaming women for not using technology then becomes part of the problem,' she points out.[12]

There is a need to overhaul infrastructure in Indian cities. But the real challenge lies in the perception of women as intruders in India's male-dominated public spaces. In India, violence against women in public spaces is often aimed at making them scurry back indoors.

'We keep hearing of projects to make women feel safer and yet I don't feel safe. I see more than one man hanging together on the street, and my pace quickens by default,' says Meera, one of the Khadar girls. 'I relax only when I reach home,' she adds. 'You know that feeling?'

I do.

I have travelled all over the country, often solo, for almost two decades now. I have travelled to remote villages and small towns and big metropolises. But I have been made to feel like an interloper in every public space I visited, though perhaps not as much as my less-privileged compatriots.

'You can make cities smarter but you cannot make them safer as long as men think it's okay to abuse women and onlookers think it's okay to look away,' says Meera.

I know what they mean. Safety is a right. Safety is a feeling of comfort. I do not feel either when I am out on the streets in my country.

Women are unwanted in public spaces in India. Along with feeling unsafe, they also feel uncomfortable because our cities are not built to support the needs of women. Do you go easy on drinking and eating if you are on a long journey whether within the city or out of it? Or hold in your pee because public women's toilets are generally unhygienic and filthy, if they are available at all? I remember the many times my mother would ask us to pee before leaving home on long journeys as toilets were so unclean that they would be impossible to use. I remember two-day-long train journeys, where I ate and drank nothing so there would be no need to use the public facilities.

'A clean India would be the best tribute India could pay to Mahatma Gandhi on his 150th birth anniversary in 2019,' Prime Minister Narendra Modi had said before the launch of the Swachh Bharat Mission at Rajpath in New Delhi on 2 October 2014.[13]

The Swachh Bharat Mission costs $20 billion and aimed to build 111 million toilets in the country in five years (2014–2019). Almost 80 million household toilets are estimated to have been built since the mission's launch in 2014.

The scope of the mission was mainly to build more toilets to end open defecation, with over 7 million Indians still defecating in the open as of 2014. The scope says, 'Priority shall be accorded pro-actively to cover households with vulnerable sections such as pensioners, girl children, pregnant and lactating mothers.'[14]

Building more public toilets for women should also have been part of this agenda. If you look at the number and quality of public toilets available to women in a city, it would seem like women are barely present in public spaces.

According to an ActionAid survey from 2016, nearly 35 per cent of public toilets in the city did not have separate sections for women. The survey was carried out in December 2016 under the People's Vision of the City (PVoC) campaign and covered a total of 229 toilets maintained by the three Municipality Corporations of Delhi (MCD) and New Delhi Municipality Corporation (NDMC), as well as those outsourced to private agencies. Of the total toilets surveyed, 149 toilets had some provisions for women but suffered from functional issues like unclean premises, lack of hygiene, and lack of safety measures. More than 66 per cent of women's toilets did not have a working flush and 53 per cent had no running water. About 61 per cent toilets did not have soap to use. The survey also found that 28 per cent toilets did not have doors, while 45 per cent toilets could not be locked from the inside. Over half of them had insufficient or no lights, either inside the toilet or outside. Around 46 per cent of toilets also lacked basic security, including guards.[15]

The lack of functional, well-maintained public toilets signals to women that public areas are not places they can, or should, traverse with ease and that women must curtail their movements when outside. This is further exacerbated during menstruation, when the need for safe and clean toilets is perhaps the greatest. But we are still not talking about this basic right enough. Over the years, there have been spirited debates about the need for period leave, but when we discuss this, we also need to discuss the right of women to clean toilets in public spaces. We need to position both these debates in the context of enabling women to be comfortable in all spaces, rather than expecting them to stop making a fuss and move on.

Some liberal feminists in this country feel that period leave will hamper gender equality at work, that it will make women look weak. This kind of argument is counter-productive because it makes women feel inadequate and inefficient. We are still trying to fit into spaces designed for men—and it's not working. The meagre female labour force participation amply highlights this. Isn't it time to instead discuss how we can create spaces keeping in mind women's different needs? I have never taken a day off work for my periods. But I have grown up with a sister who was incapacitated during her periods due to menstrual cramps. For her, menstrual leave would have been a lifesaver. Both of us are very strong, empowered women. A bodily compulsion doesn't make us weaker or stronger.

Period leave is just one small piece of the puzzle. All the other pieces (good toilets, better job opportunities, flexible hours, work from home facilities, crèches in workplaces or quality state-subsidized day care, equal division of care and domestic work at home) need to fit together to bring women back to the workplace, and retain them. We don't need to take gender out of the workplace or out of ourselves. Women don't need to be like men, they needn't hide the fact that they are built differently, and that they react to situations differently. As equal stakeholders in the nation's progress, it is our right to have all spaces fashioned in a way that accounts for our needs. We have been bringing our own chairs to the table for decades now—it's perhaps time to replace the table.

ॐ

Liberal feminism focuses too much on cancelling out gender, not so much on making the system gender-responsive. Liberal feminism is useless for most women in our country because it celebrates individual achievements and tries to impose those as norms or ideals. We need to make feminism accessible to middle-class girls and women. We need to patiently demystify feminism as a concept for middle-class women because we cannot leave out one of the largest groups of women in our country and hope to empower our lot.

Without their participation, no feminist movement can sustain itself for long. For most middle-class women, the term feminism is either scary or something that has no direct bearing on their lives. To make them understand how feminism directly affects them is a challenge we have not taken up yet. We need to push for radical change, but first we need to grow our army. We have won many battles, but the war is not going to end any time soon.

We need feminism that can align with our cultural needs and that patriarchy cannot discredit as easily. How do you make feminism palatable to middle-class women who have been led to believe that feminism is bad, and feminists are brash women who hate men? Maybe we can start by telling them that feminism is not about hating men but about loving ourselves enough to put ourselves first, that it is about making our contributions—at home and work—count, that it is about demanding to be treated with respect and to have equal say in the decision-making of our families, that it is about our right to leisure, and, most importantly, for securing a better and equal future for our daughters.

WHAT'S A WOMAN'S WORTH IN A CAPITALIST–PATRIARCHAL SOCIETY?

The thing women have yet to learn is nobody gives you power. You just take it.

—Roseanne Barr

What does women's empowerment mean in our capitalist–patriarchal society? There is no simple answer to this question. According to the book *Feminism for the 99%: A Manifesto*, capitalist societies are 'wellsprings of gender oppression', and sexism is 'hardwired' into capitalism's very structure. The inception of this can be traced back to how it separated the 'making of people' from the 'making of profit' and assigned the first job to women and with this 'capitalism simultaneously reinvented women's oppression and turned the whole world upside down'.[1]

Patriarchy demands that women stay at home or, if they must work, their jobs do not disrupt their fulfilment of household duties. Capitalism gave us the term 'homemaker' and created an indelible distinction between 'productive' and 'reproductive labour'. It colludes with patriarchy to keep women as underachievers or non-achievers because it means they have a pool of low-wage workers on stand-by. Following early marriages, unfinished education, or gaps in career owing to marriage or childbirth, when she steps out to work, a woman is either unskilled or low skilled and has to settle for low-paying jobs. Further, they have to confront various biases regarding their capabilities as workers and their natural biological functions such as menstruation and child birth are used against them to devalue their contributions. When lawmakers talk about wages for housewives, they are deepening the idea of women as homemakers. Wages for homemakers just entrenches the idea of women performing (and getting paid) for reproductive labour, housework, while playing a subservient role to men, who perform labour which is considered productive to the economy. They are the nurturers of the capitalist workforce for productive labour and so, their place is inside the house.

Not many women work in the formal sectors in India, but a majority of women do engage in home-based informal work (agricultural labour, domestic workers, small home-based businesses, tailors, seamstresses, factory workers) that is often categorized as housework. For example, it took a year-long farmers' protest in India for women to lay claim to the title of 'farmer' and to be recognized as such. Until then, agricultural work was considered an extension of housework and women farmers described themselves as housewives.[2]

The more women are relegated to the domestic sphere, the lower their skills and self-worth, which means corporations can get away with paying them a much lower salary than their male workers. The inherent gender inequalities in a patriarchal society like India also translate to fewer economic opportunities for women to begin with. A limited choice pool means that women often have to opt for either low-paying home-based jobs or jobs beneath their level of qualification and at a lower pay than men. India ranked 140 out of 156 countries in the 2021 Global Gender Gap report by the World Economic Forum (WEF). The report found the gender gap in economic opportunities for women in the country to be quite large at over 32 per cent. Women held only around 29 per cent of technical roles, and only about 14 per cent were working in senior roles and their average income was over 20 per cent less than that of men.[3] The rare occasions when I have discussed my income with male colleagues, both they and I have been surprised at the disparity in our salaries. In my first job as a correspondent in India, I was offered a measly ₹9,000 per month. I accepted the job because I hadn't been able to find another despite having a Master's in broadcast journalism and four years of work experience as a producer with the BBC World Service Radio in London. A few months after I joined, a man with a similar level of experience as me joined the organization at the same level. We became friends quickly and I found out that he was being paid 40 per cent more than me. I tried to negotiate my salary—unsuccessfully—and the overwhelming feeling I got was that

I was welcome to leave if the salary was not to my liking. Women are not just missing from the workplace, they are also dispensable in the workplace.

Women in India often compromise just to stay in the game. 'I would like nothing better than going back to my corporate career,' my friend Divya told me. 'But once I took a break, despite all my achievements and awards in corporate training, I couldn't find a suitable job.' When Divya decided to re-enter the job market, she didn't have much choice. Many corporate jobs involve night shifts. 'It was not possible for me then with small children,' she says. Finally, she gave in and rebuilt her career—this time as a schoolteacher, which offered her regular timings and longer holidays that were aligned with her sons' school holidays. While she is great at her teaching job, she has had to learn an entirely different skill set and modify her salary expectations to fit herself into a new environment. But this is not her story alone. Many women, after they have taken a break, find themselves in junior level, low-paying, low-growth jobs. Some knowingly choose them because these jobs ask less of them and they are able to achieve a better work–life balance. I decided to work as a freelance journalist after my son was born because I did not think I could balance the unreasonable demands of a newsroom with those of a newborn. But taking that decision meant that I had to let go of some of my career aspirations and my earning potential dropped in the eyes of future employers.

The pay gap is real but it is especially brutal for women who have taken a break due to pregnancies or to raise their children. The WEF report puts this in perspective. Globally, only 36 per cent of senior managers in the private sector and senior officials in the public sector are women. The presence of women on corporate boards or as top business leaders is even more limited: in India, women's representation in leadership roles is less than 14 per cent.[4] South Asia is home to 860 million people; three-fourths of them live in India. The South Asia region has closed two-thirds of its gender gap, which is the second largest in the world after the Middle East and North Africa. 'If the rate of progress of the past 15 years was to continue—a very strong hypothesis indeed—it will take seventy-one years to close [South Asia's] gender gap,' the report says.[5] The report studied 153 countries and found India to be the only country where the economic gender gap is larger than the political gender gap. Only one-quarter of women, compared with 82 per cent of men, engage actively in the labour market (working or looking for work)—one of the lowest participation rates in the world (145th). Women only account for 30 per cent of professional and technical workers. Women earn a mere one-fifth of men's income, which is also among the world's lowest (144th).[6]

The fact that patriarchy wants to keep women confined to domesticity works out well for capitalism. Many women in India who identify as housewives are actually engaged in productive labour from home. For example, there are women who work from their homes as tailors or seamstresses for entrepreneurs who wish to outsource their work at a low wage rate. Capitalism has never made an effort to address these inequalities by making workplaces gender responsible, by giving women an equal playing field—it has rather advanced the idea of housewives (even when the work done is productive) to ensure women opt for low-paying work in exchange for the relative comfort of working from home and to better manage their reproductive labour.

There is little doubt that capitalism has encouraged technological inventions—like the variety of equipment that automate housework such as washing machines, vacuum cleaners, and microwave ovens—with the potential to make women's lives far easier. But set against the backdrop of a patriarchal society and rigid gender roles, a majority of Indian women have no access to these innovations, not just because of affordability but also societal expectations. In our homes, for example, it is expected that women will make fresh food for the family no matter how late or what time of day. So, in many middle-class homes, even though there are microwave ovens that men can use to reheat their food, the wife or mother will still stay up to reheat it for him. It's touted as a labour of love, but is actually just labour. Capitalism wins when the woman buys a microwave oven (or is gifted one) and patriarchy wins when she still slaves in the kitchen instead of taking a break and letting family members reheat their meals.

Corporations, of course, are focused on maximizing profit, and when it comes to branding, women's empowerment is the goose that lays golden eggs—it keeps giving. There is an increased awareness now about empowering the country's women among the middle-classes, which in turn is an ever-increasing consumer base with spending power. In 2019, the UNDP in India assessed corporate engagement in women's economic empowerment and found that 72 per cent of BSE 100 companies (the largest Indian companies) reported an intervention in women's empowerment, meaning they diverted corporate social responsibility (CSR) funds towards women's empowerment initiatives (although its share still remained low at 4 per cent of all CSR expenditure).[7]

'Today, companies acknowledge that workplace diversity and empowering women contributes to business success,' Nadia Rasheed, Deputy Resident Representative, UNDP India, had said at the launch of the report.[8]

But while the private sector continues to invest in other complementary development priorities such as education, healthcare, and environment, investment in women's economic empowerment remained at just 8 per cent of overall CSR expenditure (2017–18). Additionally, underdeveloped states such as Bihar, Jharkhand, Assam, where this intervention is more important than in major metros, saw very little CSR intervention in women's economic empowerment.

The report also noticed that 'CSR strategies, currently, are missing certain critical aspects of the women's economic empowerment lifecycle. ...Companies are taking a siloed approach, with only 31 per cent of the businesses intervening in all three stages of prepare, enter, grow, and sustain. ...CSR support was concentrated in the Prepare and Enter stages.' The report suggested that companies look beyond their regular focus on women's initiatives and instead promote an enabling environment for women to participate and thrive in the workforce because 'when women work, it has a multiplier effect on their lives, the lives of their children, families, and communities'.[9]

At the time of the UNDP survey, women made up less than 10 per cent of the permanent workforce of the majority of BSE 100 companies. This may be because these companies are mostly in the automobile and manufacturing sectors, which have, historically, been dominated by men.[10] That it still hasn't changed says much more about corporate commitment to women's economic empowerment than anything else.

In her book *The Gender Effect*, Kathryn Moeller exposes the inherent hypocrisy of corporate investment in the empowerment of women and girls. She says corporations are focusing on women and girls to grow markets and profits. They are 'investing in, rather than transforming, existing inequities across multiple axes of difference—gender, racial, class, religious, and geographic—even as they claim to be ameliorating them'.[11]

Indian corporates have learnt that many women are now decision makers and possess purchasing power. A paper published in 2020 suggested: 'women are consuming goods not only to seek pleasure but also to reward themselves. It is therefore prudent for firms to break gender stereotypes and frame their product campaigns emphasizing development of women's personal and social self.'[12] It goes on to discuss Ariel India's advertisement campaign 'Share the Load', which attempts to show the consumer that doing laundry is not only a woman's job. They could have chosen to widen the message and urged that housework, including laundry, was not just women's work. But the brand's commitment to its product is larger than its commitment to women's empowerment; the latter functions more as a marketing gimmick. To expect that advertisements such as this are leading to some kind of revolution inside Indian homes is laughable. They are simply tools for profit making. Also, as a quick aside, it is actually fairly common among men from middle and low-income groups to wash their own clothes. During my reporting trips across India, I have come across many men from these groups washing their own clothes after taking a bath—they treat it as a part of their personal care routine.

When corporates invest in gender-sensitive campaigns, they are more focused on marketing than in bringing any serious change to the patriarchal status quo. If corporations were really becoming more gender sensitive, we wouldn't have this figure staring at us: women hold a little over 17 per cent of the board seats in India, an increase of around 9 per cent from 2014 when the Companies Act 2013 made it mandatory to have one woman member on every board. However, only about 4 per cent of the board chairs are women; this is down by 0.9 per cent since 2018. Among Indian CEOs, women comprised only around 5 per cent.[13]

Some experts argue that women are increasingly becoming decision makers at home with greater purchasing power. The annual economic survey is the best source of this information. I love reading this survey for its words of hope and gentle reprimands (to the government) and the tone-deaf reading of women's issues. The survey for the financial year 2018–19 had noted that the financial inclusion of women is an important tool of economic empowerment. At an all-India level, the proportion of women having a bank account that they themselves use has increased from 15.5 per cent in 2005–2006 to 53 per cent in 2015–16. Women's participation in household decision-making also improved significantly during this period. As per NFHS-5 (2019–2021), participation of married women in household decision-making increased to over 88 per cent from 84 per cent in 2015–16.[14]

What are these household decisions that women have an increased say in? Some women have been granted the right to make decisions on what brand of washing powder or groceries to buy (mostly with money that has been allocated to them by their spouses as household expenses). But how many women in India can make important financial decisions about investments, mortgages, and loans; decisions about buying, selling, and renovating property; and decisions about their children's education, career path, marriage?

The Indian Human Development Survey (IHDS), conducted by the University of Maryland and the National Council of Applied Economic Research, had compared data from 2004–2005 with data available for 2011–2012. The 2012 survey found only 4.99 per cent of women in India had sole control over choosing their husbands (this was 5 per cent in 2005). The 2012 survey also found that almost 80 per cent of women needed permission to visit a health centre (compared to around 74 per cent earlier). Women, however, seemed to have control over what was cooked in the house. Cooking decisions were made by about 93 per cent women, while about 50 per cent reported that the husband took part in deciding what would be cooked at home.[15]

These findings are corroborated by the NFHS-4, which considered women to be equal participants in household decisions if they made decisions alone or jointly with their husbands regarding their own healthcare, major household purchases, and visits to the woman's family or relatives. The survey found that 63 per cent of women participated in all three decisions. However, the details paint a different picture. For example, only 12 per cent of women made decisions about their own healthcare alone (as opposed to jointly with their husbands).[16]

'Women's participation in household decision making has increased substantially since NFHS-3. The greatest increase, of 21 percentage points, is observed in women's participation in decisions about major household purchases from 53 per cent in NFHS-3 to 73 per cent in NFHS-4.'[17]

The NFHS-4 findings are particularly interesting because they throw a light on men's attitudes—28 per cent of men felt they should have greater say than the women when it comes to major household purchases, and 21 per cent thought they should have a greater role in deciding whether to visit the wife's family. However, when it came to decisions about purchases for daily needs, they are happy to leave that to their wives.[18] Women's participation in their own healthcare in the ten years since NFHS-3 increased by only 13 per cent, while their participation in decisions about visits to relatives rose by just 14 per cent.[19] This slow rate of increase of women's participation in decision-making between two rounds of a decadal survey is cause for alarm. If you look at who has the purchasing power in middle-class families, you will find that it is gendered in nature. Women end up making decisions regarding the purchase of household products, essentially an extension of the work they are supposed to do at home.

'Capitalism doesn't want or promote any sort of equality whether in terms of gender or caste or income. Higher the income inequality, the better for capitalism. More unequal the society, the more corporations get away by paying less to women workers. I don't think capitalism will or can provide any help in demolishing the patriarchal system.

They want to create inequalities in the system. Because that benefits them in terms of accumulation. The more equal the distribution is the less the capitalist accumulation, in very basic terms,' economist Shiuli Vanaja told me.

Feminism for the 99% argues that capitalist societies have always divided reproductive labour along racial lines.[20] In a country like India, this division is based on caste hierarchies. Of the country's much exploited and poorly paid domestic workers, a majority are women from marginalized groups and so-called lower castes whose unappreciated and often unacknowledged labour allows more affluent women, like me, to step out of the home to work.

A paper published in 2020 on capitalism and inequality said that the ideological view of capitalism 'combines with the invisibility of structural domination to construct an entirely misguided understanding of inequality. According to the conventional view, capitalism created a complete break with the past: suddenly, all individuals were free and equal. The core of capitalist society was supposed to be competition on a level playing field for wealth. It is difficult to construct a myth that is further from the truth. The precapitalist inequalities were not abolished by capitalism and not even by the advent of democracy. And competition in capitalist societies is not about money. It is about capital but only a tiny group monopolizes capital and actually competes for it. The rest compete for means of consumption. However, capital is only a means for domination. Inequality, in reality, is about domination. Since the structures of domination are rendered invisible in capitalist societies, very little can be done about inequality.'[21]

Feminism for the 99% calls liberal feminism the 'handmaiden of capitalism' and says it has done more harm than good and 'far from providing the solution, liberal feminism is part of the problem' because it has steadfastly refused to 'address the socio-economic constraints that make freedom and empowerment impossible for the large majority of women'.[22] Many in India can relate to this. Concepts of leaning in and breaking the glass ceiling are intrinsically privileged, when for most women, especially in India, the biggest challenge is to survive everyday misogyny and patriarchy to acquire their most basic rights.

Liberal feminism loves to focus on the individual, the book says. In a country like India, we need to focus on the group. Its focus on individual advancement can be seen best among social media celebrity which 'confuses feminism with the ascent of individual women' and 'in that world, feminism risks becoming a trending hashtag and a vehicle of self-promotion, deployed less to liberate the many than to elevate the few'.[23]

For the 99 per cent, the interplay of capitalism and patriarchy has created a vicious cycle. There is a constant pull between their roles as workers and as homemakers or nurturers. Let's try and answer a simple question—why do corporations in India try to romanticize patriarchal festivals such as Karva Chauth where a woman fasts for an entire day to pray for her husband's long life? These advertisements serve a dual purpose. They convince women that such acts of sacrifice are undertaken all for love and, hence, are beyond reproach, which in turn keeps these festivals alive and the coffers of businesses full.

But why do women fast? Women who are otherwise modern and educated, why do they fall into such patriarchal traps? My mother undertook a similar fast for Shiboratri (for Lord Shiva), a ritual where she had to fast from sunrise to sundown without even drinking a drop of water. And my mother, who rejected every other traditional imposition, couldn't say no to this because she didn't want to risk being criticized by her sisters-in-law or mother-in-law. Hungry and thirsty, she would leave home at 9 a.m., take three trains and two ferries and come home late in the evening looking exhausted. Then she would pick up her tray of offerings for the god and run to the nearest temple with me. All the other women would have arrived in their bridal finery, but my poor mother would be in a crumpled cotton sari, her hair dishevelled, her face pale and thin. She would hurry the priest to take her offering and pour the water on the shiva lingam. Then, we would leave. She didn't even want to do it. 'Why do you do it?' I had asked her once.

'It's a tradition.'

'But you don't like traditions.'

'I don't. But it's better to keep the peace at home. If I don't do it your father will sulk. And your aunts will come over specially to taunt me.'

These traditions should have been left to die a natural death. But rather than disappearing, we have been seeing a revival for many. Corporations, one may argue, are simply fulfilling consumer demands— if they stopped catering to these patriarchal festivals, will these festivals go away? Of course they won't, but reinventing them and broadcasting them through innumerable advertisements is surely delaying the process of their natural demise.

The other medium that has been consistently sending out gender-regressive messages is the television. Soaps and Bollywood films, after a series of progressive 80s and 90s content, have become increasingly regressive. Television soaps relentlessly stereotype women as stay-at-home, subservient beings, highlighting the breadwinner–homemaker binary, while most mainstream Bollywood films have disturbingly continued to portray the heroes as larger-than-life macho figures and the women as mere sidekicks.

These gender roles are also reinforced and introduced to our children through our epics. Most Indian epics portray men as heroic and brave, while the women are weak and vulnerable, completely at the mercy of the men in their lives. For centuries now these epics have propagated the idea that women are weaker. Epics like the Ramayana, reflect Indian families, where men should ideally have the last word and women are expected to be seen, and not heard. They also give edicts on how a woman should behave with propriety. In the Ramayana, for example, Rama is a virtuous prince. His father Dasarath is a helpless old man bewitched by his beautiful wife Kaikeyi. Kaikeyi is portrayed as devious and conniving, but also someone who is so gullible that she agrees to a plan hatched by her aide. Rama's mother Kausalya is powerless to stop the events that unfold because she is old and hence, not the king's favourite anymore. They end up living in the forest where Sita is abducted by the demon king Ravana and finally rescued by Rama with the help of his loyal follower Hanuman and his army of monkeys. Sita is celebrated as the ideal wife and daughter-in-law who sacrifices her happiness for the sake of her family. She submits herself to every decision made by her male relatives and her elders. When these epics are televised, as they often are, they propagate the same regressive values to millions.

If you happen to browse through some of the matrimonial ads online and in our country's newspapers, you will see that parents are looking for Sitas for their sons—pretty, subservient, same caste, same class brides.

As more women attain education and some social norms are weakened owing to relentless feminist advocacy, corporations and the entertainment industry have a responsibility to position themselves on the right side of gender equality.

∽

Today, there is a need to go back to Marxist literature, especially because the manner in which it defines women's labour is why traditionalists are opposed to it—it can disturb the status quo and interfere with the family structure that has emerged as a refuge for men. Marx defined housework as 'petty, stultifying, and degrading', while Engels said that with the 'emergence of private property and class, society had began grouping men as breadwinners and women as housewives—and therein had began women's oppression. ...Therein lies the great historical defeat of the female sex.' The Irish socialist republican James Connolly had said that if men were the slaves of a capitalist society, the housewives were 'the slave of the slave'.[24]

'Capitalism has placed on the shoulders of the woman a burden which crushes her: it has made her a wage worker without having lessened her cares as a housekeeper and mother,' Alexandra Kollontai, a Russian revolutionary, politician, diplomat, and Marxist theoretician had pointed out in an article in 1920.[25] This still holds true.

But then should Indian housewives demand wages for housework? Would that make their work visible and hence valued as Marxist feminists have argued? In 1975, Silvia Federici wrote that while capitalism exploited every worker, 'the wage at least recognizes that you are a worker, and you can bargain and struggle around and against the terms and the quantity of that wage, the terms and the quantity of that work'. But housework, she pointed out, was considered something that came naturally to women, 'an internal need, an aspiration, supposedly coming from the depth of our female character'.[26]

'Yet just how natural it is to be a housewife is shown by the fact that it takes at least twenty years of socialization—day-to-day training, performed by an unwaged mother—to prepare a woman for this role, to convince her that children and [a] husband are the best she can expect from life. Even so, it hardly succeeds. No matter how well-trained we are, few are the women who do not feel cheated when the bride's day is over and they find themselves in front of a dirty sink.'[27] Federici was one of the founders of the International Wages for Housework Campaign that started in Italy in 1972 under Selma James. The campaign demanded that housework should be compensated because it was the basis of industrial work.

'In fact, to demand wages for housework does not mean to say that if we are paid, we will continue to do it. It means precisely the opposite. To say that we want money for housework is the first step towards refusing to do it, because the demand for a wage makes our work visible,' she wrote.[28]

When Marxist feminists argue for wages for housework, they are putting the onus on the government to recognize housework as productive labour. But in India, when the debate began in earnest, it began on the wrong foot where it still remains. In 2012, Krishna Tirath, the then Women and Child Development minister, had said she was considering a proposal to quantify the work a housewife does at home and make it mandatory for men to share a certain percentage of their income with their stay-at-home wives.[29] But when you put the onus of paying a wage on the husband, you are basically entrenching the idea of him as the 'master'.

Monetizing housework will more than likely increase women's exploitation inside their homes and might even increase abuse and violence because in such a scenario she is a formalized wage earner, working under the man of the house. Intimate partner violence is 'far from being accidental' and 'grounded in the basic institutional structure of a capitalist society'. 'Often fuelled by alcohol, shame, and anxiety about maintaining dominance, this sort of gender violence is found in every period of capitalist development.'[30]

We do not need house 'wife' salaries but rather house 'work' salaries. The onus should be on the state, not on the husband. Only then can unpaid labour acquire the status of productive work. Either spouse could decide to stay home and earn a salary for caregiving duties. But we are not there yet.

'There are societies in India which are not as patriarchal as other societies. Secondly, the inter-generational as well as inter-gender relations are different in different parts of India. Not all women in India face "capitalism". There may be rural areas where there are self-reliant farms, there may be communities in, for example, Uttarakhand and other places where there is a form of agriculture industry which has less of the patriarchal attitudes. I think patriarchy and capitalism perhaps work as a poison or double whammy for Indian women in urban areas and perhaps amongst the better off,' feminist economist Devaki Jain told me over email.

That is true, but capitalism has reached most corners of our country riding on the wave of development. The more buildings we build, the more we need cheap labour. This cheap labour likely comes from farming communities. Farmers are distraught over debts and bad crops and for a part of the year, many farmers migrate to cities and towns to work at construction sites to make some extra money. When they move to the cities to work, the onus of both tilling the land and looking after the family falls on the women. In Uttarakhand, where I spend half the year, I see women shouldering a bulk of the farm work alongside household chores and care work. They are as overworked as women in urban areas. So, while capitalism lures the men to the towns and cities to work as construction labourers or as messengers or drivers, the burden of farm work is left to the women, including labour-intensive work like weeding.

Jashoda, one of my neighbours in a village in Uttarakhand called Parvada, begins her day at 4 a.m. A widow, she lives in the neighbouring village with a school-going daughter. Her son works in a shop in a nearby town, so the responsibility of looking after the land falls squarely on her. She also works as an anganwadi worker for the local government crèche and lends her labour in other people's fields. While she is out the whole day, her fifteen-year-old daughter takes care of the cooking in the morning and when she gets back home from school in the afternoons. Could one blame her daughter if she decided one fine day that it was all too much for her and dropped out of school? Capitalism has not left out even lower-income women from its web of exploitation, especially when it comes to the informal economy, which is run overwhelmingly by women. From the domestic workers who make it possible for some of us to step out to work, to community health workers whose contribution to public health, especially during the pandemic, has been monumental—our country runs on the underappreciated labour of women, including unpaid labour at home. Even if there were to be studies about the superwoman syndrome or the burden of the double shift, these women, just like a vast majority of middle-class women, would be left out of the count. But the fact is that they suffer this syndrome just as much as those of us who are part of the formal labour force. Their work is invisible, their overwork is invisible—but the fallout cannot be any different, can it?

Covid-19, despite the devastation it has wrought in its various waves, has blown the lid off women's paid and unpaid care burden. When I began writing this book in 2013, I struggled to find reports and studies to back up my own analyses, but in 2022, when I was working on the final edits, I was amazed at just how varied the available literature was. There is a spotlight on women's double shift, their burden of housework and caregiving as well as the various other factors that are standing in the way of their true empowerment. This is truly a watershed moment in history and the only turn we can take from here is towards a gender-responsive world. I say gender responsive and not gender equal because that goal is still unattainable in our lifetimes. While the pandemic put a spotlight on the struggles of women worldwide, it also stalled advances being made towards a gender-equal world—South Asia can now only hope to achieve gender parity in two centuries.[31]

WHY ARE WOMEN NOT WORKING?

*When a man gives his opinion, he's a man. When a woman gives her opinion,
she's a bitch.*

—Bette Davis

The day Divya completed three months at her new job, she was
at a team meeting, impatiently tapping her pen on her mobile
phone. One eye on the screen of her phone—seven missed
calls. Her surreptitious glances were not enough for her to gauge who
was calling, but she was pretty sure it was one of her sons. She needed
to be home for her elder son's birthday party. But the meeting didn't
seem to be ending any time soon. She looked at her watch again.

Her husband was picking up the cake but the rest was all her
responsibility. On top of that, she had to take an early flight to
Hyderabad the next morning to attend a conference.

She felt physically sick. The nanny had been briefed about the
birthday party and her travel schedule many times and she had agreed
to the extra hours. And yet Divya was anxious and those seven missed
calls were only making her stress worse. This was her first outstation
assignment; she could no longer make up excuses to get out of them
just because she couldn't manage to organize childcare. Her husband
was almost always on call. She wouldn't want to jeopardize his
career over hers. Divya believed that she was merely supplementing
her husband's earnings. She had never thought to put herself, her
career, her desires, and wants above that of her husband. He was the
breadwinner; she was the supporting spouse.

'If only my mother had not passed away so soon,' she thought
to herself for the hundredth time that day.

'Divya?'

She returned to the meeting with a start.

'Yes?'

'I said, any questions?'

'No, none.'

'Hope you're not thinking of an excuse to get out of tomorrow's workshop?' Her line manager joked. But Divya didn't like the joke. It sounded like a dig. She knew it was.

'Lucky are those women who can either afford or find suitable live-in nannies,' she thought gloomily, picking up her folder with one hand and dialling home with the other.

That day there had been no emergency. Her boys just wanted to talk to her about the birthday party and wanted to know when she would be home. But she was never short on emergencies—every day without one was another bullet dodged.

Divya went to her out-of-town assignment, worrying through it all about her children and the home. She knew she couldn't keep doing it. Once she completed her assignment, she handed in her resignation.

'It was too much stress,' she told me. 'I just was not able to do it all. I was anxious. I felt like I was going to have a nervous breakdown. I cried all the time and I thought of ending my life, too, often.'

Divya did not share her struggle to balance work and her personal life with her manager, who incidentally was also a woman, because she knew it would do her no favours. It is an unwritten rule of women's emancipation in our country to never talk about your struggles. Hide them. Stew in them. But put on a brave face and soldier ahead.

Divya's concerns were not unfounded. In December 2021, a woman Delhi High Court judge had advised women lawyers to cope without complaining and to manage their time competently, the implication being that women were not already doing that. She had gone on to urge women to hire help, which is not just a financial but also a societal privilege. She criticized women's 'sacrificial mentality' without delving into the origins of such mentality. She asked women lawyers not to 'seek sympathy from the court or from lawyers on the other side or even your clerk. You don't have to tell them that my child is unwell, I have to pick up my daughter from school. Please don't do that…. That stereotypes you.'[1] But this mentality doesn't exist in a vacuum, neither can it be decimated in one. Women take such advice as the only way to move forward in their careers and suffer in silence or leave the workforce when it becomes too much for them to cope. The overwhelming message being sent to us by senior women professionals, whom we hold up as ideals, is that women will have to work *around* the patriarchy. The onus is always on us. Our seniors teach us to compromise and not negotiate, they teach us to tip-toe around patriarchy instead of calling it out and demolishing it in our homes and workplaces. And we follow in their footsteps, modelling our careers on their advice, playing by men's rules in the workplace; kow-towing to patriarchy, not extricating ourselves from it.

If it was as simple as hiring a driver and a cook for women to continue to work, then our formal labour force would look more balanced. A lack of understanding and empathy is what drives women to the brink—to be expected to do it all and do so without expecting any institutional support is appalling.

In 2018, I visited a village in Noida called Uchagaon. Lying cocooned between glitzy shopping malls and skyscrapers, the village was a prosperous one, an urban village. The residents came from a mix of rural and urban backgrounds, which was evident from their clothes, the way they talked, the things that made up their lifestyle. I camped at the house of a former village council chief. His wife was an energetic woman. She wore the sari the modern way with the pallu hanging behind her, only partially covering her head. Their house was spacious with a large courtyard and a shed for livestock where a couple of cows were masticating nonchalantly. She introduced me to her daughter-in-law, Varsha. 'She has done her master's in economics,' she informed me.

'You don't want her to work?' I had picked up on some pride in her voice as she told me of her daughter-in-law's educational achievements and felt confident to say this to her directly.

'No, no! Why would she work? We don't need the money. My son works in the city. She's in charge of the household and she does a wonderful job of it,' the mother-in-law told me, while beaming at the young woman. 'All that education has made her very smart. We depend on her for everything.' She asked Varsha to key in my number on her phone. 'I don't know how to use it so she handles it for me.' Varsha was in her mid-twenties. She was dressed in a simple cotton salwar kameez. As we were chatting inside the house, and her father-in-law was sitting out on the courtyard, her face was bare. We had a brief conversation—she was indeed smart but knew her limits well enough to not press to be allowed to work. 'Our society is a little different,' she told me. 'Some things are just not done here.' Varsha is among the 17 per cent of women graduates who are not available to work in our country because of household responsibilities.[2]

The fall in women's labour force participation rate (for those aged twenty-five to fifty-four) in India and the country's aspirations to become a $5 trillion economy are at odds with each other. Women's labour force participation has stagnated in urban areas since the late 1980s and has seen a concentrated decline among younger (aged twenty-five to forty) married women in rural areas. The Progress of the World's Women report in 2019 suggested that this drop could be because 'family incomes have stabilized as men have shifted from casualized forms of work to regular wage earning, thereby encouraging women's withdrawal from paid work'.[3] Poor quality of available paid work combined with long hours of unpaid household work and caregiving might be deterring women from finding paid work once the household's income has improved. The report also found that 'rural married women aged twenty-five to forty are more likely to have school-age children; with girls' rising rates of secondary school attendance, women are less likely to have their daughters' help with unpaid domestic responsibilities and thus are more likely to forgo paid employment themselves'.[4]

A United Nations development study in 2015 had estimated unpaid care work in India at 39 per cent of the GDP, adding that 'women have no choice but to give priority to unpaid work and stay out of the labour force, they make large sacrifices, perhaps missing the chance to expand their capabilities in the workplace. They also lose opportunities for economic independence'.[5] According to latest figures, only a little over 22 per cent of Indian women participate in the labour market, translating to a gender gap of more than 70 per cent. Illiteracy, lack of decent jobs, and the burden of household responsibilities—none of these stressors have improved in the last few decades to improve women's economic participation. Our contribution to our country's GDP has remained at 18 per cent, one of the lowest in the world. Increasing 'women's access to digital technologies and financial products' and reducing the time women spend on unpaid care work 'by filling gaps in essential infrastructure, including childcare, and promoting labour-saving technologies such as clean cooking stoves' are some ways this could be addressed.[6]

In a patriarchal society like ours, it is not enough to just create programmes and policies (and laws) without sustained efforts to change mindsets and, hence, normative behaviour. Following the Global Gender Gap report in 2021, the Indian government listed out the measures it currently has in place to address gender inequality, including initiatives such as Beti Bachao, Beti Padhao, which ensures the protection, survival, and education of the girl child; the National Crèche Scheme, which ensures that women take up gainful employment by providing a safe, secure, and stimulating environment for their children; Pradhan Mantri Awaas Yojana, which aims to provide affordable housing to women and their families; skill training provided to women under the Skill India Mission; the various financial schemes aimed at encouraging entrepreneurship among women; and the Women's Studies Centres that have been established in educational institutions to undertake research and develop curricula in the areas of gender equity, economic self-reliance of women, girls' education, etc.[7] The Kasturba Gandhi Balika Vidyalaya Scheme was launched in 2004 to provide residential schools at the upper primary level for girls from disadvantaged groups or communities, which was extended to senior secondary in 2018–19. As of 2018, there were, however, only around 3,700 schools under the scheme.[8] India has some of the world's best plans and programmes for women and girls but their implementation has left much to be desired. Changing deeply embedded patriarchal attitudes would allow a larger number of women and girls to have access to these schemes.

Even in 2020, nine out of ten Indians believed that the wife must always obey the husband—a shocking statistic. Four in ten Indians also believed that husbands should be responsible for providing for the family, while the wives should focus on the home. These figures are from a Pew Research Centre study, published in March 2022. While there are some occasional rays of hope—62 per cent of adults said both men and women should be responsible for taking care of children—the overall statistics paint a bleak picture—around 34 per cent of adults felt that childcare is a woman's sole responsibility. A little over half of those interviewed said both men and women should be responsible for the family income, but 43 per cent saw this as a largely male obligation. Eight in ten Indians felt that when there's a scarcity of jobs, men should have greater rights to employment than women. The survey also underlined a son preference, and that parents felt their sons should have greater rights to inheritance as they are expected to look after the parents in their old age. A vast majority of Indians surveyed also did not feel that women are discriminated against. The study concluded what we have known for a while: 'These attitudes, combined with a scarcity of jobs, may be one reason why India has one of the lowest female labour force participation rates in the world.'[9]

So much has changed in India since my mother stepped out to work. But two things have remained unchanged—women's lives and empowerment and men's control over them. When my mother's generation stepped out to work, the 'working woman' was such a new concept that while they faced resistance at home, at work they were patronized by male colleagues and bosses. This show of benevolent patriarchy made their working lives easier because they were excused from tougher assignments or those that involved travelling out of town or night shifts. This benevolence is no longer present. Women have emerged as worthy competitors and the stranglehold of patriarchal control has tightened to keep them subservient to men, in the home and outside.

Working in an office is still considered a masculine activity. 'In India there are different stereotypes. Men are allowed to be dominant, while women are expected to be deferential. Women have to ensure they are authoritative but likeable,' Joan Williams, founding director of the US-based Center for WorkLife Law, told me. 'If she is likeable, she is incompetent. He is assertive, but she is aggressive,' she adds. At the workplace, across the world, women have to walk the tightrope between what is traditionally considered masculine and feminine behaviour. And across societies, across cultures, across countries, (most) men have perfected the art of undermining and sidelining women who challenge them, and they get away with it as the system is designed to protect them. This has never been truer than in India's uber-patriarchal society.

'The idea of a worker is someone who is always available. An ideal mother and an ideal worker do not align together well,' Williams continues. The gender bias women face at work, Williams says, is pretty similar in India and the US. Women have to provide more evidence of their competence, it takes longer for them to get promoted; men are judged on potential, while women are judged purely on performance. This is leading to a kind of fatigue, at least in India. Women are exiting silently, unable to handle the unfair demands at home and the harassment at work. They are tired of putting way more effort than their male counterparts for only a fraction of the rewards, both in terms of money as well as career growth. As Williams says, 'If you have to be twice as good, you will only go half as far.'

'After a while, you do ask yourself how much more of this can I take?' says Divya. I am surrounded by women friends who are struggling to find jobs after being victimized by male colleagues or women employers, who willingly perpetuate the patriarchy to stay in the game. In India, this is even more pronounced. Women bail on women in India. They bail on themselves, choosing silence over speaking out against abuses, their own or a co-worker's. Our empowerment is so fragile that we are forever walking on eggshells, lest we lose our hard-earned freedom. After struggling to fit in, to stay afloat purely on the basis of my capabilities for over two decades, and achieving possibly just a quarter of my potential in my career, while being a superwoman and a supermom, I no longer care about doing it all.

The insistence on doing it all in a country like ours, with so many different forces at play, adds to the existing pressure on working women. As they say, we have to learn to walk before we run.

Take 'Lean In Circles'. Lean In believes in the power of women to drive change through the Lean In Circles. At the time of writing this book, there were more than 50,000 Lean In Circles in 184 countries. The Circles are peer groups that give women a place where they can set goals, practice skills such as negotiating and interviewing, and find inspiration and support. The organization came out of Facebook COO Sheryl Sandberg's book by the same name. In her book, Sandberg devotes only three chapters to work–family balance and through the rest of the book talks about how women are capable of taking control of their careers and forging ahead. She has been criticized for placing the onus of overcoming gender biases on women. 'We lower our own expectations of what we can achieve,' she wrote.[10] This is not something women do deliberately. Our professional successes are not dependent on something as simple as deciding to take control of one's life and career or to look in the mirror and practice self-worth or even self-love. Given the fact that so few Indian women are part of the formal workforce in our country, many women are what the Lean In organization calls 'onlies'.

'When you are the only woman in the room or on the team, and we know from our research that onlies feel left out, under pressure to perform, excluded. They are also more likely to experience micro aggressions, more likely to be sexually harassed in their career, and they are one and a half times more likely to leave their jobs. In corporate US, only one in five women are an only—but here, given that there are so many fewer women in the workplace, the only experience is very real. When I talk about the only experience in our circles in India, I see a lot of heads nodding in agreement. The shared experiences make you feel how much harder it is to succeed as a woman in India and hence the urgent need to cheer on women who are successful,' Rachel Thomas told me during a visit to India in 2019.

She had noticed more self-doubt and a larger confidence gap among Indian women. 'When we speak to women in the US or in Europe, this always comes up as a core part of being a woman in the workplace but in India it is so, so essential—women don't feel comfortable speaking up, they don't feel comfortable asking for more or even asking something [like a raise or a promotion] for themselves.'

But then again, she says, the way the word 'confidence' is bandied about in our society and in workplaces is a 'disservice to women'.

'When you say things like why women can't be more confident or why can't women be as confident as men, you are putting the onus of being confident on the women, when actually it is a reaction to the culture,' Thomas says.

During her interactions with women in the Circles, the things that struck Thomas the most were that while the experiences of being in the workplace—self-doubt, impostor syndrome, sexist bosses, harassment—felt similar, the dynamics were unique to India. 'It is not just difficult for women to get into the workforce but also to retain their employment. Women face more of a headwind and get much less support at home than say, for example, women in the US,' Thomas said.

In a study in 2011, Dr Karine Schomer found that issues faced by women are often similar in every part of the world, especially when it came to work–life balance.[11] She identified these issues as long work hours, challenging schedules, time-consuming commutes, need for childcare and eldercare support systems, the burden of household responsibilities, career path demands versus family demands, stress-related health problems, and societal attitudes towards women and work. The study noted that the US is one of the few countries in the world that does not have federal laws guaranteeing paid maternity leave, paternity leave, a minimum number of paid sick days a year, or the right to breastfeed a child in the workplace. In contrast, India has progressive national laws and governmental policies in all these areas, although there is not much emphasis on their implementation. What worked to the advantage of Indian working women, according to the study, was the availability of low-wage labour. Most middle-class Indian homes have either live-in servants or household help that come daily to do cleaning, cooking, and other household chores. In the United States, this is a luxury available only to the wealthy. The report also argued that in India, women have the support of the extended family system, though, as has been discussed earlier, this support has dwindled following the breakdown of the joint family. Institutional resources for social welfare needs, such as childcare and eldercare are more extensive in the US, infrastructure for commuting and flexible work arrangements are more advanced, and both food preparation and house cleaning are more mechanized as compared to India.

In Europe, childcare coverage is enviable and shows what we should aim for. In 2019, 89.6 per cent of children in the EU aged between three years and the minimum compulsory school age received formal childcare, compared with 96.7 per cent for those aged between the minimum compulsory school age and twelve years of age. In Denmark, parents pay 25 per cent of the cost for their children attending day care, and if they decide to hire a nanny, the government pays for that, too.[12] India, on the other hand, does not have a system of public funding for preschool childcare, although education for children between six and fourteen years is free in government-run schools. The one point of similarity between all developed nations is that they provide women with options to outsource housework and caregiving duties to professional institutions, leaving them free to join the formal workforce. Conversely, one could argue that in India these systems are still not in place because the government still does not envision women as productive workers who can contribute to the GDP of the country but rather as support systems for productive workers—the men. India may aim to become a trillion-dollar economy but it is unlikely to happen until it makes provisions that allow women to work as full-time productive workers in the formal workforce without being burdened by overwork.

While Indian women have made enormous progress in higher education enrolment, workforce participation, and career advancement within recent years, and many cultural attitudes are catching up with this new reality, they are still battling age-old ideas about who they are supposed to be.

And yet, change is on the horizon.

During her India visit, Rachel Thomas had an interesting interaction with a company executive. 'A male leader in a company meeting asked us what companies can do to make sure women are getting more support at home. It was a beautiful question showing awareness about the dynamics here. In the US, they do not think about what happens at home. Their influence typically stops within the four walls of their organizations....' In the US, support for women workers, Thomas says, is generally restricted to flexible timings, paid family leave, and support during and after maternity leave. So, she was surprised that workplaces in India were willing to go beyond the workspace and work with the families to support their employees.

Thomas was surprised to find that human resources, too, were asking about how to bring about changes at home. She was then told about initiatives such as '"bring your mother or mother-in-law to work", to instil pride in them that their daughter or daughters-in-law were doing something worthwhile, and I realized this is a much more layered problem than just getting women to join the workforce.'

THE HOUSEWIFE CONUNDRUM

Some women marry houses.

—Anne Sexton, 'Housewife'

In 2017, Indra Nooyi, president of PepsiCo had shared an illuminating post on LinkedIn about work–life balance. When I read the post, I interpreted it somewhat differently. Yes, it was about work–life balance but it was also about women's perceived role in their households. In her post, she wrote about how in 2001, when she was appointed the president of the company, she ran home to share the good news with her mother, who was visiting from India. The promotion was a rare honour for a woman, that too a woman of Indian origin. She had come a long way, bursting through corporate glass ceilings. For a woman from India, she had climbed mountains, traversed deserts, battled prejudice and preconceived notions and patriarchy. But when she reached home that day, her mother had ignored her enthusiasm and instead asked her to quickly go out to the store because they had run out of milk.

'So, I go out and get milk. And when I come back, I'm hopping mad. I say, "I had great news for you. I've just been named President of PepsiCo. And all you want me to do is go out and get milk." Then she says, "Let me explain something to you. You may be President of PepsiCo. But when you step into this house, you're a wife and mother first. Nobody can take that place. So, leave that crown in the garage."'[1]

Nooyi, undoubtedly one of India's biggest success stories among women achievers, took a lesson from this incident. She says, she thought her mother was right: 'No matter who we are, or what we do, nobody can take our place in our families.'

'Now, I'll admit, I've found it's rarely possible to be the kind of mother, wife, employee, and person you want to be—all at the same time. Often, you need to make a choice, and that's especially true if you want to be CEO. There's no way around it,' Nooyi had added in her post. She talks of the painful choices she and her husband made so she could carry on with her ambition while knowing that many women did not have extended family to help with childcare or jobs that give them the financial means to pay for additional support. While she never spoke about it publicly, the choices they made had an impact. She understood the gender imbalance that Indian women have to struggle against no matter who they are. As the CEO of one of the world's largest multinationals, she created systems that would support employees—especially women—who are caring for young children, aging parents, or both. Under her aegis, PepsiCo started offering on-site childcare at their headquarters in Purchase, New York and near-site childcare for employees in Plano, Texas. 'And we offer access to quality childcare for employees in certain markets around the world. That's just part of our larger effort to make sure we're supporting our working caregivers in every way we can and empowering people to build not just a career, but a life.'

Indra Nooyi, born Indra Krishnamurthy, was raised mostly in Chennai, India. Nooyi has consistently ranked among the world's 100 most powerful women. In 2008, *TIME* listed her among the 100 most influential people in the world.[2] She was ranked by the Fortune list in 2015 as the world's second most powerful woman.[3] As the CEO of PepsiCo, in 2011, Nooyi earned $17 million, including a base salary of $1.9 million, a cash bonus of $2.5 million, and pension value and deferred remuneration of $3 million. In 2014, she earned $19,087,832, including $5.5 million of equity.[4]

And yet, she has to leave her crown in the garage. It's a reminder of how even the most powerful of women have to put their role within the family structure first. This raises a question—why do trailblazers like Nooyi never call out this misogyny for what it is? If even women with their reach have to tiptoe around patriarchy, what hope is there for the rest of us?

The year after Nooyi was asked to leave her crown in the garage, I met many superwomen on wheels—the 'working' housewives of Mumbai locals. Many miles and oceans and privileges separate them, and yet they are united in the fact that all are expected to be homemakers first.

A woman I met on a Mumbai local train in 2002 told me, 'Once you are in the house, you are the mother and the wife. Your family looks to you to feed them and look after them. That's how it is.' This was my second day in the city, my first day taking the local train to work. My morning and evening train rides soon became a study in gender roles. On Mumbai's efficient network of overcrowded local trains, I discovered superwomen daily.

That evening I found myself in the presence of super industrious women, cutting and chopping vegetables, kneading dough. Some women bought the vegetables from roving train vendors and fished out chopping boards and knives from their bags. I was a bit taken aback—I hadn't seen anything like this before. The women were laughing and gossiping with each other while swiftly working in a running train with no space to even breathe. 'What are you doing?' I asked curiously of my neighbour. 'What does it look like?' She laughed at me.

'We are getting a headstart on dinner preparations,' one of them told me. 'I have an hour to kill. By the time I get home, it will be late and everyone will be hungry and waiting for dinner. This way I can get dinner going as soon as I get home.'

'What about your husband, can't he help?' I asked, to amazed laughter once more.

'Where are you from, girl? Which husbands cook? Anyway, the kitchen is a woman's responsibility. Does it look good if a man is cooking there?' an elderly woman responded.

In the mornings, when these women start out, the women's coach is almost empty. There's still no space to sit but no breathless crowds either. As the train starts on its route, the coach fills up with women making their way to the city to work, their hair wet from a hurried shower. Their saris are smartly starched, salwar suits neatly pinned and tucked. Some are attired in tops and trousers. In the evenings, their sarees are crumpled; there are shadows under their kohl-rimmed eyes.

I did not ask any of the women their names. I didn't need to.

They were every Indian woman.

The housewife conundrum takes on new forms for women who work informally. They are considered housewives even though they do perform productive labour. If there ever was to be a detailed study on the superwoman syndrome in India, these women would be left out of the count.

Take for example Kusum, a beauty therapist from Faridabad. A gregarious, quirky person, she's always wrapped up in socks and gloves—even in the peak of summer—as she roams the city nearly from dawn till dusk visiting her clients at their homes on her red scooter. Kusum was born in a small village a few kilometres from Varanasi. Her elder brother had moved to Delhi and set up a prosperous business. Kusum and her siblings came to live with him. All of them enrolled themselves in various vocational courses. Kusum chose to train in make-up and beauty. However, Kusum was too tall, too dark, too plump and she was married off to a man who didn't have a stable job. The husband's family constantly demanded money and gifts from her brothers until Kusum put her foot down. She lodged a complaint against her husband and in-laws at the local police station. That stopped the demands and the mental and physical torture.

Kusum had given up her job at a beauty salon when her marriage was arranged. After a few years of marriage, however, she realized that she needed to start working again to support the family because her husband was constantly in-between jobs. She set up her own beauty business but decided on something that wouldn't be very capital intensive. She painstakingly built up her home salon business, gave birth to two children, built her own house, sent her children to good schools. But she also worked almost eighteen hours a day to make this happen. Kusum worked until the seventh month of both her pregnancies. 'If I had taken a break, how would we have managed at home? My husband never had a stable job,' she told me. It was not a complaint, but a mere statement of fact. Even today, she spends twelve hours working with her clients. She devotes another six hours to unpaid work around the house—cooking, cleaning, and helping the children with homework.

One day, rushing to get to her last appointment before she could go home, Kusum met with an accident. A car crashed into her scooter and she fell over, but she got up almost immediately, grabbed her things, and tried restarting her scooter. It was at this moment that a man came up to her and handed her something—it was half of her little finger. She hadn't even realized that her finger had been sliced off when she fell. She stared at the finger for a while, and then at the bloody stump on her hand. Then, clutching the little finger in her hands, she called her husband to take her back home.

'It was just getting really late and I kept thinking of all the dishes in the kitchen waiting to be cleaned, the dinner that needed to be cooked, the cleaning up, and then waking up again next morning as early as possible—I was just not thinking. I just wanted to reach home at the earliest! The sooner I reached, the sooner I would be done with all the work and the sooner I would be able to go to sleep.'

Later, she had to get the finger grafted. The procedure left a permanent scar. I briefly wondered: what made her, and other women like her, keep going?

'Don't you get tired roaming around constantly? Why don't you open a salon?' I had asked her. 'Opening a shop means investment. I cannot afford that. I have the children's future to look after. A house to build. So much to do.'

The day she lost her little finger, she never made it to her last appointment. But she was back at work after a month, although, ideally, she should have rested for much longer.

'Who has the time to rest? Who will do the housework? Or the cleaning? My husband won't eat if I don't cook. So, I was up and about. Then I thought, why shouldn't I come to work?' she told me. She couldn't afford to not work for a long time at a stretch. Her husband, though usually out of work, didn't share household duties. Kusum wouldn't dream of asking her husband to share her chores.

'It might happen in your city, sister, but not in the villages,' Rama, a farmer from Mukteshwar in Uttarakhand had said to me.

I was visiting the quiet hill station for the weekend and had earlier noticed three women labouring up the hill, heavy loads on their heads, their shadows growing longer as the day wore on. They had been at it for almost ten hours. I offered them tea and learnt their names—Surbhi, Maya, and Rama. The three women lived in a nearby village. Over tea, we talked about their lives. The three of them had near identical lives.

Maya is thirty years old. She has been married for over ten years and has two sons and two daughters. She wakes up every morning at 4 a.m. She sweeps the house, feeds the livestock, and then fires up the mud oven. She makes tea, wakes up her children and her husband. By this time, her in-laws are also up. She serves them fresh tea and biscuits and gets into the kitchen with her cup of tea, which she gulps down as she chops her way through mounds of vegetables, rolling out rotis, and making curries while shouting at her children to get ready. The mornings are always a blur. Once she has packed their lunch boxes and seen them out the door, she can relax—but only for a few seconds. Next, she must give her in-laws their medicines, then start preparing lunch for the family. For her own breakfast, she hurriedly eats a little bit of food, swallowing it down with more tea.

Surbhi is twenty-five years old. She has been married for over five years and has two sons. Rama is twenty-one years old and has been married for a year. She does not have any children yet. They, too, wake up before dawn and feed the livestock, their families, cook lunch, and shove some food down their throats. At 7 a.m., the women meet. They then carry loads of organic waste to the compost pit. They do this non-stop for eight to ten hours every day. Sitting down for a while to exchange a laugh, a little gossip. They have a hurried lunch at around 1 p.m. before returning to work on the fields. They get home at 7 p.m. and clean the house, cook dinner, put away the livestock. At 11 p.m., they finally call it a day.

The three women all own a little patch of land where they grow seasonal vegetables. The patch they were working on the day I met them belonged to Surbhi's husband's family. Women in rural areas often handle agricultural labour on top of their household chores. It is often their responsibility to sow and reap and produce, but the money they earn is given to their families. Surbhi, Maya, and Rama—unable to hire labourers—did what many women in the region do and began taking turns to work on each other's fields. This way they had the necessary help without having to depend on anyone else. Rama, the youngest of the three, is more talkative than her friends. On the day I meet her, she is dressed in a black salwar and a red kurta, her hair covered by a black scarf. Her face carries a constant weary expression, except for when she smiles. But just like my mother, she doesn't smile often. Her husband works in the city selling life insurance policies. Her friends' husbands are real estate agents.

'What do they do the whole day?'

'They hang around in the town for work.'

'Do they not help with the farming?'

'They help sometimes in sowing the seeds but generally we do it. They are busy. We stay at home.'

'But you also work?'

'This is not work. These are household duties.'

'But you do get tired, right?'

'Yes, but we manage.'

'Have you ever asked your husbands for help with housework?'

They look at me incredulously. Then at each other. Then they burst out laughing.

'If I don't do the work I do, no one else is going to do it. I cannot see the house in disarray, I cannot see the dishes piling up in the kitchen, or the laundry building up. If I let these things slide, I will be severely criticized. I am judged every minute of the day—at work, at home. It's exhausting,' Divya told me. It is exhausting because housework consumes women's lives in India, whether they live in the cities or in rural areas. Divya, too, had stepped out to work with an unwritten undertaking that she would also continue to take care of the house. Divya's husband helped sometimes when she was overwhelmed—and asked for his help. But often he just didn't notice that she was struggling to get everything done. The result was that she had to resign from her job after just a few months of joining. Her husband left for work early and came back late at night. Coping with two children, their schoolwork, cooking, remembering important dates, playing the ideal

wife, daughter-in-law, mother—Divya was struggling to balance all
the roles. She had a nanny to look after her sons, but the days she
didn't turn up for work, Divya couldn't either. Who will look after
her children? She tried out day care centres for children despite the
fact that they were prohibitively expensive and the services were not
really up to the mark. But even day care centres don't keep children
beyond 7 p.m. Divya went through her life battling strong emotions
of anger, frustration, despair, and resignation. At the time, giving up
her job felt more like a relief to her, rather than a sacrifice. Back in
Mukteshwar, I asked my new farmer friends a serious question about
their husbands.

'What do they do when they get back home?'

'Watch television,' they say in unison.

'Or hang out with friends, or sleep,' Rama adds.

'Same, same,' the other two add.

The term 'housewife' in India is a misleading term. Its simple
definition of a married woman who cares for the home, is not entirely
applicable in the Indian context. Married Indian women are always
housewives, but, as mentioned earlier, this doesn't mean that all of
them carry out purely unpaid care duties—many of them are also
women who work in the informal sector. And those who cannot step
out of their homes for work have now found an innovative way to
monetize the very experience that has for long reduced and devalued
them.

DOCUMENTING THE HOUSEWIFE EXPERIENCE

No woman gets an orgasm from shining the kitchen floor.

—Betty Friedan

'I am pregnant'—the title of the YouTube video screamed in all caps. As I press play, the screen fills with the face of a rosy-cheeked young woman in a nightie. She is schoolgirl pretty. Face flushed, she rambles on for long minutes before announcing the good news. Tina, the host of the channel, is a housewife based in a village in West Bengal. Her YouTube channel, 'My Village Life Tina', where she posts videos of her daily routine of housework, cooking, and caregiving duties, has more than 156,000 followers.[1] Middle-class Indian housewives like Tina are among a growing breed of Indian YouTube vloggers, from across the middle classes (lower to upper middle class, and rural to urban) who bring to their followers the drudgery of unending housework and caregiving. These vlogs have been inspiring women from similar backgrounds, mostly other housewives, to enter the space of content creation. Their vlog channels have become complete ecosystems in themselves, standing in for missing support networks in the lives of many viewers. The women discuss everything from their marital problems to the general tediousness of their lives while documenting the sameness of each day. In that sameness, they make visible the invisibility of care work and their role in it.

There must be hundreds of these daily routine vlogs by women who stay at home—women who have never worked but wanted to or women who have given up work after marriage and children, according to their own admissions in these vlogs. Some of them are educated, some even highly-educated, but their lives now are just a maze of cooking, cleaning, and serving their husbands and families.

They have hundreds of thousands of followers who watch their vlogs where they chronicle their daily lives, which consist of long hours of looking after their families. These vlogs are immensely popular—the majority of the audience appears to be other housewives, as I gathered from reading through comments, women who draw strength from knowing others are going through the same trials as themselves—the comments sections of these vlogs are ample proof of that. The content of these vlogs also presents a striking sociocultural exposé. They take us right into the heart of an Indian family, usually a space that is closed and guarded, where outsiders are not allowed.

With each of her episodes, Tina lets viewers into her world without any compunctions; she shares every small detail of her life. There are episodes where she attends weddings or visits her relatives, shares her beauty routines or a challenge she's facing with one of the family members. But most of the content is about her daily life as a housewife—minutes of footage of her cooking, cleaning, or helping her mother-in-law cook and clean. Her day starts early and the grind continues until late at night.

In early 2022, Tina's YouTube channel had thousands of subscribers. Hers is not a one-off success story, but part of an amazing feat achieved by many middle-class Indian women, one that has created a living document of gender roles within our homes, the unequal distribution of housework and caregiving, and the secondary role of women in their families.

These women, in their twenties, thirties, forties, are all middle-class housewives, who fill up their followers' screens daily with their mops and kitchen knives, sweating it out in the kitchen, washing and drying clothes, sweeping and mopping and being constantly at the beck and call of their family members, serving their husbands and children—every day. But if you look beyond the shaky videos with choppy transitions and the amateur voice-overs, you will hear the story they are telling.

Do these women know they are documenting the daily misogyny of Indian families that finds place in annual gender parity reports in terms of alarming statistics but has never been worthy of sustained outrage?

They don't.

But what drives them is a deep sense of injustice that often boils over into their videos. And of course, in their lives with limited choices, these videos have brought a lucrative economic opportunity like no other. With hundreds of thousands of followers, the women don't just earn from YouTube ads every month but also from product placements.

co

It was early 2020 when I chanced upon these housewife vloggers. During one of my 3 a.m. staring-at-the-ceiling moments, I came across a video by someone I thought was a mommy vlogger. But I was a little surprised because Payal, of 'Simple Living Wise Thinking', was not one of those sharply turned-out mommy vloggers, in perfectly matched clothes and make-up, sharing fitness, self-care, and parenting tips and tricks, speaking in perfect English or Hindi.[2]

Payal seemed earthy and approachable, and simple. She spoke Hindi with a heavy Bengali accent and had no qualms about vlogging in her nightie, an article of clothing that screams middle class like no other. And Payal is the quintessential middle-class Indian housewife, although she lives in the United States. She is adorable in her simplicity and her acceptance of her life where she is solely responsible for housework and caregiving. It doesn't matter that she lives in the US, where there is a semblance of equality between spouses when it comes to housework. She is often self-deprecatory and accepts the sheer drudgery of being an Indian housewife—solely responsible for cooking, cleaning, and child-rearing—with annoying compliance.

Payal's daily routine vlog led me to Tina's, and to many others like hers. Payal shares recipes, challenge videos, and some tips to better manage daily life but mostly her viewers can watch her chat away while she does her housework. Her videos opened up the world of India's housewife vloggers for me.

Was I surprised by what I saw? Not really. I grew up in a middle-class household. I keenly observe the lives of my mostly middle-class friends.

These women in nighties, cooking, sweeping, cleaning, sharing their beauty routines, sometimes advertising beauty products or clothes or kitchen equipment, their make-up loud, clothes sometimes garish and mismatched, sometimes pretty and simple, their conversations unrehearsed and often abrupt, are everywoman. They are great examples of the conservative modernity of India's middle classes. These videos are a living project, a testimony to how the majority of women in this country live, and the inequalities they battle with throughout their lives.

Vlogger Tina's sister-in-law, her husband's sister, Soumali, is also a very popular daily life vlogger. She has a channel in Hindi, simply called 'India Vlogger Soumali' (597,000 subscribers),[3] one in Bengali called 'Hichk!' (130,000 subscribers),[4] and an eponymous channel 'Soumali Adhikary' (1.13 million subscribers).[5] Soumali is an example of a woman in an upwardly-mobile middle-class family who gave up her career because her husband was earning enough to support their affluent lifestyle. Her life is a far cry from that of her sister-in-law in rural West Bengal. But the two women are connected by the expectations on them to prioritize their roles as supporting actors in their spouse's lives. These also go a long way in highlighting the various injustices and discriminations women face from their girlhood. In one of the videos, Soumali reveals a startling fact—that her grandparents had sent her away to live with her mother's family because they did not want a girl child.

'It was not my father's decision as many of you seem to think,' she says in one of her vlogs, looking downcast. Her viewers had expressed concerns that if Tina, her sister-in-law, gave birth to a girl, her father-in-law (Soumali's father) might send the child away too, as he had sent away Soumali. 'My father didn't send me away but he didn't oppose it either. My brother is a different man. He won't let that happen to his daughter....'*

In one of her episodes, Tina shows her viewers a huge bunch of raw bananas that fell from the tree and shares her sadness that a little bird had built a nest there and laid three eggs—but one of the eggs

---

*Translation mine.

fell and broke. This one video made me pause and take another look at all her previous videos. These were not just daily routine videos—they were a window into her inner life, a life that, until lately, held no great interest for anyone else.

Sometimes these videos are just an attempt to be heard, to know that someone is listening to them, and empathizing with them. These women and their lives are invisible to everyone, sometimes even to their own families.

And they know it.

But now they have built a community where people are interested in what they have to say.

'Most of my followers say that their lives have changed after seeing my videos. They say no one cared about their innermost feelings but when they watch me, they feel I know what they are going through,' Ruchi, whose vlog 'indian youtuber ruchi' has 164,000 subscribers on YouTube,[6] told me during a conversation.

'Women are so alone. I felt alone too for a huge part of my life till I began this vlogging journey. My journey inspires other housewives. I am no different than them. I am also struggling with the same problems and today I have found a space to share my feelings and emotions. I feel heard and understood.

'When I make a vlog, I know I am contributing something to another woman's life. I am showing her my life, with all its problems and shortcomings so she knows she is not alone. And this feeling is priceless,'* she explained.

∽

Ruchi, who lives in Gujarat, was married before she turned seventeen, and was soon sucked into a vortex of childcare and housework.

The bubbly mother of two was always driven by a desire to do something for herself, apart from the role of a homemaker and mother that she found herself confined to so early in her life. She developed an interest in photography due to her husband, a freelance photographer.

---

*Translations mine.

Soon, she was working as one too, but photography assignments meant her children had to manage on their own while she was away. 'My children were suffering because of this.'

And then she chanced upon a daily routine vlog by another woman. At first, she was surprised. 'I thought to myself, what is this, showing people what you are eating, doing housework. But as I watched more episodes, I could feel myself getting addicted.'

When Ruchi began her journey as a vlogger, there were naysayers who would call up her husband and ask him, 'What is she doing? It is so embarrassing!' But Ruchi did not let that deter her. By then she had followers who found her 'inspiring' and 'impressive.' And she felt an obligation towards the women who looked out for her vlogs every day.

'All around me I saw women who were overworked and depressed. Housewives do everything at home and yet no one cares about them because domestic work is not important and housewives are less than nothing. We are constantly reminded that our work is not important,' she told me in a mix of Hindi and English.

Appreciation is, however, hard to come by. 'People think what's there in cooking or housework—it's not rocket science. We cook three times a day all year long, even in the oppressive heat of the summer months,' she tells me. 'My husband didn't help before but now he does, maybe because he thinks, now that I am "working", I need help. But the point is that I needed help before too. But whatever, I am glad he helps me now. When I upload videos of him helping me, there are comments on my vlog shaming me for making my husband work at home,' she laughs.

Some of the videos lay bare how women have learnt to accept toxic masculinity. Rama Singh Jadaun's YouTube channel, 'Ayan Mom and Beauty', with over a million subscribers,[7] is a testament to how women are taught to live with male entitlement. Rama is a pretty, slightly-built woman with silky, straight hair, and twinkling eyes. She is a livewire, often seen shaking a leg to a Bollywood tune in her videos, and speaking with a charming rustic twang. She lives in Andhra Pradesh with her husband and her toddler son. The description box of her channel reads: 'I am a Graduate of Bundelkhand University Jhansi and also pursued polytechnic diploma in Information and Technology. Afterwards I worked in various Organizations related to Women and Child welfare for almost 6 years before my Marriage. After Marriage I had to leave the job because of posting of my Husband.'[8]

When I speak to her, her husband keeps interrupting. The first time he corrects her is when she tells me her age.

'I am twenty-eight,' she tells me.

'I am sorry to interrupt,' he says, taking the phone from Rama. 'But she is actually twenty-seven.'

When I talk to him, I cannot help but notice how he constantly puts her down, perhaps unconsciously, while also claiming to be proud of her. I have noticed this passive-aggressive casual sexism in too many Indian homes.

But there's a spark that I can see in Rama's videos, a spark that can be harnessed to change things inside our homes. In one of her videos, her husband calls himself her 'god'. Rama's expressions are mixed. After he finishes talking, she looks at him quietly and says with a smile, 'I appreciate you but I don't think you are my god.'

From the videos, and during our conversation, it becomes obvious that he admires Rama for her success. But he is also trapped in the uber masculine role that the patriarchy has imposed on him, which doesn't allow him to fully express this admiration—to her or to others. I am reminded of Kamla Bhasin's repeated assertions that men are as much victims of patriarchy as women. Such interactions between husband and wife with all their inherent misogyny and cautious sparks of autonomy are worth exploring more if we are to correct historical power imbalances, and these women have unwittingly taken the first step. They have opened up their houses for all to see their overworked lives and how they are controlled by their partners, and sometimes even ridiculed.

'When I was studying, I had a different life, but I still had to do housework. When I began working, nothing much changed because I stayed with my brother and I had to cook and clean for him. After marriage, of course, your responsibilities increase even more because you are a wife and a daughter-in-law and there are certain expectations from these roles. Housework, cooking, caregiving—we do it throughout our lives. After marriage, it's just that we do it in a different family,' Rama told me.*

Rama manages to post a vlog every day despite the unending housework only by staying up late in the night, when she edits and readies her videos to be published the next day. But she doesn't mind—the vlogs have given her an additional purpose in life and an income with which she can now support her family in Bundelkhand—a drought-ravaged, poverty-stricken part of India.

Indian housewife vloggers are secretive about their earnings, but most reportedly earn way more than they would working in an office. The money they earn supplements the family income—they are still considered homemakers with a hobby.

Vlogger Radhika, with over 400,000 subscribers, is a housewife whose husband drives an auto-rickshaw.[9] She explains in one of her videos that her YouTube income is a 'dream come true'. The money she earns from her YouTube channel 'Radhika Real Vlogs', product placements, and brand endorsements has ensured she can afford little luxuries for her children and herself. These women are every brand's dream—low-paid endorsers with a large, targeted audience. These vloggers help brands reach one of India's largest consumer sectors, the middle class, while accepting payment that is perhaps a fraction of what these corporates would pay for celebrity endorsements. While one cannot ignore the capitalist exploitation of women, at least they are beneficial to some extent. These women have no negotiating power, which is why even though some of them have followers that can rival that of a minor celebrity's, they settle for much less for product placements.

These women are discussing pertinent problems that women in India face. Yes, they do it while washing vegetables, or sweeping the floor, or brushing their hair, but the epiphanies they share are just as real and surprising in a country where women are rarely encouraged to talk about their feelings and emotions publicly. Women are even

---

*Translations mine.

hesitant to talk about their innermost thoughts within their closest friends for fear of being misjudged and misunderstood. One of the most honest vloggers I came across during my sojourn in this part of YouTube was Mamon (Happy with MAMON), a woman in her early forties from West Bengal.[10] In one of her videos posted during the peak of the Covid-19 lockdown, she says, 'everyone is having a great time because they don't have to go to work. But for us housewives, we are still at work and our work has increased manifold.'*

I have been trying to document and quantify the work women do at home for years now and here it was being documented one day at a time, in a better way than any case studies or reports could do.

This tribe of housewife vloggers on YouTube is increasing owing to the easy availability of cheap smartphones. It also has a domino effect, with one vlogger empowering many others to start their own channels. Some of the housewife vloggers are from rural areas in India where women have close to no personal freedom, and little agency—one of the only ways they can have a life away from housework and caregiving duties is through these videos. The families play along, indulging this as a hobby that also makes them money while not coming in the way of their duties to the home and family.

'I would say it's middle-class, upper-caste Hindu women who have been left out of the feminist discourse because of their deep alignment with patriarchy and role in caste subjugation,' sociologist Pallavi Banerjee told me. 'The grassroots feminist movement in India has never found an ally in middle-class women and the elite feminists do not see [middle-class women] as worth "saving".'

But these women vloggers are powerhouse influencers. And it is time to harness the power of the middle-class women.

These women all boast hundreds of thousands of followers—they have obviously struck a chord. Sometimes I read the comments on their vlogs and the overwhelming response seems to be from other women who feel relieved to know they are not alone in their plight. There is a newfound awareness among middle-class women about the

---

*Translation mine.

thousand indignities of their lives and a strong desire for a different, more equal life for their daughters.

In one of her vlogs, Soumali spends the entire day cooking for her husband's friends. When they come, she serves them at the table. Once this is done, at 3.30 p.m., she tells her followers 'I am going to eat now in the bedroom today with you all. I am so tired.' She accepts it as a simple fact of life that she is not expected to sit down with her guests to eat, that she should serve them and then eat alone in the bedroom. From what I have seen in her videos, her husband is a lovely, supportive man. And that is the tragedy—even the most lovely and supportive of men in this country are sometimes oblivious to how they perpetrate these inequalities in their homes.

'We have not come a long way by any measure,' Banerjee says. 'Less than 25 per cent of Indian women are part of the labour force, we know the rape statistics and femicide rates in India and the million other ways in which women are denied basic rights. What we have instead is a neoliberal and capitalist rhetoric of gender equality that is fashionable for both men and women to espouse to stake a claim to modernity.'

When Ruchi's husband lost his business owing to the national lockdown, it was Ruchi's YouTube earnings that sustained them. But her YouTube channel means more than a livelihood to her.

'In these videos we are chronicling our days, quantifying the work that we do in a day—work that sustains our families but that is dismissed as nothing. When our family watches our videos, we hope they realize the amount of work we do throughout the day. We are a community. We interact, share, engage, and listen to each other. In a country where no one listens to a woman, this matters,' Ruchi says to me.

In one of the vlogs on the channel 'Pakhi family vlogs', the eponymous vlogger is shown sleeping on a divan; the camera is being operated by her husband. He says, 'She deserves to sleep. She has been working since 6 a.m. Now she is sleeping, and I am doing what I need to do—reading. When she gets up, she will get busy with cooking and housework again and I guess I will go to the terrace and have a stroll. She never gets time to go to the terrace for a stroll.'[11]

He sees her exhaustion yet doesn't realize that he can help mitigate it by actually sharing the housework.

These vlogs all began as an attempt to be heard, to be seen. The reason these vloggers have such large followings is purely because the daily grind they show in their videos is so universal that it speaks to a majority of women in this country. These vlogs, unbeknownst to their creators, are documenting something important—they are visibilizing what has so far been invisible. They are all time use surveys in motion.

MIRROR, MIRROR ON THE WALL, WHO'S THE LAZIEST OF THEM ALL?

Of course I am not worried about intimidating men. The type of man who will be intimidated by me is exactly the type of man I have no interest in.

—Chimamanda Ngozi Adichie

'My grandfather was a well-known champion of women's rights and he would encourage girls to study, to be strong. But at home, he didn't lift a finger and my grandmother did it all. But it never struck me as wrong. I am thinking about it now while you are asking me these questions.' Iqbal Abhimanyu works for an international news agency and is a Spanish language expert. His commitment to gender equality is staunch but he is quick to admit that some things at home were so normalized that they never stood out as wrong, like his grandmother sending him out to the shops while asking for his sister's help in the kitchen. When Abhimanyu began dating a Danish woman, he had to rethink gender roles at home.

'There was no option. I had to. I learnt,' he says, laughing. 'It's not so bad. Or hard.'

But when he was growing up with his grandparents, his grandmother doing all the housework was normal. 'I never thought to help her out. And she wouldn't allow me in the kitchen anyway. And it is true when we went to our relatives' houses, my sister would immediately be called into the kitchen, while I would hang out outside with the men.'

'Nobody ever asked me to go to the kitchen but I would feel compelled to go and help the women working; you feel that way when you are a girl or a woman growing up in a patriarchal society,' Shiuli Vanaja, who is his sister, tells me later.

In their house, Abhimanyu's mother, a staunch feminist, ensured his father did an equal share of the housework. 'However, all that changed when he came to visit his mother,' Abhimanyu remembers. 'My grandmother would grumble: at home you work, but here you just watch TV. Not that she would have allowed him to work in the kitchen,' he remembers.

The patriarchal nature of Indian society conditions Indian men in two ways. The first group of men have the best intentions, and want to share in the housework, but they are just not trained to do so. While almost every Indian girl ends up receiving some training from the older women of the family in housework and often in cooking, men are hardly ever taught to do these things, despite the fact that both are life skills. When men do help around the house, it is an exception, not the rule.

For example, Subhayu, a man in his early thirties who has lived in hostels throughout his life, loves to cook. A travel enthusiast, he has friends who enjoy cooking, too. 'But would they consider cooking regularly at home?'

'That I don't know.'

'Would you?'

'I don't know. But I did grow up in a family where I saw my father sharing cooking duties with my mother. So, for me it's not a huge deal. But in many parts of India, I believe it would be. Men would do occasional cooking like cook meat or something but not everyday cooking.'

In many parts of India, women do not cook or touch non-vegetarian food. In such cases, the men have no qualms cooking meat with their friends. But when it comes to everyday household chores, Indian men are just not brought up to consider lending a hand. But they will go to any extent to ensure that women do not bail on housework.

I asked many men in my circle and out of it as to why this doesn't bother them. The default answer, especially among younger men was, 'We never thought about it.'

'It seemed normal.'

I have grown up seeing my father lazing around when he was

not working. He worked long hours but in his downtime, he would watch television, read newspapers, or just hang out with his friends. We had a room on the ground floor that was set aside for my father to entertain his friends, and they would start trickling in after 6 p.m. And the minute my mother was home, on hearing her key turn in the door, my father would call out to her, 'Can you send down some tea?' Some of the other men would pipe up, 'Something to eat too please, Bhabi.' My mother would force a smile, and instead of changing her sweaty clothes and taking a bath to wash off the grime and dirt of the day, she would go into the kitchen and start sending down kettles of steaming tea, and sweets, biscuits, and omelettes.

It is also not always that Indian men do not know how to cook or care, or that they cannot learn how to. It is just that they think of it as a past-time, something to indulge in occasionally rather than a shared chore. In India, men are averse to housework because they have grown up believing that housework is a woman's domain. That doing household chores is somehow effeminate. They have never been taught how to do housework. Their mothers have pampered them, even actively dissuaded them from lending a hand around the house, and they expect the same of their wives.

'My father is more dominating—my mother and I are expected to play a subservient role and this despite the fact that I come from an upper middle-class family. Both my parents are well-educated,' a seventeen-year-old girl from Kolkata told me.

'He will never take water on his own. We always have to serve him water. My brother does the same. My father never cooks. During the lockdown in 2020, he tried to clean the house a few times but it was very stressful because me and my mum had to make it easy for him by removing all the furniture in his way.'

'Gender difference is so normalized in our house that my mother finds nothing wrong in his behaviour,' she adds.

Perhaps only women can change things at home by putting their foot down when it comes to toxic masculine behaviour.

'Unexpected guests were always turning up at our home and my mother used to get annoyed that she was not informed beforehand

and refused to cook the extra meals. My father would cook the extra lunch and dinner. He would show no resentment or annoyance for that,' Shiuli remembered.

'That is what I have grown up seeing, so I get annoyed with men and women when they don't insist on more gender equal participation in housework,' she adds.

I ask her playfully about her brother. 'I don't know how he is with his girlfriend. Men behave differently with their family members and in their [romantic] relationships,' she answers with a laugh.

Her answer is playful, but hides the constant anxiety that Indian women carry around with them about the men in their lives. My biggest fear is that my son will grow up to be sexist and patriarchal, and so right from the age when he couldn't even speak properly, I found myself constantly watching him for toxic behaviour. It was exhausting for both of us. The day he declared pink was his favourite colour, the day he had a fight in school because someone called him effeminate for wearing pink socks ('I told them colour has no gender,' he said) were the proudest moments of my life. And while it's exhausting, I can't afford to look away, not even for a second.

In my many conversations with woke men in the country, I have been repeatedly told that 'things are changing'. Are they?

Things have not changed for the majority of Indian women. When men don't change how they approach something as basic as housework, what good is empowering our daughters? Because if other young men have not had the same upbringing, how will this empowered daughter's life be any different from her mother's?

For some time, I have felt that we should not be wasting time trying to turn men into allies to bring about the change we deserve. Gender rights activist Ginny Srivastava agrees. 'In their heart of hearts, men also know this is wrong. I think it's a waste of time. The men already know it's not right—they still do it. If we have tons of resources and tons of patience, it would be something we could do. But given the lack of resources, we should focus on women.'

We should direct every available resource to ensure that our girls benefit from existing public programmes so that we are empowering mothers along with daughters, because just empowering the latter leaves the work half-finished. If I have learnt anything from my own life, it is that it is ultimately our mothers who will help us reach the finish line. And we have to pay it forward. We have to campaign relentlessly to change the mindset of a society that doesn't really value its daughters. This change will have to come from us, and it will have to begin inside our homes.

IN THE NAME OF WOMEN

Women's potential remains as an untapped resource in the country.
Despite significant strides, India's growth story has ignored women.

—'Powering the Economy with Her'

When you walk into a village, no matter how remote, you are assailed by messages of Beti Bachao, Beti Padhao. The sad part is that these messages are everywhere, even in villages where there's only a barely functional primary school and the nearest secondary school is a few kilometres away, which makes it difficult for many girls to continue to high schools.

The Beti Bachao, Beti Padhao initiative was launched to change the way Indian society viewed girl children, to discourage sex selective abortions, foeticides, and encourage parents to educate and empower girls. The government claims that these efforts have borne fruit and the sex ratio at birth improved in 104 districts among those identified as gender-sensitive.[1]

But when it comes to educating the girl child, as already has been discussed, progress has been slow.

Every village I visited in Bundelkhand has walls painted with messages of 'Beti Bachao, Beti Padhao'. But the government forgot to provide high schools to actually make this a reality. Girls who drop out after primary school can use a smartphone, say hello and thank you, and dress in Western clothes, but they are not empowered enough to voice their opinion.

In the village of Deora, for example, not only is there no high school, but the anganwadi centre, too, has been defunct for over five years.

'There has been no development in this village, sister. There's no anganwadi. Where will the children go to study? The school is also only till Class V and the quality of teachers not good,' Rajesh Kumari, a cooperative worker, whispers to me. 'Girls drop out of school because the high school is too far away. It's not safe for the girls to walk to the high school especially during monsoon.'

The second part of the catchy slogan has remained just that in villages across India. According to the government's own estimates, almost 56 per cent of the fund was used in simply advertising the programme. In 2019, the government, in response to a question posed in the Lok Sabha, revealed that out of the ₹684 crore allocated by the government for the programme, only ₹159 crore was distributed to different states and districts.[2]

That is a lot of money—money that could have been used to build more schools. If our aim is to educate more girls, each village in India should have a primary and high school and a community college. However, since the education of a girl child is dependent on so many different variable factors, there exists a need to think out of the box. Could we, for example, consider mandatory residential schools for girls? After years of ground reporting on the condition of women and children in our country, I strongly believe that to give girls a level playing field, we need to take them out of a system where they are considered either burdens or, at best, much-loved guests. We need to pluck them from environments where they grow up seeing their mothers in subservient roles, from home environments that indoctrinate them to believe that their entire worth lies in whom they marry and how well they run their households. Of course, there is still a lot more that needs to be done in terms of sensitizing educators and stripping them of their patriarchal attitudes. It is perhaps impossible to rid an entire society of patriarchal thinking but there could be checks and balances to redress such issues. A girl, when she is given equal opportunities, may also then have the confidence to challenge institutional patriarchy in her community.

Earlier that day, Kumari had invited me into her home, where she had gathered a few other women to talk to me about their issues. These women have opinions, but they still hesitate to voice them because of the highly patriarchal nature of the region where women remain constrained to their homes, in purdah. They continue to be kept out of schools and colleges and married off early. Politics has remained a male bastion and women are shunted out of every sector where their participation could make a difference to their own future. This organized segregation is so deep-seated that women often unconsciously take a backseat—and sometimes they feel relieved to be able to do so. With this being the reality of the situation, I am baffled when our government promises 'not just women's development but women-led development'.[3]

If merely launching a slew of programmes for girls and women was enough to kick-start women-led development, then we wouldn't still be centuries away from achieving global gender parity. We are still at a nascent stage of women's development and to talk about women-led development is not just myopic but may also be considered a clever rhetoric to pull focus from the hundreds and thousands of ways women are being failed in our country every day.

And the question remains—where are these women who would be leading this development?

Now, women's development (I have not yet dared to progress to women-led development) rests on education, employment, entrepreneurship, and political participation, and as a country, we have failed to tick every one of those boxes.

Apart from the Beti Bachao, Beti Padhao initiative, the government had also launched the Sukanya Samriddhi Yojana, which encourages parents to open a savings account for their daughters (to save for a daughter's education and marriage) that can remain operational until the girl is twenty-one. The number of new accounts opened under the scheme from 1 April 2018 to 31 October 2021 was 14,273,910.[4] The initial investment in the savings account, which can be opened in either post offices or designated private and public banks, can start from ₹250 and go up to ₹150,000. The initial hook for this initiative was that it's a high-interest account with an 8.5 per cent interest rate, though the rates have fallen since its inception.[5]

In India, because women are culturally conditioned not to stand up to men, it is very easy for men to appropriate these rights. Indian men have been able to turn women's development into a women's disenfranchisement process, while the government has looked away. Most parents do not think twice about appropriating a girl's bicycle—a benefit provided by the government in many states to allow girls to go to school—for her brother, or registering a business or property in a woman's name to take advantage of women-specific subsidies (ensuring that she signs away those rights in a separate set of documents).

So, if I open an account for my daughter and start saving for her education and marriage, who's monitoring if I am just using her name for the high interest rate or if I am saving up for her dowry? How many parents are actually saving for their daughter's education? Obviously, in a country where credible data is hard to come by, it is impossible to actually figure out how these accounts are being used. But if I hazard an informed guess as a journalist and an observer, the scheme is likely being used to save for girls' marriages.

Financial inclusion is an important part of bringing about women-led development. The government says the Jan Dhan Yojana scheme has allowed over 18 crore women, both in rural and urban areas, to access formal banking and various financial services for the first time.[6] But according to media reports, as of 2018, a sizeable 20 per cent of these accounts were lying defunct.[7] Opening an account in the name of a woman is the easiest thing to do but to actually empower the woman to learn to operate the account and to allow her the autonomy to manage her own money calls for deeper engagement with their empowerment.

You go to any local market, you will see there are people who offer account management services for a little fee. Government banks generally have a designated employee who helps women open and operate their accounts—the emphasis is not on empowering them to do it themselves.

According to the government's own data, as many as 15 per cent of the accounts were at zero balance as of 23 January 2019. Additionally, 84 per cent of the accounts were merely 'operative', having only been used infrequently.[8]

So, facilitating women to open bank accounts has remained a merely symbolic gesture.

Women-led development is also dependent on entrepreneurship and participation in the labour force. The Mudra Yojana was launched to provide collateral-free loans to entrepreneurs. This is important for women entrepreneurs as most women have no property that they can use as collateral. So, naturally it comes as no surprise when the government claims that women constitute over 70 per cent of Mudra's beneficiaries.[9]

But according to the *Indian Express*'s assessment of the government's claims, the number of Mudra beneficiaries starting a new business was low. Only one of five beneficiaries used the loan to start a new business while the remaining applicants used the Mudra money for expanding their existing business.[10] It should be noted that it is an open secret in India that many men register businesses in the name of their female relatives to reap the rewards of subsidies that women enjoy. The Stand Up India scheme also provides entrepreneurship loans of up to ₹1 crore to women entrepreneurs from all backgrounds. The government claims over 10 crore women have availed entrepreneurship loans jointly from MUDRA and Stand Up India.[11]

Now let's look at some numbers again: according to the Economic Survey 2019–20, only 43 per cent of the 27,084 recognized start-ups in India had a woman director as of 8 January 2020.[12] In the Index of Women Entrepreneurs 2021, India ranked fifty-second out of the fifty-seven surveyed countries.[13] Only about 14 per cent of Indian women own or run businesses, according to the sixth economic census, conducted in 2014. More than 90 per cent of companies run by women are microenterprises, and about 79 per cent are self-financed.[14] According to Innoven Capital, a venture debt and lending platform, the number of funded start-ups with at least one female co-founder declined from 17 per cent in 2018 to 12 per cent in 2019.[15] A report released in 2019 by Bain & Company in partnership with Google noted that India's growth story 'left behind a key demographic: women'.[16] The report highlighted the fact that women's contribution to the country's socio-economic progress remained unrecognized and most 'women work as unpaid caregivers, household managers, or in other home-based positions; only a minority work outside the house'.[17] Improvements in social parameters did not translate to their economic inclusion and development. In fact, women's participation in the labour force is expected to decline further because of 'labour trends, technological disruption, and constraining social barriers'.[18]

Entrepreneurship among women is key not just to boost the economy but also to transform a woman's position in the society and her home.

Take Kusum, the mobile salon girl, for example, who runs her business with a precision and grit that can only be called entrepreneurial. She maintains a client base, she does sales and marketing calls when she comes home, and she manages to sell a few more services. But when I ask her why she doesn't set up a physical beauty salon while maintaining her mobile salons, 'It's too risky,' is always her response. She has the potential to build up her business and employ more people but she doesn't have the social or institutional support to take such a risk, or to build on her natural entrepreneurial talent.

As of 2019, India had more than 15 million women-owned enterprises, representing 20 per cent of all enterprises but with the potential to create 30 million women-owned enterprises by 2030. While this number might seem large, the Bain & Company report had warned that most of these are single person enterprises, which provide direct employment for an estimated 22 to 27 million people.[19]

As noted earlier, a number of enterprises reported as women-owned are not in fact controlled or run by women. 'A combination of financial and administrative reasons leads to women being "on paper" owners with little role to play.'[20]

The report had underlined what we already know and which countless reports and studies have highlighted over the years, that while women are now better educated, and have better access to healthcare than before, they continue to face 'structural, social, and economic barriers to paid employment. That limits women's individual economic advancement and constrains India's social and economic progress. Women's potential remains as an untapped resource in the country.'[21]

Men control almost all resources in our country. What they cannot control, they have no qualms in seizing from women.

THE FIRST HUSBANDS

The fact that these 'Pradhan Patis' operate openly and meet government officials, administrative staff, and the police means that this practice is accepted and allowed by one and all.

—Vimlesh Kumari

Earlier in 2019, a petition was launched on Change.org. In the petition, a woman village head had asked for the 'Pradhan Pati' system of administration in rural India to come to an end. What this means is that even though a village might elect a woman as their chief, her husband will represent her in all public dealings. Vimlesh Kumari had said in her petition that she was 'one of the first Mahila Pradhan who is actively heading village affairs. Unlike my dear predecessors who were as capable as I but were unfortunately undermined and not allowed to do their job.'[1]

'A vast majority of Women Pradhans have been left powerless by a shameful practice called "Pradhan Pati". Simply put: Women Pradhans exist only on paper. Once elected, they are sidelined and left being a mute spectator by their husbands or male members of the family, who preside over meetings, take decisions, meet higher officials on her behalf,' she wrote in her petition. 'The fact that these "Pradhan Patis" operate openly and meet government officials, administrative staff, and the police means that this practice is accepted and allowed by one and all. No wonder it is so rampant and continues to thrive,' the petition added.[2] Vimlesh says Indian authorities accept this tradition and allow it to flourish. I witnessed this when I travelled across Uttar Pradesh and Madhya Pradesh, two of India's largest states, in 2018. In Deora, a village near Uttar Pradesh's border with Madhya Pradesh, I met and interacted with a man who I thought was the village chief because he was the one I was introduced to when I had requested to meet the sarpanch. After a long conversation about the village's development and other issues, we said our goodbyes. On my way out of the village, I saw a hoarding with the picture of a woman called Ram Devi—the village chief of Deora. I turned back and asked around to confirm the identity of the village chief. After asking around for a whole day I found out that Ram Devi was the village head of Deora, but she did not live in Deora. She lived in a nearby village called Sijhari with her husband. Her original address was in Deora, which allowed her to contest the village council elections. And as soon as she won, she made her son the de-facto head and went back to Sijhari. In Deora, nobody has really seen Ram Devi. As far as they are concerned, her son is their village head and they go to him with their problems and issues. 'She is a woman. Who goes to a woman with problems? She can't also just roam around the village. She has household responsibilities,' a villager told me.

In the face of such deeply entrenched ideas of what a woman can and must do, it is no wonder that women pradhans are rarely empowered to take on leadership roles. The government has also been trying to reserve 33 per cent of seats in the Parliament for women, a move that has been viciously opposed by various political parties.[3]

But even if we get the reservation—will things change for women? Will they have more of a voice and will there be more women ministers or leaders? The experience of women's reservation in panchayats does not paint a very hopeful picture.

Instead of transforming existing normative behaviour, successive governments have fallen in with the patriarchal status-quo because men are vote banks, and women can be expected to vote as per the wishes of their fathers, brothers, husbands, or fathers-in-law.

'We are not educated. What do we understand about politics? We vote as their father tells us,' Kasturi Devi, a fifty-five-year-old woman farmer, who lives in Mauranipur, Jhansi, in UP's Bundelkhand, told me, nodding at her son.

Earlier that day, I had negotiated the uneven road into a haphazard colony of mostly makeshift and a few concrete houses in Mauranipur. The lanes were narrow, the sewers were blocked with fallen leaves and sludgy water. Cows masticated on a sliver of ground visible from between two houses. I stopped at the house of Kasturi and Mishraji, who run a kirana store, a mom-and-pop store, in the colony. Their daughters-in-law, Sangeeta and Bipan, were hunched over a mud stove in the courtyard, rolling out perfectly round rotis and cooking them directly over the coal fire. When I met them, the state was gearing up for an election. I asked Sangeeta if she will vote; she gave me a strong yes. And then I asked her whom she will vote for and on what issues. 'That he will tell me at the time,' she told me with a smile, nodding towards her husband, who was standing a few feet away.

'We vote according to the elders. We have to respect their decisions,' Suman, a woman farmer, a few villages away told me. In her home, the elder is her mother-in-law, who will vote on the advice of her son, Suman's husband.

In 2019, Lokniti–Centre for the Study of Developing Societies, in partnership with the German Foundation Konrad Adenauer Stiftung, had interviewed over 6,348 women from Bihar, Gujarat, Haryana, Punjab, Kerala, Mizoram, Odisha, West Bengal, Jharkhand, Telangana, and the Delhi National Capital Region. It found two in three women in India reported having no freedom at all when it came to political participation. They needed permission from their elders to attend political events, including protests or demonstrations or village meetings. Only one in ten women said they had a lot of freedom. Over a quarter said they were keen on a political career, while six in ten did not even entertain the idea. The survey then asked if a woman should not contest against a man if she knew she had limited chances of winning. Two out of five women had said that women should contest elections even if their chances of winning were limited. Four out of ten women said that Indian voters were more likely to vote for a man than a woman, while six out of ten felt politics was the privilege of wealthy, upper-caste women. The study also found that 'the culture and environment at the home had the potential to create visible barriers to women's participation in politics. Absence of a fair share in decision making at home was an important variable that impacted on the activeness of women's interest and participation in politics. Women in urban areas reported enjoying a greater say in decision making in the family and also demonstrated greater interest in politics.'[4]

The study concluded that the Women's Reservation Bill providing for reservation in state assemblies and the parliament has not yet been passed because male elected representatives fear it will adversely affect their chances of getting elected. It added that political parties have made only 'vague commitments to enhance women's representation in elected bodies but have done precious little to nominate a larger number of women candidates when finalizing their nominees when distributing the party ticket' claiming no one would vote for women.[5]

Many may point at women's participation in social media as an indicator of women's increasing awareness about politics but the Lokniti study found that 83 per cent of the women surveyed had zero social media participation, 8 per cent of the women had low participation, 6 per cent had moderate participation, and only 3 per cent of the women were highly active on social media with regard to politics.[6]

The Lokniti study also found that 'unlike active political participation, political participation through online platforms saw women from privileged groups to be more participative. Women living in urban areas, women with higher levels of education, and younger women were more participative or active on online platforms for political activities as compared to rural women, women having no access to education, and elderly women respectively. But like active participation, women from higher socio-economic groups were also found to be active on online platforms. The possible reason for this could be the availability and ease to understand and use technology for the privileged sections of the society.'[7]

Why were the surveyed women not interested in a political career? The biggest obstacles according to them were societal expectations. Around 13 per cent of women also attributed it to household responsibilities. The rest cited a lack of interest and awareness and educational backwardness. Around 7 per cent of women said their lack of interest was owing to cultural barriers—the fact that women are not supposed to talk to other men, the purdah system, and no freedom of mobility.[8]

Indian politicians with different ideological persuasions all come together and bat for the patriarchy when it comes to giving women a share in the resources that they unambiguously control.

Take for example Lalu Prasad Yadav, the former chief minister of Bihar. After he was charge-sheeted in a fodder scam, he had anointed his wife—a political greenhorn—as the CM just to retain control over the state. It's not unlike how Indian households work, where women are always picking up after men and the rights they enjoy are bestowed as a gift that the men have allowed them to enjoy. Incidentally, Yadav was also one of the politicians who vociferously opposed a 33 per cent reservation for women in the Indian parliament.[9] Social activist Sunil Jaglan's voice echoes in my ears, 'Men are actually scared of the power of women.'

A former village head of the Bibipur village in Haryana, Jaglan brought in sweeping changes to the condition of women and girls in the village during his tenure. His initiative, now referred to as the Bibipur model, is currently running in a hundred villages across India, although you won't hear too much about it. There was a time when Jaglan and his initiatives were celebrated but, as with most women's empowerment initiatives, the interest died down soon and a model that should have been adopted throughout the country is now scarcely acknowledged.

In 2012, Jaglan became a father to a daughter. At the hospital when the nurse came out to give him the news, he noticed she was very subdued. Very quietly, she said, 'it's a girl,' and then went away, refusing to take the money that Jaglan tried to give her to show his happiness at the news. Jaglan was surprised but he didn't think too much of it, until he saw similar behaviour from others in the village.

'I would try to give sweets to the elders and they would grab my hands and say, don't worry, the next one will be a son,' he told me. In villages across India, when a son is born, the news is usually celebrated by beating utensils or drums. 'No one does it for a daughter. When my sister began to beat a plate after my first daughter was born, people called us mad.'

Despite the uber patriarchal nature of Haryana, Jaglan's father was progressive and as enthusiastic about educating his daughters as his son. 'We were treated equally,' Jaglan says. 'But there was always a difference between us which I didn't identify while I was growing up—but now I do. Like for example if the three of us were sitting down for a meal and mid-meal I needed water or something else, it would always be one of my sisters who would get up to get it. My mother was brought up in a hugely patriarchal set-up and she preferred me to my sisters and thought I should be educated not them. She was just carrying on the traditions passed on to her.

'I also grew up believing that I was more important than my sisters,' he admits.

But everything changed in 2012.

After his daughter was born, Jaglan suddenly became an object of pity. It bothered him and he began to read up on gender inequality and female foeticide and began aligning his experiences with what he was reading. 'Suddenly, I understood why some pregnant women never had their babies,' he told me. 'One day they were pregnant, the next they were not.' One day, he strode into his local health centre to check on the sex at birth ratio. What he found shocked him—there were only thirty-seven girls being born in Bibipur against fifty-nine boys.

Jaglan, who was the sarpanch of Bibipur at the time, gathered the women of the village in the chaupal (village hub) and after four hours of discussion that day, they admitted that female foeticide was a usual practice in the village. 'Women play along owing to social pressure. A daughter-in-law is valued only when she produces a male heir,' Jaglan said. 'This behaviour is so normalized in our society, it doesn't bother us. I couldn't identify how wrong it was till I became a father to a daughter myself.'

The next two years saw Jaglan, now the father of two daughters, starting a mahila gram sabha—a separate village council for women—where, for the first time in Bibipur, women were encouraged to speak up. They were also allowed to gather at the chaupal, where women are usually not allowed as it is considered a meeting point for the men of the village. He had also joined the khap—a parallel village council that was outlawed by the Supreme Court in 2018,[10] which operates in the hinterlands of uber-patriarchal states like Uttar Pradesh and Haryana, and is known for its regressive anti-women diktats. Khaps have been known to order bans on mobile phones for women or wearing Western clothes. Some khaps are even more aggressive, ordering honour killings and revenge rapes.[11]

'The khap is a centuries old tradition in villages in these regions. If I tried to build a new system, who would listen to me, or allow me? I needed to be a part of the khap so I could initiate reforms within the system. I couldn't ignore their social reach and influence—even government authorities reach out to them to resolve disputes in villages,' Jaglan says.

Jaglan became a khap leader the same year his first daughter was born. Soon after, he did the unthinkable—he organized a maha khap panchayat where women, including his unmarried sister, spoke.

'An unmarried, single woman speaking at a khap meeting, no one could imagine it,' Jaglan said. No one could imagine a khap gathering where women would be speaking about sex determination, male heir preference, or female foeticide either.

'My reason to try and change society was very personal. I never spared a thought about the inequalities my sisters faced, but as a father I felt them strongly,' told me.

Jaglan's approach was simple—he began by changing things that could be seen. This included moves like naming a pathway that the Bibipur women used to bring harvest to their homes from the fields 'Lado Marg' (little girls are affectionately called 'lado', the word originating from 'lad', meaning love), renaming the village square as 'Mahila Shakti Sthal' or women's power hub, and creating 'Selfie with Daughter', a viral social media campaign where village councils sent out formal congratulations to families for the birth of a daughter by planting trees in their name.

'These are symbolic gestures but it gives women a sense of belonging, of being wanted,' he told me. 'For centuries we have made women feel unwanted and unnecessary. It's time to change that and symbols like these mean much more than we can even imagine in terms of emotional empowerment,' he said.

But away from the optics, he also organized door-to-door campaigns against female foeticide and set up committees to monitor pregnancies in the village to stop the practice. He also set up a library with more than 900 books by women, about women.

Two years later, Jaglan told me, the at-birth sex ratio in his village had improved to fifty-one girls against forty-five boys.

The Bibipur model is very simple: it looks at every aspect of gender inequality in a region and addresses it. Jaglan never wanted to change things overnight or clash with traditions. 'It is impossible to break down centuries-old traditions and systems but you can get in the system and reform it and that's what I did,' Jaglan, who was the village sarpanch from 2010 to 2015, says.

The Bibipur model encouraged villages to build libraries for women, to name lanes and roads after them, to create meeting points for women in the village to grant them the right to public spaces, and to abolish the purdah system—where women have to keep their faces covered in front of men—in traditional households. It focused on computer literacy among women, on banning the use of misogynistic abusive words used by men, and on giving women property rights. The last is especially important considering the fact that in 2015–16, more men than women aged fifteen to forty-nine owned property— only 28 per cent of women owned land, either alone or jointly with someone else, as opposed to 49 per cent of men.[12]

The model also encouraged women to vote for politicians or parties that were committed to gender rights. Further, it focused on empowerment programmes for housewives, breaking the taboo around menstruation, and motivating women to take part in household decision-making, especially when it came to financial gains and losses. Jaglan also bought two machines to make sanitary napkins in the village so that women could make their own sanitary pads (women between the ages of twenty and twenty-five were trained) and didn't have to depend on anyone else.

There's a saying in villages in Haryana and Uttar Pradesh: 'Agar dadi chahegi, toh poti ayegi' (Only if a grandmother wants can a granddaughter be born). Jaglan's model encouraged conversations between grandmothers and granddaughters so the former would not insist on sex selective abortions or foeticides, creating a ripple effect of societal change. The campaign that really made Jaglan famous was Selfie with Daughter, which went viral when Prime Minister Narendra Modi mentioned it in his radio programme.

'We called it "Beti Bachao, Selfie Banao"—the idea was simple, if the smiles of the parents matched their daughters in their love and sincerity, the parents would win an award,' Jaglan told me. 'I was bothered because I hardly saw parents in villages taking smiling photos with their daughters. It disturbed me.'

Jaglan says men are not making an effort to change society as a whole, even though they might be changing their attitude towards their own daughters in their own families or households.

'There are many men who have joined me in my campaigns. There are many men who have transformed their thought processes but there are not enough movements led by men against gender inequalities,' he says, adding that, 'some men run NGOs with their wives, organize a few functions a year. I always tell them a few events a year won't help.'

'And this psychology begins at home because when a girl is standing up on a stage and giving a fiery speech, everyone claps, even her father. But when she speaks up at home, she is asked to shut up and told not to bring her fire inside the house.'

The full name of Bibipur village is Women's World—Bibipur. Jaglan wanted to change the name of the village formally but the authorities turned down his request. However, that is how he names the village on his business cards and at the entrance of the village is a gate that welcomes you to Women's World—Bibipur.

'Men are actually often worried—I will admit that I have felt the insecurity myself, too, sometimes. They are fearful of women's power, and they are even more scared of being stripped of their own power over women. Men symbolize power in our society. They are concerned about holding maximum power in their households. They are worried about listening to their wives because what will people say. Men are actually weak. They need proper psychological guidance to understand that it's not just men who matter. Women do too.'

In 2019, I was invited to speak at a panel on women's safety in urban spaces in New Delhi. The panel had representatives from law enforcement agencies, government officials, and corporates. As the discussions began, I noted, with mounting disbelief, how the male panellists reiterated the fact that India was not unsafe for women and that surveys that call India the most dangerous country for women should be taken with a pinch of salt. They seemed to genuinely believe what they were saying. 'Look at our religious texts,' one of them said, reciting one, 'how much women are respected in this country.' As he was reciting the text, I wanted to interject with a section from the Manusmriti where it says women, animals, and lower caste people should be beaten to be kept under control. One man called the Thomson Reuters 2018 report, which stated that India was the most dangerous country for women in the world, an exaggeration and went on to give the example of how he treats his daughters. I have heard similar arguments from many Indian men over the years, as though if they treat their daughters well, all is well and equality has been achieved. But how are others treating their daughters? And, most importantly, how are they treating their wives?

The morning after the panel, I woke up to #RIPPriyankaReddy trending on social media. Reddy, a twenty-six-year-old veterinary doctor based in Hyderabad was returning home the evening of the panel when her scooter broke down. A few men had come forward to help repair her scooter. They raped her and then set her alight.[13] I briefly wondered what thoughts, if any, went through the minds of my fellow panellists from the previous night. Did the news burst the bubble of their delusions?

Not many women can afford a private-car-backed empowerment. True empowerment can come only when our public transport and streets are safe and our homes are safe and equal.

One key reason we are unable to ensure the safety of this country's women is because how women look at safety and how men look at women's safety are completely different, as has been discussed earlier. For most women, safety is a feeling, something in the present. For most men, safety is CCTV cameras, police posts, rapid action teams, fast-track courts. As they do not understand that safety is a feeling, male policymakers are incapable of mounting an intervention against their brethren. If men and women are equal stakeholders in society, then it should not just be the responsibility of the women to teach men to behave. Yet most sensitization programmes are driven by women or women's groups. The average Indian male's contribution to women's safety is exactly zero!

We are in a state of gender emergency in this country right now. And men have chosen to be bystanders. In 2014, UN Women appointed Bollywood actor Farhan Akhtar as its first male Goodwill Ambassador for South Asia.[14] Akhtar had started his own campaign, MARD—Men Against Rape and Discrimination—to sensitize men and create awareness about the safety of women.

'None of this: Eighteen-inch biceps. A moustache that supposedly proclaims your virility. "Showing appreciation" by leering at girls on the streets. And stalking and harassing a woman until she "falls in love" with you or hitting your wife or your partner; none of this defines a "mard", which is the Hindi word for "man",' Akhtar had written in an article for the UN.

'Here's what does define a "mard", a real man, though. Showing respect. Supporting her choices. Standing up for a woman's right to live free from violence, from the fear of violence. Speaking up when that right is violated, and interrupting the cycle of discrimination she faces.'[15]

'That kind of engagement is essential,' the then UN Women Executive Director, Phumzile Mlambo-Ngcuka had said. 'We need creative and committed men like Farhan to push the gender equality and women's empowerment agenda.' Around the same time UN Women had also launched the HeForShe campaign—an initiative aimed at placing men at the centre of activism and dialogue to end gender discrimination around the world.[16]

'Men as a group have not only not been proactive in the fight for gender equality...I recently came across men's rights groups in India. They are organizing on the other side and nothing can be more dangerous. Yeah, so not much stride there. We are not openly and legally burning women on the stake or with their [dead] husbands but that's about it,' the sociologist Banerjee said.

We have come some distance but we still have miles to go.

IS THIS ALL THERE IS?

How unhappy does one have to be before living seems worse than dying?

—Deborah Curtis, *Touching from a Distance*

For a few years after Divya handed in her resignation, she travelled around the country with her husband as he bounced from one job to another, before a sudden tragedy befell them and the family was back in Delhi, living with her husband's parents. All these years she stayed away from working, looking after her children and the home. She often thought of how she was wasting her education, but there was not much else she could do. But education is never wasted—as she would find out soon enough. While they were away from Delhi, Divya's husband was diagnosed with a life-threatening illness.

As she entered the room, the doctor looked grave. He indicated for her to sit down.

'Is everything okay?' Divya asked tentatively, as her heart thumped.

I am afraid I have bad news…. 'Your husband's kidneys have failed.'

'Both?' She whispered.

The doctor nodded yes.

'He will need a transplant. Immediately.'

When he told her the cost of the procedure, her heart almost stopped. But she listened carefully to the doctor, and with a storm raging in her heart and mind, she went home.

A few weeks after this, her mind was made up. She had decided to donate one of her kidneys to her husband. She had decided they would move back home and she would get a job.

She managed to save her husband's life, but was soon fighting another battle. The months of struggle leading to the donation, trying to balance being a breadwinner as well as a carer, while clamping down on rising resentment against her husband and her in-laws for years of emotional abuse overwhelmed her. 'My mother-in-law made me feel like I should be grateful to them that they paid for my medicines and the surgery.... They went ahead with the surgery even though the doctors had warned them that it could be fatal for me because of the position of my kidney.

'I feel like I am invisible. There is no appreciation, no acknowledgement. I have no life and what life I did have, I had to give up because I have been taught since childhood that home is a woman's priority,' she says.

'I do not mind the work. I can do this and way more than this. I just feel like a little bit of acknowledgement would be nice. There are days when everything is so dark. And no one understands. I do not even have the time to meet my friends and speak to them to unburden the heaviness that sits in my heart like a rock,' she continued.

'I cook, clean, go out to work, look after everyone's comfort, never ask for anything in return—well, nothing huge at least—but some days, just some days I am troubled by a thought...is this all?'

She has attempted suicide twice. She thinks of killing herself worryingly frequently. She goes through most days in a haze, feeling an emptiness she can neither understand nor articulate.

'I don't like talking about it much,' she says. 'What's the point? This feeling hangs over me like a dark cloud. I don't think it will ever disperse—not while I am alive at least.'

Over the two years of the pandemic, Divya was mostly distraught. Working from her small home, with her children attending online classes, she had no space to call her own.

The pandemic has done a good job of lifting the veil off exactly how household responsibilities affect women in India. The pandemic increased women's housework and caregiving burden across the world. In a recent study, 78 per cent of Indian women (as compared to 66 per cent globally) claimed that their burden of household chores had increased. These responsibilities may continue to impact women's lives after the pandemic. 'Over one-quarter of Indian women (26 per cent) say they are less likely than their spouse to return to the office when it is safe to do so.'[1]

Overwork is a huge cause of depression among Indian women, as it is worldwide, and, as the WHO says, there's need for more research on this. In India, we need to start talking about it in our homes first and foremost. Overwork is what most women can point to as a cause of their depression, but in a majority of women it is merely the straw that broke the camel's back. The feelings they are struggling with have built up over time—every slight, every humiliation, every discrimination that women face inside their homes, right from their childhood.

Of the thousands of women who die by suicide in India every year, around a third are victims of domestic violence. As the connection between depression and domestic violence is well-established,[2] it is safe to say a majority of them would have been suffering from depressive or anxiety disorders.

Saira's life had hit a nadir after her son was born in 2009. The violence in the home increased. Her depression deepened. There was no one she could talk to. She didn't know if anyone would understand. Finally, the dark hole of despair got the better of her and she swallowed a handful of pills. 'This is where things end. This is where things start getting better,' she thought in her mind. Things happened very fast after that. She swallowed the wrong pills. Her husband, she alleges, hatched a plan to get rid of her by declaring her mentally unstable. She ended up locked in a mental asylum for three days. By the time she made it back out, her husband had left. She was alone, with two children to look after and no income. She felt alone, scared, lost. One day, she called her husband to ask for help. He asked her very calmly if there was a ceiling fan in the room where she was making the call.

'I said yes,' Saira tells me.

'And?'

'He told me to go and hang myself from that fan.'

In 1992, Anima had fled her marital home with her four-year-old son, unable to put up with the daily abuse.

'I couldn't take it any more and I took refuge in a friend's house. The next day, my in-laws came and took me back but as soon as we got home, they started abusing me for bringing shame to the family,' Anima told me. 'It was unbearable. I couldn't tolerate it. I drank pesticide to end it all permanently.'

Such incessant abuse in the home pushes women to a point where they believe their only way of escape is death. The feeling of being cornered is a very common feeling among middle-class women, I have found. Women are supposed to stay quiet and get on with it without complaining because violence and discrimination as well as overwork are normalized in our homes. Anima put up with so much abuse in her relationship because she didn't know any better. She had grown up seeing her mother stay quiet in the face of physical and emotional abuse by her father and her grandparents. After she was married, her mother-in-law would gaslight her into believing that she was being abused due to her own shortcomings. 'What do you do? Where do you go? You are financially and emotionally ruined. Physically you are exhausted. You educate a daughter, make them doctors and engineers and then you ask them to bear with the abuse—how does that work?' Anima asks me. And I have no answer. I have pondered these questions often enough myself. My mother didn't leave because she had nowhere to go—how is it that women still have such limited choices?

'Women are brought up with the understanding that we are not capable of rational and logical thinking, that we are only capable of being selfless and sacrificial beings,' Anima continues. 'And then, it all begins to clash with your education and the rational thinking that comes with it. And you just die from trying to understand who you really are. Which is why you will see that most women who are committing suicides in India are educated women.'

A 2015 study pointed out that 'one of the most consistent findings in suicide research is that women make more suicide attempts than men, though men are more likely to die in their attempts than women'.[3] This is the gender paradox of suicide, where more women have suicidal thoughts, while more men actually follow through. However, not many studies focus on this paradox or try to explain this. The above study had speculated that it may be because 'there has been a tendency to view suicidal behaviour in women as manipulative and, ultimately, non-serious (despite evidence of intent, lethality, and hospitalization), and to describe their attempts as "unsuccessful", "failed", or attention-seeking as if to imply that women's suicidal behaviour is inept or incompetent.'[4]

Anima tried to kill herself again when she was fifty-two and while she was being treated for depression.

'It's like a bottomless ditch and you keep falling and falling—no one listens to you. No one wants to listen to you,' she says.

Depression among women is on the rise in India. Most women who are suffering from depression are likely to die by suicide according to a study published in the *Lancet*. The study, the first comprehensive estimate of sufferers of mental health disorders across India, found that from between the years 1990 and 2017, the share of mental health disorders in the country had doubled. The prevalence of depressive disorders stood at 3.9 per cent among women; about the same percentage of women reported anxiety disorders.[5] It is worrisome because depression and suicides are becoming an epidemic among Indian women.

A study published in the *Indian Journal of Psychiatry* in 2013 had summarized the various reasons women might be killing themselves in India. The study cited the work of sociologist Susan Wadley, who had examined the identity of women in folklore, myths, and legends rooted in history, and found that the Indian woman is 'constantly made to adopt contradictory roles—the nurturing roles as daughters, mothers, wives, and as daughters-in-law, and the stereotyped role of a weak and helpless woman. The latter is fostered to ensure complete dependence on the male sex. Consequently, the constant movement from strength to passivity leads to enormous stress placing the woman's mental health under constant threat.'[6]

The above study had examined existing data in suicide research and found that mental distress was higher among married women, especially housewives, when compared to married men or single women because within Indian marriages, 'the traditional role of the female is limiting, restricting and even boring, which may lead to depression. Moreover, in traditional Hindu families there is a rigid code of conduct for women which prevents communication and expression of emotions, especially negative ones, because of which there is higher prevalence of internalizing disorders such as depression in women compared to men.'[7]

This is true of all patriarchal societies in South Asia, more so than in Western societies. 'Cultural attitudes towards the woman's role in marriage may also partially explain the comparatively higher ratio of female to male suicides found in Asian countries as compared to Europe and the United States of America. In countries like India, Pakistan, and Sri Lanka, where arranged marriages are common, the social and familial pressure on a woman to stay married even in abusive relationships appears to be one of the factors that increases the risk of suicide in women.'[8]

The study also identified dowry to be complicating the problem because 'when dowry expectations are not met, young brides can be harassed to the point where they are driven to suicide. In some cases, families oppose the marriage of young couples, who face the unsolvable conflict of either living apart or severing ties with their families; choose suicide—either together or alone.'[9]

A survey of women treated in hospital emergency rooms after a suicide attempt revealed that over 40 per cent were young rural women, fifteen to thirty-four years of age; an unhappy marriage (over 60 per cent), financial problems (over 40 per cent), and having been beaten by a spouse (almost 40 per cent) were the most frequently cited stressful events they had experienced. 'Harassment by in-laws on issues related to dowry is characteristic of the Indian setting. It has emerged as a risk factor for poor mental health. This age-old practice continues to survive and has been a significant factor that has driven many women to suicide.'[10]

'It is difficult to generalize why women are dying by suicide in our country. If you ask me if it's [because of] a lack of support, I will say it's a possibility. If you say it's domestic violence, I will again say, it's possible,' Soumitra Pathare, a consultant psychiatrist and director of Centre for Mental Health Law & Policy, told me, adding that suicide prevention will have to be designed with care.

According to Pathare, 'Most men who die by suicide do so because of a history of alcohol addiction. A third of women who die by suicide have a history of domestic violence. Alcohol and domestic violence are very closely linked. Again, suicide, domestic violence, and alcohol addiction have a close relationship and men and women fall into it through their own circumstances. Which is why suicide prevention requires a lot of nuancing depending on the subgroup we are dealing with. Right now, we are focused on suicide prevention at the point where the person might die. That's sometimes too late and we should look at much distant interventions to prevent it. Between the path to suicide and end point there are multiple points where we can intervene.'

There was a 126 per cent rise in suicides among women between the ages of fifteen and forty-nine in India between 1990 and 2010.[11] In 2018, the *Lancet*, in an analysis of suicide deaths in India between 1990 and 2016, found the death rate among women to be 2.1 times higher than the global average in 2016.[12] In the book *Suicide and Society in India*, Peter Mayer, a professor of politics at the University of Adelaide, along with his co-researchers, found that women in India are particularly prone to suicides when they are between thirty and forty years of age.[13]

When you look at the figures published by the NCRB, you will see that the number of men committing suicides is far higher than women. But these figures often do not take into account that most suicides by women are not reported as suicides by family members because of the stigma attached to mental illnesses and suicides, especially when it's related to domestic abuse or dowry harassment. Suicide is considered a shameful act for all in India, but women's suicides bring additional shame onto the family and the larger community. A suicide in the family also creates a link to mental illness which could affect the marital prospects of a woman's other female relatives—sisters or daughters.

It is the reason why my mother did not talk about her mother's suicide for over five decades. 'People judge you by that one incident that you had no control over,' she told me. 'Nobody talked about my mother's suicide and we understood it was not something we should talk about.'

Both men and women need therapy in this country, therapy that is contextualized and customized to our society and its peculiarities. But India has only 0.75 psychiatrists, instead of the desirable three, per 1 lakh people, rendering this a distant dream.[14] According to 2017 figures, there were only 0.15 psychologists per 1 lakh of the population.[15]

Not many women I spoke to for this book had sought the help of a psychiatrist, and those who had often came away feeling even more confused.

Divya went to one psychiatrist, then another. She couldn't connect with anyone. They didn't understand what was ailing her. 'They want to hear something from me...and I feel what I say is not something they are comfortable with, so they try to fix me in ways that I don't want to be fixed. I want them to understand me as a woman but they see me only as a wife and a mother and they diagnose my problems from that lens. There is no effort to understand or help me understand my emotions. And then there are the medicines. I don't want medicine. I just want to talk. And I want someone to listen to what I have to say without judging me.

'Also they are so expensive,' she adds. 'For middle-class women, it's impossible to continue with regular sessions.'

So, Divya found solace in traditional healers, astrologers, sometimes alternative healing. I have tried some of them, too, including past life regression, and they have helped me more than any of my psychiatrists.

My past life regression therapist was such an empathetic woman that she would listen to me for hours after my session was over. She would let me sit there with her in silence, let me cry it out. She helped me more than anyone else. When she made me open that door and enter my past lives, she unlocked a knot in my heart. I am not sure how much of what I saw was my imagination but her empathy stayed with me. Her empathy healed me way more than any happy pills could. But again, alternative healing such as past regression therapy or reiki is expensive and, of course, often dismissed as bogus. But it is perhaps a reminder of how ineffective our mental healthcare sector is that women are willing to try it all, even untested procedures just to find some mental clarity. This includes spiritual healers.

This was why I found myself walking into the Sunday gathering of a much sought-after traditional healer in Delhi NCR.

∽

Mataji's round face is all screwed up with concentration. A woman bows down respectfully and places a bowl of uncooked rice in front of her. Mataji keeps touching the rice and chanting. Slowly, her body moves as if in a trance. As the momentum of her movement increases, the coconut oil in her hair seeps onto her forehead, mixing with sticky, greasy sweat. As she works herself into a frenzy, her devotees move close to her, touch her; they are in tears. The goddess is in the room. They all want to be blessed. Mataji is now in a full trance. As she shouts and screams, the shawl slips from her shoulders, and her hair comes undone from the rough bun it is in. She pulls a woman into a bear hug and starts patting her back violently. Both of them are sobbing, choking over huge gulps of tears.

'You are very troubled, child,' she says. 'But don't worry, all will be well. It's just physical ailments. They will go away with time,' she says, putting her hand on the woman's head, whose body is now wracked with sobs.

After half an hour, she is spent, and she just sits there. She looks calm. As I stare at her, she smiles at me and nods. 'It's all going to be fine,' she whispers to me. 'Mataji will make the pain go away.'

Mataji is a god-woman. Her devotees believe she possesses divine powers to drive away evil forces. Sundays are the days she graces her devotees with home visits, to ward off evil spirits or perform prayers. Her Sundays are booked six months in advance.

Later, Mataji slowly enters another trance. Once again, she brings back the goddess into the room. The heady smell of burning camphor stings my eyes. The devotees' chants reach a crescendo as Mataji shrieks and shouts. The goddess has come to visit, her assistants whisper. Ask whatever you want. In a minute, the smiling face of Mataji is contorted in pain. She shakes and cries as the ululation, the music, the songs, all swirl around her. And then, as suddenly as she had entered the trance, she is back again. She slumps forward in a heap. When she rises back up, she is pleasant, calm. There's a throng of devotees lying at her feet. She blesses them all.

On that Sunday, I met a roomful of women struggling to make sense of their lives, battling depression, and trying to find answers in the divine because seeking help for mental illnesses is cumbersome in India. Most women won't even admit to being depressed. My mother never did. And I know exactly why they feel this way.

Studies say that while incidences of suicides among married men were less, that was not so among women. This seems to be particularly the case for young women in developing countries in Asia who are more vulnerable to suicides or suicidal behaviour owing to arranged and early marriage, young motherhood, low social status, domestic violence, and economic dependence. Social, cultural, and religious constraints may discourage women from employment, careers, and financial and social independence, and encourage them to remain within unhappy marriages in dependent living arrangements with extended family.[16] What is not discussed as often is the effect of the childhood trauma of watching our mothers deal with emotional and physical abuse and the continuing discrimination that we face in our adult lives. But where can we get the help we need to address our mental health issues?

'I do not think you can dismiss traditional or alternative healing as nonsense. From a cultural, social perspective it is less stigmatizing for women. Alternate healing is actually quite effective, some traditional healers, too, do a great job. Of course, they are not a uniform category and they range from absolutely rubbish to sensitive and empathetic. But traditional healers are much more acceptable in our society,' Pathare told me.

But there is hope. Women, especially younger women, have a new understanding of the realities of their homes, which they do not want to sweep under the rug. Instead, they are trying to find ways to make their mothers' lives better and, in the process, they are also choosing a different path for themselves.

I conducted an informal, spur-of-the-moment online survey in 2019, trying to identify patriarchal micro-aggressions or 'passive-aggressive patriarchy' in our daily lives and how men and women perceive patriarchal attitudes and institutions in this country.

In the survey, I had asked a few very specific questions, and although there were only around nineteen responses, they were interesting. I found a wide difference between the answers given by men and women. There is a communication gap between the two and it is as important to address that as it is to address all other issues of inequalities. It is also interesting that the men and women surveyed were all educated and smart and yet the responses to the questions showed how they were still shouldering the burden of age-old, archaic notions of gender.

When I had asked about their views on marriage, most women said it was an outdated institution that feeds patriarchy and dumps responsibilities on the women.

Others felt it could be celebrated as love and union but 'only when it's not coerced like in arranged marriages. The union has to be consensual and both must agree to it.' But most respondents felt that it was less about love and more about being a societal affair or a milestone.

Men, on the other hand, only had good things to say about marriages. For most it symbolized 'love and commitment'.

It gets interesting when we come to questions about housework. The women's bitterness was obvious in their responses. Most of the men who took part in the survey said women were mostly responsible for housework, while some disagreed. But women unanimously responded saying that the current distribution of housework is unequal.

One respondent said that while it should be equal 'even in marriages involving the most progressive men, it is not.'

'Caregiving duties are shouldered almost exclusively by women', they felt. 'The default assumption is that the woman will handle it. I feel the need to factor this in while dating, to try to be with someone who is on the same wavelength as me about this that it should be equal. And I have seen marriages where it's equal and normal but it's weird that this equality is not our default setting.'

To a question about what the men and women in their families did first in the morning and last at night, one man said his sister 'fed the kids first thing in the morning and the last thing she did was to get them to sleep'. First thing in the morning, most women made tea, took out the trash, cooked breakfast, and the last thing most of them did was 'cleaning up before going to bed'.

Men sometimes made tea for their partners, but mostly reported scrolling through their phones, or watching television while eating breakfast.

Most of the women were of the opinion that cooking was a burden that was dumped on them—it was at best an obligation.

Men said it was a bit of both—women do love cooking but were often dumped with the responsibility too. 'I do think most of the women though would like to rest deservedly than [cook] a vegetable!' one male respondent wrote.

'There are many women who love cooking and possibly an equal number who are dumped with the responsibility,' another said.

In answer to the question if women should be out at night, most women were emphatic in saying that they should. 'If you love to be out, you should be able to go out. I love my night outs,' one woman said.

'If that's what they want to do. Because people (not men, not women, all people. Everyone.) should be able to do whatever they want,' another said. Men, while agreed it was a choice, were quick to add that they would 'be worried if it's someone close to me. Coz, it's certainly more unsafe for women than men'.

'It is true late night is unsafe for women and they shall be careful but not avoid it,' another said.

'For all you "it's not safe"ers—MAKE IT SAFE,' one woman said.

For most women, the question of safety was embedded in a patriarchal structure where men wielded power over women. 'Women are expected to comply with socially mandated behaviours. When they don't, they are punished, usually by violence, which is not necessarily physical,' one respondent said. Women don't feel safe because of the 'sexual violence perpetrated by men, and the role played by patriarchy, police'.

'Men are conditioned in a certain way. Patriarchal society and system geared against women including law and order. A lot of factors come into play but all have their origin in patriarchy and treating women like objects for sex,' one respondent said.

Most women blamed it on patriarchy and the patriarchal attitudes of the policy makers and the police. 'Men in politics and police don't think it's okay for women to be out at night time or even otherwise. Men and women raised and taught by patriarchy that don't let them see women's struggle for independence as something normal.'

'Because men think that "izzat" lies in a woman's vagina and the best way to show your dominance is to attack her "izzat". Because even the well-intentioned men don't stop the horrid jokes on their whatsapp groups but tell their female relatives to not go out alone after dark.'

Another respondent said our government 'keeps saying "beti bachao, beti padhao" but has nothing to say when said beti is violated. Because women have been reduced to beti, maa, behen, etc. and not addressed as equal citizens.'

To the next question—'Women are respected in India more than anywhere else in the world. Would you agree? If yes, why?'—the response was that when men say women are respected in India, they mean women 'who stay strictly within the bounds of patriarchy and don't question tradition or rock the boat by asking for better treatment'.

'Theoretically yes, but practically many women are supposed to be subservient to their husband or in-laws' wishes,' one woman said, while another wrote that 'women have never been respected in India'.

While most of the male respondents agreed, some were ambivalent. 'Society in general needs to learn to give and demand respect from each other, be it class, caste, or gender,' one said.

But women were truly vocal on this question. 'Women are respected when it's convenient. They're respected for their achievements and stature, but they are not treated as equals,' one woman wrote in the form.

'Respect for women here is only as per convenience.'

'My outfit will change people's perspective on whether they should respect me,' another wrote.

'I mean, in my urban elite 6 per cent echo chamber, yes. But despite our privilege, my mom (and us kids) were abused by her in-laws and husband pre-divorce so there's that. And there's always fear that something will go wrong. The underlying fear is constant—which means respect isn't the default,' another woman wrote.

Men continued being ambivalent. 'There's talk of respecting women and it's also supposedly part of our culture. But there's a general lack of respect for human life in our country and women fare much worse than men.'

When it came to safety, for men it was 'a sense of being free to do as you want to (not in terms of creating havoc, but in terms of living your best life for yourself, for others you care for, and for your society). When you can express yourself (verbally, physically, emotionally, financially, etc.) without fear of repercussion or the need to explain yourself.'

For women safety was more a physical fear, than a metaphysical sense of being.

I asked—what can we do to make streets safer for women?

Women said:

'More women need to be out on the streets.'

'Bringing up our sons not to be rapists.'

'Better policing and legal remedies.'

'Education in schools, at home that women are not meant to be oppressed, touched without consent, etc. Crackdown on cops and hold them accountable for crimes against women, sensitize them on how to treat victims of such crimes. Also short term—lighting in dark corners, shame those who commit crimes against women publicly.'

'Educating society. Better patrolling, more camera are secondary. Also, there should be absolutely no moral policing.'

Men were all about 'more neighbourhood watch schemes, CCTV cameras, swift punishment of violent offenders, increased patrolling, better street lights, better public transport especially night services'.

But as a woman responder had summarized it, 'Well-lit streets and privacy reducing CCTV and gender sensitive police can all be effective up to a certain extent. What we need is a society built on better values.'

When I asked about their father's contribution in daily life to understand if care duties are shared or not, the responses I got were:

'Emotionally abusive in the past; a Mansplainer.' (capital deliberate)

'He is a combination of a progressive as well as regressive man.'

'He is a victim of patriarchy. One who never wanted to be the breadwinner. Laidback and only attacks when attacked. Is sadly caught in shackles he can't break.'

'Loving, involved, selfless as a father. Needs to be a better husband.'

'He is [a] very amazing person. His world centres around his family. Though he is always going to be concerned with what society has to say about our lifestyle, he has always done right by himself for both his daughters.'

'He has been supportive but not very involved in my life, he leaves the child rearing and household responsibilities to my mother.'

Mothers were 'caregivers, self-sacrificing, loving, constantly multitasking, and unfortunate victims of patriarchy. One who had toiled day and night, at work and at home. Single-handedly doing all the physical and mental labour of running and providing for a family.'

While a few women said their mothers were opinionated and rebellious, most described them as 'a submissive victim' who rarely stood up to their husbands.

'Could have done so much more if she hadn't married, or married later,' one woman had written of her mother.

The two most important takeaways for me from this quick survey were that these responses were from my own echo chambers—mostly liberal-progressive, educated, middle-class people who have an online presence. These answers make it clear that gender equality statistics cannot be dismissed because one believes that such inequalities only exist in families belonging to the lower socio-economic strata.

The second takeaway was how most respondents tried to justify their father's shortcomings by using words such as 'loving', 'selfless', and 'victim' before criticizing them. This is something I, too, have struggled with all my life. My father is also a loving and caring man, and yet I have seen how unkind he could be towards my mother. Throughout my life I have battled to reconcile myself with the two images of him as a father and a husband. Today he is ill and bed-ridden, but still horrible to my mother. He treats her like his personal attendant, as he has always done. Some things never change. We continue to struggle with the trauma of being the daughters of patriarchs—a reality that is hard to accept and harder to live with, especially when the victims are our mothers.

MIDDLE-CLASS MORALITY AND THE GODDESS SYNDROME

Our culture has created two almost irreconcilable descriptions of a 'good woman'. The first is the individual achiever; the second, the self-sacrificing domestic goddess.

—Martha Beck, *O, The Oprah Magazine*

In the middle of 2020, the Gauhati High Court granted divorce to a man on the grounds that his wife did not wear any of the marks of a married Hindu woman (conch shell bangles, sindoor).[1] The court took the absence of these markers to mean that the wife was not committed to the marriage and stated this amounted to harassment of her husband and in-laws. 'Such a categorical stand of the respondent [the wife] points to the clear intention that she is unwilling to continue her conjugal life with the appellant [the husband],' the judges had said in a judgment passed on 19 June. Just a few days later, a judge in Karnataka, ruling in a rape case, had said 'the explanation offered by her [the victim] that after the perpetration of the act she was tired and fell asleep is unbecoming of an Indian woman,' adding that it was 'not the way our women react when they are ravished'.[2] After widespread outrage, he deleted these comments from his judgment. These two judgments make it clearer why Goddess Kali needs to take over India.

I have lived through a few momentous occasions in India's feminist history including the aftermath of the infamous Delhi gang rape in 2012, which increased the focus on gender rights in India and brought about some much-needed policy changes. We called it a watershed and hoped things would only get better from then onwards. For the years that followed, it did seem India was becoming, or at least trying to become, a better country for its women.

But even as the facade becomes more ornate—liberal, permissive, modern—the chains are tightening underneath.

Don't go by what you see or read—empowerment is still an individual achievement in this country. Most Indian women are battling it out in their homes, without access to social media or the internet. Some, who have access to the digital world, have never been intellectually empowered to call out the daily injustices in their lives.

Sure, financial empowerment can go some way in sustaining women but without intellectual empowerment, women will remain in a position of disadvantage. The small library Jaglan built in his village went a great distance to inspire the women and girls in Bibipur. This is why the intellectual empowerment of women should be emphasized.

For as long as I can remember, a small, square photograph of the Indian goddess Kali has travelled with me around the world. When I left for London in 1999 to study for my master's degree, my absolutely non-religious mother had slipped it into my suitcase, unnoticed. I was twenty-one and the hidden symbolism of it was lost on me. Over the next three years, that photograph attracted much attention from my flatmates in the hostel where I lived. They were from various parts of the world—China, Greece, the US, Spain—but all of them were enamoured with the image of Kali. One student in particular—George—who was studying law, was obsessed with her. We spent hours talking about Kali. It was such an unusual experience for me. I think it was here that, for the first time, I began to look at her with new eyes, and to understand why my mother put her photo in my suitcase and why I have clung to that photo throughout my life. I am not a temple goer, I am not religious—I believe in a higher power, and mostly I believe in the universe, but I have always drawn strength from the image of Kali, from her untameable nature. My European friends wanted to know more about this goddess who challenged their perception of demure Indian women who lived behind the veil.

Kali doesn't care to conform to what's expected of her. She hangs out in cremation grounds and drinks alcohol from a skull. She could teach Indian women a thing or two about having fun. Kali is a badass goddess who embodies sexual energy and destruction. She is uncontrollable; she threatens and challenges the status quo.

Perhaps this is why she is not widely worshipped in India apart from in Bengal, where a mildly muted version of patriarchy exists. In India, Kali is more of an antagonist, a black magic goddess, worshipped by shamans and occult practitioners. She should be worshipped as a feminist idol.

In India, women are often labelled with the term 'goddess'. Goddesses are beyond reproach, and women in India are expected to live a life beyond reproach—symbolizing unending love, virtue, and sacrifice. Really to be little Ms Nobodies who can only be mothers, sisters, wives.

Remember Irom Sharmila? The world's longest hunger striker, Sharmila was protesting against a draconian law that gives the army impunity in a region wracked by insurgencies. All hell broke loose when the activist decided to break her fast and resume normal life. During the sixteen years of her fast, her home had been a narrow hospital cot. Her frail form, with a gaunt face surrounded by dark curly hair, and a tube on the bridge of her nose through which she was being force fed by the state, became an indelible image of an unparalleled protest. She was called the Iron lady of Manipur, revered, worshipped as a goddess. But when she decided to take back her life and live it according to her own choices (she was in love and wished to marry her long-time partner, the British-born Desmond Coutinho), she became an instant pariah. After ending her fast, she had no home to which she could go back. She went back to her narrow cot, in her impersonal hospital room. Solitary, lonely, and defeated.* *The goddess had fallen.*

The iron lady of Manipur, who had put her life on hold in 2000 for her people, had been feeling the pressure of being a goddess for a long time. In a letter that she had smuggled out to me with the help of a German journalist in 2010, she wrote, 'once you become a public figure for a cause for the greater good, you will never again be free from criticism about your behaviour. Your admirers will like

---

*She married Coutinho in 2017 and now lives in Bangalore with her husband and twin daughters.

to decide and interfere with your destiny and your personal life.' She didn't say it—she didn't have to—but this judgment is stronger and sharper if the object of reverence is a woman.

In my letter to her, I had asked her who Sharmila was and what she dreamt of. She replied that she dreamt of enjoying good health, happiness, and prosperity, and wished to travel the world with her life partner. And if she had been allowed this small dream, perhaps she wouldn't have withdrawn so totally from activism and politics.

The late writer and human rights activist Mahasweta Devi was also a goddess to many, a title she had never agreed to because it limited her choices as a woman. She lived life completely on her own terms, even if it meant going against the diktats of society or the wishes of her loved ones.

She fought against all kinds of labels throughout her life—especially labels that wanted to limit her as a woman. She didn't let society limit her sexual choices or personal freedom. She has, from public podiums, asserted many a time that she hated what she called the 'fake Indian morality' where everything is suppressed. She had once told me in her abrupt manner. 'I make mistakes, I own my mistakes, I am a human being.'

But women in our society are expected to be perfect, like goddesses. A thousand years back a Sanskrit sloka had described the essential qualities of women as 'Karyeshu Dasi, Karaneshu Mantri; Bhojeshu Mata, Shayaneshu Rambha, Roopeshu Lakshmi, Kshamayeshu Dharitri, Shat Dharmayukta, Kuladharma Patni.'[3] (The ideal wife should work hard like a slave, be wily like a minister, caring like a mother, skilled in bed, beautiful like Goddess Lakshmi, forgiving like Mother Earth.)

We are still nudging women towards achieving such perfection, which is why Indian women are always compared to Goddess Durga and not Kali. Durga has ten hands. Four children. She is fair and extremely beautiful. She slays demons. She panders to her children, keeps her husband's temper in check, and all without any complaints and with a sweet smile on her face. For years, goddesses like her have been models for young Hindu Indian women. Meek, subservient, multitaskers. She is revered so much that when a film titled *Sexy*

Durga was released in 2017, it created huge outrage in the country. How can a word associated with physical love, passion, and desire be used to describe a goddess? We like our goddesses (and our women) to be beautiful and desirable, but divested of any personal desires. To never talk back, never look their elders in the eye, never demand their rights, be lifeless, sexless beings. Domestic goddesses.

In *Devi*, a seminal film by Oscar-winning filmmaker Satyajit Ray, a young girl, Dayamoyee, is worshipped as a goddess after her father-in-law dreams that she is a reincarnation of the goddess Kali. Soon, she is trapped inside this image of herself as a goddess and ends up losing her mind. The original short story by Prabhat Kumar Mukhopadhyay was written in 1899, then made into a film in 1960. It is sad that it is still as relevant today.

My mother's ma had killed herself when she was only two years shy of hitting forty. It's a wound my mother has been carrying for most of her life. 'She was widowed at twenty-five. Society imposed all these restrictions on her. White sari, she ate just boiled rice on most days, she was a shadow of my book-reading, strict mother,' my mother told me, her voice thick with emotion. 'She must have had her desires too...she was so young. She must have been suffering. Her mind must have been in flux. But nobody cares about what a woman is going through. We are supposed to fix it and get going.'

This repressive culture was bound to explode some day or the other. And it has, though surreptitiously, through a French extramarital dating app launched in India in 2017.

An Indian woman using the app called Gleeden had written in a testimonial (shared with me by the company in 2020):

Dear Gleeden,

I am a 36 years old woman and I'm the mother of two children. I have been married for 7 years and I have always been faithful. Until now...I was caught between his complete lack of interest and the violence of the fights I continuously started to make him acknowledge me. Then I discovered Gleeden. I wanted to feel again those butterflies in the stomach when you meet somebody that you like and then you discover that he likes you back.... I subscribed and almost immediately I collected requests from lots of men very different from one another. I was flabbergasted by the number of married men who were on the website without their wives knowing. I met a few. Sometimes at a restaurant. Sometimes in hotels. I felt beautiful, seductive, and powerful.

The same year, Gleeden released the results of a survey* which found that 56 per cent of Indian women had already cheated on their spouses and 49 per cent confessed to an intimate relationship with someone other than their spouse. Indian women were also the most uninhibited towards infidelity—53 per cent admitted to having an intimate relationship outside their marriage. 'Indian women seem particularly open minded about infidelity, especially when it involves romance,' Gleeden's marketing director Solene Paillet had said at a press conference.[4] This is a telling criticism of Indian marriages, defined as they are by duty and responsibilities rather than love, romance, and, most importantly, respect and companionship.

When the app was released in India, they were overwhelmed with the number of people that signed up. Today, it has 13 lakh active users. In 2019, they released a survey on why men and women cheat, and the results were surprising. According to the survey, part of a press release shared with me, seven out of ten women cheated on their husbands because they didn't share the household chores or caregiving duties. Women were cheating in India because they were not treated as equals by their husbands, because they felt underappreciated, unloved, and ignored.

'I do not know what I was doing—I was just moving from one affair to another. It didn't make me feel good but it was a respite from my mundane life where at the best of times I felt like a machine. These encounters were exciting, something to look forward to in my life. I

---

*The survey was conducted online on a sample size of over 1,500 people from across major cities like Delhi, Mumbai, Chennai, Bangalore, Hyderabad, Kolkata, Pune, and Ahmedabad. The respondents were married individuals between the ages of twenty-five and fifty years.

was important to someone not as a mother or a wife or a daughter but as a lover, as a human being,' a woman in her early forties, who chose to be anonymous for obvious reasons, told me. She had found herself entangled in a few extramarital affairs after she turned forty. It soon became an obsession, an addiction for her. 'It made me feel good at that moment. Later I felt horrible. But it was worth it in that moment. I felt seen.'

A friend had once very excitedly told me that she was being sought out by attractive young men on social media. As she talked about it, I could sense the excitement and happiness that was taking over her generally serious and focused persona. She was a few years older than me and I had wondered about the origin of her feelings. She loved her husband and her children, and she loved her life, but she felt like life owed her a little bit more. This feeling has been haunting Indian women for too long now.

The company says 'Gleeden responds to an urge that is very present within the Indian society, especially in the big metropolitan areas which have been growing non-stop over the past two and a half years. India is our fastest growing country today. This study helps us to better understand the Indian society and its perspective towards infidelity and online extramarital dating.'[5]

A recent press release, shared with me by Gleeden's PR team, said the app saw a steady increase in traffic as India went into a lockdown to combat the Covid-19 pandemic. During March and April in 2020, it recorded an increase of over 166 per cent in new subscriptions. Most of the new subscribers are women, according to the company, which put the ratio of men and women users at 36:64, close to the composition in Europe. Most of the new users were from Bengaluru, Mumbai, Kolkata, and Delhi, and were young professionals.

'What is even more pleasing is the rise in [our] women user base in the country. Gleeden has always strived to be a platform that wishes to comfort women who are strangled in unwanted relationships,' the company said in its latest statement.[6]

What this essentially means is that women are now questioning the very sanctity of marriages that they are solely responsible for upholding, often at the cost of their sanity and desires.

Women in India, like their Western counterparts, have been questioning the institution of marriage simply because it is skewed in favour of men all over the world. Maintaining a marital relationship in this country is more emotional and physically back-breaking work. Divorce is not just a dirty word but often an impossible feat to achieve in India. During a rocky phase in a friend's marriage some years back, I had taken her to meet a woman lawyer. After hearing her out, the lawyer was candid. 'Get him to sign the papers and agree to a mutual divorce otherwise this will carry on for years if he decides to contest. That's how this country still works unfortunately.'

Yes. Unfortunately.

Even when you are done, you are not done—not until the man says so.

And middle-class morality plays a huge part in this decision, too. 'When I shared with my father that I was contemplating divorce,' a friend had once confided in me, 'his first reaction was you can't do that. What will people say. Think about your children. Every woman has to compromise. It's nothing new that you have to do.'

All over the world, people are rethinking the institution of marriage, which in its traditional form only deepens gender inequalities and keeps women away from realizing their full potential. From live-in relationships to the lesser-known beta marriages or short-term renewable marriages (proposed in countries such as the Philippines, Mexico, Germany),[7] young people are trying to redefine love and companionship. In India, after years of being a taboo, live-in relationships are now less so. Indian millennials and centennials today prefer to enter live-in relationships before they take the plunge. In 2019, a BW Businessworld and X Billion Skills Lab study found that a majority of young men and women in India (seventeen to twenty-two years of age) preferred live-in relationships. The survey was conducted among 5,217 young people in twenty cities across India.[8]

According to Inshorts' Pulse of the Nation poll, around 80 per cent women aged between eighteen to thirty-five years in India support live-in relationships and 26 per cent had said they would prefer lifelong live-ins over marriage.[9] Further, in 2013, the Supreme Court brought live-in relationships under the ambit of the Domestic Violence Act.[10] The poll had surveyed the responses of 1.4 lakh Indians from urban and rural areas. However, there are other surveys, too, that point to young people preferring arranged marriages and staying in joint families. For example, MTV's 'Mera Bharat Amazeballs' survey in 2020 that included responses from over 25,000 people between ages fifteen and twenty-five from 400 towns across India found that more than 60 per cent of young Indians prefer arranged marriages.[11] It is hard to reconcile the difference in the findings of these surveys. To me, it seems like our young people are going through a period of transition—they are still trying to figure out their lives while fighting the expectations of their families and society. But what I find the most hopeful in this chaos of contradictions is that they are thinking, rethinking, and questioning the status-quo.

Marriages, being patriarchal institutions, are inherently linked to inequalities in countries like India. Prodded by feminist mothers, the next generation has already started their work.

In 2020, I came across a very interesting school project by a seventeen-year-old girl. She had asked two very important questions in a survey she put together for a school project, which she had posted on social media.

They were, 'Are gender roles in open relationships different from gender roles in monogamous relationships?' and 'Do the functions of marriage differ between open relationships and monogamous relationships?'

She found that while most couples in open relationships had been together for a long time (many for more than ten years), the monogamous couples who responded had been in relationships of varying lengths, but usually less than a decade. She also noticed that in most open relationships both partners had equal control of their finances, whereas in most monogamous relationships both men and women admitted that financial control lay with the men. A similar pattern was seen when it came to housework, with approximately 80 per cent of people in open relationships reporting that both partners shared the load equally, as opposed to the unequal distribution of labour among monogamous couples.

Her final question was about happiness, something that most Indian men and women compromise on. Her findings went against the idea of happiness and conjugal bliss that is fed to us—men and women in open relationships reported to be significantly happier than people in monogamous relationships.

In this young woman's questions, I could see the change that is occurring in women's perceptions of an ideal marriage. Middle-class women are embracing this shift almost discreetly, focusing more on passing on these ideas to their daughters than creating lasting change in their lives in the present.

THE ECONOMICS OF EQUALITY

Equality is not just the right thing to do. It's smart economics. How can an economy achieve full potential if it ignores, sidelines, or fails to invest in half its population?

—Robert Zoellick

In 2015–2016, the global media reported an unusual phenomenon in Maharashtra. The state has been drought-hit for years, reporting the highest number of farmer suicides in the country. The Reuters news agency reported on a drought-hit village called Denganmal, more than 100 kilometres from Mumbai, where the only water comes from 'two wells at the foot of a nearby rocky hill, a spot so crowded that the sweltering walk and wait can take hours'.[1] The article told the story of Sakharam Bhagat, who has three water wives, also known as 'paniwali bais'—literally water maids. 'Bhagat, sixty-six, now has three wives, two of whom he married solely to ensure that his household has water to drink and cook,' the Reuters piece continued. In water-scarce regions it is almost always the women who walk long miles to fetch water. In this drought-stricken part of Maharashtra it had made sense for the men to marry more than once to ensure their households ran smoothly.

Towards the end of 2015, the non-profit ActionAid also released a short film on the water wives of Maharashtra. In the film, the story unfolds around an old man who informs his first wife, who is fanning him while serving him food, that he has finalized the arrangements for his third marriage. His second wife, who is pregnant and making chapattis, looks on angrily. He is heard saying in the film, 'Talk to her, explain to her that I am marrying for the third time only to help you two out.' Towards the end of the movie, the second wife is looking after the children, while the third wife, a much, much younger woman is shown balancing a multitude of vessels on her head for the long walk to the nearest water source.[2]

This practice is also seen in other parts of the country. In Derasar, a small village in Rajasthan's Barmer district with a population of about 600 people, men usually have two wives. The reason? When the first wife gets pregnant, they need another woman to do the household chores and fetch water.

The film on the water wives ended with the message: 'They exist everywhere, in our homes, our workplaces, in our minds. Where a woman is unpaid, unheard, and unrecognized.'[3]

Another non-profit WaterAid noted, 'Although the village says these marriages are a social good, giving homes to the second and third wives who are usually widows or have been abandoned by their husbands, these women do not have the same rights as the "legitimate" first and most senior wife. The junior wives do not have conjugal rights, nor are they eligible to inherit their husband's property after his death. Their sole role in the household is to fetch water from a distant source. For this, they are given food, shelter, and the semi-respectability of being married. This arrangement is an example of communities finding ways to adapt to extreme difficulties, and a stark reminder of how much work is still needed to ensure gender-equal, easy access to safe drinking water in India, especially in rural areas.'[4]

Such practices clearly do not arise out of an altruistic idea of making sure more women get the protection and respectability of marriage. For instance, in Denganmal, the practice of water wives is now considered folklore, local activist Dasrath Bhelke told me during our conversation. The change came about when the village with a population of about seventy families got a well and piped water.

In 2015, Denganmal had hit the headlines with stories of women being exploited. Today, it is a case study in how ensuring basic rights, such as access to safe, potable water, can improve women's lives.

'People are educated now, they don't believe in such regressive practices. And more than anything else they have water now. The region also began to get good rainfall in recent times,' Bhelke told me. 'They send their girls to schools and colleges. No one can think of repeating such a practice.' Bhelke says the village is a prime example of how much difference water availability can make in improving the lives of women.

In India, as in any other developing country, women and girls are responsible for collecting water. While in urban India, women spend hours queuing up at common taps to fill their cans and pots, in rural India, especially in water-scarce regions, women and girls travel miles to collect water for daily use. According to the National Commission for Women, a rural woman walks around 14,000 kilometres a year just to collect water for her family.[5]

Photographs of women carrying tall towers of vessels on their heads lead people (mostly men) to exclaim over the beauty and skill that this demonstrates. But in reality, this is back-breaking work and women in many parts of India spend an inordinate amount of time collecting, transporting, and managing water. Girls often drop out of school to help their mothers in this daily water haul, which is, of course, part of housework and hence considered unproductive labour.

Women and girls across the world spend a whopping 200 million hours every day collecting water. The UNICEF called it a 'colossal waste of their valuable time' in a statement in 2016.[6]

'Just imagine: 200 million hours is 8.3 million days, or over 22,800 years,' UNICEF's global head of water, sanitation, and hygiene, Sanjay Wijesekera, said in the same statement. 'It would be as if a woman started with her empty bucket in the Stone Age and didn't arrive home with water until 2016. Think how much the world has advanced in that time. Think how much women could have achieved in that time. …When water is not on the premises and needs to be collected, it's our women and girls who are mostly paying with their time and lost opportunities.'[7]

The UN's Sustainable Development Goal for water and sanitation, 'Goal 6', calls for universal and equitable access to safe and affordable drinking water by 2030. The first step is providing everyone with a basic service within a thirty-minute round trip, and the long-term goal is to ensure everyone has safe water available at home. However, UN estimates are that in sub-Saharan Africa, for example, for 29 per cent of the population (37 per cent in rural areas and 14 per cent in urban areas), improved drinking water sources are thirty minutes or more away. One round trip to collect water is thirty-three minutes on average in rural areas and twenty-five minutes in urban areas. In Asia, the numbers are twenty-one minutes and nineteen minutes respectively.[8]

One can imagine how much of an impact piped water could have on women and girls. As Wijesekera said, 'No matter where you look, access to clean drinking water makes a difference in the lives of people.'[9]

There are success stories from India, too. In 2013, a WaterAid project managed to bring piped water to each house in the village of Padariya, in Dindori district in Madhya Pradesh. It has changed the life of young girls in the village. A case study from the project tells the story of Saraswati, who told WaterAid that the time she saves now goes into studying or just relaxing.[10]

'Earlier, I used to fill water from a hand pump before going to school. Filling two utensils in two rounds took an hour as there are long queues in the mornings. It was too heavy to carry and there were days when I used to be late for school,' Saraswati had explained.

Saraswati, who was then studying in Class VII, had many responsibilities, like washing utensils, cleaning, and cooking as her parents worked in their agricultural plot all day long.

'Earlier, I also had to fill water in the evening and hardly got time to study. As the village had limited number of hand pumps, there were always queues in the peak morning and evening hours,' she adds.

During her PhD research in Jharkhand, feminist economist Shiuli Vanaja also found that women had no leisure time because of their water-fetching responsibilities. Women were spending almost two hours every day collecting water. Piped water could mean they would have those extra two hours a day to spend on childcare or farm labour and, from an economic perspective, this would result in an increase in productivity, increase in incomes, and a positive cumulative effect on children's education.

ActionAid also reported that improved access to water has demonstrable effects on health outcomes of children and school attendance of girls while sounding a note of caution that 'contradictory conclusions have emerged on the whether time saved by improved water supply leads to more time spent on market work. It notes the possibility that time saved in collecting water is reallocated to improving family welfare. More studies are clearly required before generalizations can be made and regional differences can be understood.'[11]

That is where it all comes to a halt—there are just not enough focused studies around. And this is why studies like Vanaja's are interesting because they are trying to go beyond the obvious and look at different aspects of women's overwork. Vanaja looks at it from the lens of leisure, for example.

'It's difficult to quantify leisure because women do not want to talk about leisure, so it is difficult to analyse it,' she says.

McKinsey, in its Power of Parity report 2018, asserted that India has one of the largest opportunities in the world to boost GDP by advancing women's equality—$770 billion could be added to the GDP by 2025. An *IndiaSpend* report in 2017 had surveyed women in Rajasthan's Udaipur district and found that mothers with children in the one- to six-year-old age group spent an average of 9.4 hours a day on household chores and only seventeen minutes on paid work.[12]

'Today, companies acknowledge that workplace diversity and empowering women contributes to business success. This is also important for the Sustainable Development Goals—when women work, it has a multiplier effect on their lives, the lives of their children, families, and communities,' Nadia Rasheed, Deputy Resident Representative, UNDP India, said at the launch of a new report on corporate engagement in women's economic empowerment.[13]

In Bhuira, Rajgarh tehsil in Sirmaur district in Himachal Pradesh, a small jam factory stands testimony to what can change if we provide women with adequate and equal opportunities. But this jam factory is just one example. Himachal Pradesh has been a success story not just in poverty reduction but also providing better access to markets and services to women and other disadvantaged groups.

A World Bank study in 2015 found that in 2011–12, about 63 per cent of rural women in Himachal Pradesh reported themselves as being employed, placing the state second in female labour force participation in the country after Sikkim, and significantly above the all-India average of 27 per cent. 'In urban areas, the female labour force participation rate in Himachal Pradesh was much lower, at 28 per cent in 2011, in keeping with the "classic" Indian pattern, but was nonetheless, double that of neighbouring states. In fact, urban women's employment in Himachal Pradesh was at exactly the same level as those in urban areas of Kerala and Tamil Nadu. Much of this is driven by the fact that women in rural areas in Himachal Pradesh are more than twice as likely as their male counterparts to report themselves as being self-employed in agriculture. But urban women are also more likely than their counterparts in neighbouring states to have regular salaried jobs. One-fifth of urban women in Himachal Pradesh had regular salaried jobs in 2011.'[14]

The World Bank study concluded that girls born in the state enjoyed better access to health and education, participation in the labour market, and in community decision-making. 'Availability of water and fuel sources in remote areas probably translated into reduced time for women and girls in fetching these resources, allowing more time on well-being enhancing activities.'[15]

The state also invested in programmes specifically targeting the welfare of women and creating 'safety nets for widows and poor women,' the study found.[16]

Giving more political agency to women empowers other women in the community. Despite the fact that many women village chiefs are mere puppets, those who work actively in their roles are likely to inspire other women in the community. The Indian government in 1993 reserved a certain proportion of all council chief or village head seats in its villages for women. Each five-year election cycle, one-third of the villages are randomly selected to appoint a female village chief. After these quotas were implemented, the study found that there was an increase in the proportion of women as village leaders from 5 per cent in 1992 to over 40 per cent in 2000. The presence of a female village council chief had a modelling effect, the study said, adding that it led to increased career aspirations and educational attainment among

10 per cent of girls and reduced the time they spent on household chores. In villages that had two female village chiefs, girls were 8.3 per cent less inclined to want to be a housewife or to allow their in-laws to choose an occupation for them; 8.6 per cent were more likely to desire a job that requires an education; and 8.8 per cent were more likely to want to get married after the age of eighteen. In villages with female council chiefs for two election cycles, the gender gap in adolescent educational attainment was erased, with the percentage of girls reading, writing, and attending school equal to or surpassing that of boys. In these villages, the gap in time spent on household chores among genders also decreased by eighteen minutes a day as compared to villages that never reserved a female council chief seat.[17]

This should provide the necessary motivation for policymakers to weed out the regressive Pradhan Pati practice that makes the government's efforts to politically empower women useless. Another study also found that corruption was less severe where there were more women parliamentarians. In 2000, a group of researchers found that 'women are less involved in bribery, and are less likely to condone bribe taking. Cross-country data show that corruption is less severe where women hold a larger share of parliamentary seats and senior positions in the government bureaucracy, and comprise a larger share of the labour force.'[18] A survey conducted in Maharashtra in 2008 found that 'the availability of basic public services was found to be significantly higher in female-sarpanch villages as compared to male-sarpanch villages, in cases where the election had been held 3–3.5 years prior to the survey.'[19] In 2016, another study found that 'women legislators are less likely to be criminal and corrupt, more efficient at completing projects, and less vulnerable to political opportunism.' The study examined data from 4,265 assembly constituencies in India and found that 'women legislators can increase economic growth.'[20]

Can a nation progress far leaving behind half its population? The time for small changes is far gone—we now have to address widening gender gaps on a war footing.

In June 2020, Unstereotype Alliance, an industry-led initiative convened by UN Women, found in a study that increased equality for women is essential to a country's success. According to the study, globally only 53 per cent think most women feel moderately safe to very safe in their home, one in four men still believe there are circumstances where it is acceptable to hit a spouse, and two in three male respondents think women should be paid the same as men for doing the same job. Despite differences in attitudes towards women in different countries, there was consensus that gender equality is important for progress.[21]

Phumzile Mlambo-Ngcuka, then the executive director of UN Women said, 'Discriminatory social norms underpin the persistence of human rights violations. Women are paying a high price for that. Those norms systematically deny women's equal access to political participation, employment, education, and justice, and expose women and girls to violence. The Gender Equality Attitudes Study shows that most people see gender equality as important, but there is clearly more work to do to connect it to the reality of women's rights.'[22]

What women can do with greater political agency has been demonstrated in the way women leaders have led their countries during the Covid-19 pandemic.

From Germany to New Zealand and Denmark to Iceland, women controlled the pandemic with strong leadership, empathy, and compassion.[23] Her Excellency Vjosa Osmani, the first woman assembly president in Kosovo, has been praised for her professionalism in leading the assembly during the crisis; she told UN Women in an interview that 'when women participate in high-ranking political and state level circles they contribute to more balanced, gender-sensitive, environmentally considerate, and forward-looking policies. It is only through such a policymaking approach that we stand a chance in meeting the Sustainable Development Goals and in making this a genuine #DecadeOfAction and a #GenerationEquality.'[24]

Women leaders, she told the UN Women, 'have been able to unify the public and to engage people on the importance of changing their everyday behaviours to help contain the virus' spread and to flatten the curve. Although the burden of the pandemic falls heavily on everyone, there are several aspects that require a specific gender-centred approach, such as securing safe childbirth and controlling maternal mortality;

the impact of school closure on women as primary caretakers; and its connection to workplace activities. In my capacity as assembly president, I am advocating for a continuous gender-sensitive approach so that women are given a sustained and long term equal treatment.'[25]

If housework and caregiving become shared responsibilities inside our homes and practical steps such as providing piped water to households are ensured, it can free up women to participate in the labour force, which will only create positive change in our society and economy. We need to make this country work on a fifty-fifty model. This will also go a long way in keeping women in the workforce and allow them some work–life balance.

We cannot commit to bringing more women into the workforce without providing them a workplace that understands their many daily commitments. It is an open secret that women worldwide shoulder the greater burden of housework and caregiving. In India, of course, as discussed earlier this has become a deathtrap for many women. But women are expected to carry on, hustle through life, and somehow get to the end of every day without losing their sanity. Hustling has become a way of life, constant busyness a virtue, being a superwoman a goal, and 'having it all' a disease. We never stop to ask what is the virtue in having it all? Why doesn't this concept apply to men? What is, after all, having it all?

Women are encouraged to 'lean in' at work but without taking into consideration that all women have different realities depending on what their home life looks like. Expecting them to compete at the same level as men speaks of a narrow vision. Women are not better or worse than men, nor are they more or less capable—they are just different. Companies cannot provide them a one-size-fits-all solution. A direct consequence of this culture is that women have, themselves, started frowning upon leisure. The concept of leisure among Indian women is nearly non-existent. 'I don't even have time to die,' is a refrain I have heard many women utter.

'Women know the negative connotation,' Vanaja says. 'If you are sitting and doing nothing, you will be branded a lazy woman. But leisure is important for women's well-being.'

For working women, there is just never enough time for leisure. I barely get to meet my friends—maybe once a month and even then we are always looking at our watches—there's always something that needs to be done at home or somewhere else we need to be.

Women's lives in India make me think of the Japanese term 'karoshi'—literally 'overwork death'. Today articles talk about it as a global phenomenon[26] but Indian women have been battling it for decades.

According to the WHO, working for over fifty-five hours a week leads to a 35 per cent higher risk of stroke and 17 per cent higher risk of dying from heart disease.[27] In my estimation, Indian women end up working at least sixty to seventy hours every week—and this is a conservative estimate. I work at least twelve to eighteen hours every day in paid and unpaid work which takes my average work week to way over eighty-five hours. If I add the weekend to it as I often work through the weekends, the total would be around ninety-six hours a week. If I didn't have the burden of housework and caregiving, I could perhaps restrict my work time to forty hours a week.

In Japan, the concept of overwork was institutionalized after the oil crisis in 1973. Since then, the seventy-hour work week has been normalized. News of employees dying by suicide or dying at work owing to overwork has become common. This is not too different in India, save for the fact that most of the victims are women.

The Japanese Ministry of Health legally recognized the existence of karoshi in 1987 as a severe social problem and set up a helpline for victims. The helpline reportedly receives over 300 calls every year.[28] More recently, the Japanese government's Work Style Reform Bill 2018 was passed to offer some respite to workers.[29] The first global study that looked at the effects of long work hours found that this can increase deaths from cardiac arrests. Globally, overwork and work-related stress led to 745,000 deaths from stroke and ischemic heart disease in 2016.[30] And these deaths, the study said, can occur even decades after the source of stress has been left in the past, so after workers have officially retired.

'Working fifty-five hours or more per week is a serious health hazard,' Maria Neira, director of the department of environment, climate change, and health, at the WHO had said in a statement that accompanied the report. 'It's time that we all, governments, employers, and employees wake up to the fact that long working hours can lead to premature death.'[31]

Hopefully, as the pandemic forces us to focus on how we work, we take a step forward and connect our problem of overwork and pre-existing gender inequalities to rising suicides and depression among women in our country.

MOBILIZING MIDDLE-CLASS WOMEN

You need women when you know the fight is going to be long and hard. That is the speciality of a women-led movement—they are indomitable, indefatigable.

—Medha Patkar

'I will now go home and make lunch, after that I will fetch my daughter from school, leave her at home and then come back here again. I will be here till 3 a.m. Then I'll go home and wash clothes, pack my daughter's school bag, and make preparations for breakfast and lunch.'

I had met Nusrat Ara, a tall, heavyset woman, a long-time resident of Shaheen Bagh, a conservative, middle-class, Muslim-majority neighbourhood along the borders of New Delhi. Ara, along with several other housewives, was fronting one of the largest women-led sit-ins in recent times in India.

Shaheen Bagh is a no-frills, congested, working-class neighbourhood in South Delhi, a popular haunt for bargain shoppers owing to rows of factory outlet shops on both sides of the main road. The local population is mostly middle-class, a bunch of people who go about their daily business of living and surviving from day to day.

But on the night of 15 December 2019 something shifted, as a group of unassuming and quiet Muslim women in hijabs and burqas came out of their homes for a peaceful candlelight vigil on the main road, silently protesting police brutality on their children.

On 12 December, the Indian government had passed the Citizenship Amendment Act (CAA) that aims to provide citizenship to all non-Muslim refugees from Afghanistan, Pakistan, and Bangladesh who came to India before 2015. This was preceded by the implementation of the National Register of Citizens (NRC) in Assam, to identify illegal immigrants. The exercise, as I found while working on an article for *Foreign Policy*, had stripped 19 lakh people of their citizenship, including over 13 lakh Hindus and around 6 lakh Muslims—69 per cent were women.[1]

The first wave of protests against these exercises began in colleges and universities in India, including in the nearby Jamia Millia Islamia University, a Muslim-majority university, where many young people from Shaheen Bagh study. On the night of 15 December 2019, the Delhi Police stormed into the university's campus, fired tear gas, bullets, and brutally beat up students to curb protests over the CAA and NRC.[2] However, following wide outcry after the crackdown on the students, the government took a step back on the NRC only to announce the National Population Register (NPR), which critics have alleged will be collecting data for NRC, although the Indian government denies it.[3]

'I have no idea where my birth certificate is or where my degrees are. Why just me—most women here don't even have these documents. They probably got left behind in our father's houses when we left after marriage. Must be gathering dust in some old suitcase, if they have not been eaten up by insects,' Ara, who is exactly my age, told me. The World Bank in 2018 said that as many as 1 billion people in the world live without any official proof of identity and 81 per cent of them live in Sub-Saharan Africa and South Asia. One in two women in low-income countries is undocumented.[4]

As women are not really expected to 'do anything' with their education, neither they, nor their families pay much importance to keeping these documents safe. Just like Ara above, I have heard from many other women that their documents were left behind in their parents' home after marriage or never updated as they moved around the country with their spouses. Not many parents bother getting a birth certificate, and school or college certificates often find no place in the bridal trousseau that their daughters can take with them to their new homes.

'We didn't sleep the entire night of the Jamia crackdown,' Shahjahan, one of the protesters, says with a catch in her voice.

Ara and her friends had first occupied the streets as mothers but the protest and the movement that grew around it made them realize they were strong, independent women who were not afraid to speak their mind, and take on the police and the authorities.

'Women have a hundred responsibilities at home and all of them are non-negotiable. A majority of us live in the city with our husbands and our mothers-in-law are in the villages. So, we have to do everything single-handedly. But that has not deterred us. God has given us a lot of strength. We can look after the home as well as be on the streets fighting for our future.'

The women of Shaheen Bagh determinedly occupied a main road that connects the Indian capital to Noida, a satellite town of the capital, for months, demanding a recall of the CAA, NRC, and NPR, until they had to disperse owing to the Covid-19 pandemic. I spent many days with them during the protest and always came away feeling energized and motivated by their indomitable spirit.

It is not true that middle-class women cannot be mobilized. Over the decades, they have been mobilized over and over again but it is always for a cause surrounding either their children's futures or their livelihood. But the Shaheen Bagh protests, and later the farmers' protest in 2020–21, have shown that it is absolutely possible to bring middle-class women out on the streets in protest. But the feminist movement has been unable to bring them together, maybe because the middle class has so many divisions of income and differences in cultural attitudes. Feminism has remained such an elite concept (in terms of class, caste, and religion) in India that women like Ara, Shahjahan, or Ruchi, the housewife vlogger, feel like outsiders. Feminism will need to be simplified, broken down into models that can unite these women in their environment, talking in their language. Empowerment will not be the result of an outright rejection of patriarchy, but will arise from a much more gradual process.

At the Shaheen Bagh protest I met many housewives like Ara, who had never thought they would step out of their houses to take part in a protest or stand shoulder to shoulder with men.

'I have lost all my fears,' sixty-five-year-old Shabnam told me, looking away for a brief moment to raise her voice and repeat a slogan raised by a speaker on stage. 'I have never raised a slogan before.' She said with a sheepish smile.

'But now I want to change the world!'

Rahimunnisa, a local school principal sat on a chair, right next to Shabnam. She had weak knees and needed to be carried out from her house. But she came to the protest everyday—sitting in a corner, rolling her prayer beads and listening keenly. 'We are purdah-observing people,' she told me. 'We are here out of a sense of responsibility towards our families and our community.'

Women like her have always stepped up when their communities have needed them.

Rewind to 1984, Bhopal, Madhya Pradesh, when mostly Muslim women discarded purdah to take to the streets and seek justice for themselves and their families, victims of an industrial gas leak. That year, almost forty tonnes of poisonous gas had leaked out from a pesticide plant in Bhopal, killing around 20,000 people. Several thousands were taken seriously ill. Till today, children in Bhopal are born with birth defects and various other disorders. The Bhopal Gas Tragedy, which marked its thirty-sixth year on 3 December 2021, may have fallen off our radar, but the women have not abandoned their fight against one of the largest multinationals in the world.[5]

'In the beginning the men came, too, but in a couple of years, the movement was being dominated by the women,' Rachna Dhingra, a member of the Bhopal Group for Information and Action, who played a defining role in mobilizing the women, told me.

'Women who were in purdah came out on the streets. They are still fighting; they have kept the movement alive. They are still protesting to secure just compensation, raising awareness about the continuing effects of contamination on the children,' she added. 'Whatever little we could achieve in the last thirty-five years was because of them. They just do not give up.'

'You need women when you know the fight is going to be long and hard. That is the speciality of a women-led movement—they are indomitable, indefatigable,' veteran activist Medha Patkar and lead campaigner of the thirty-four-year-old Narmada Bachao Andolan (Save Narmada Movement) told me in 2021.

The Narmada Bachao Andolan, perhaps the longest non-violent movement in the history of the world, was led by women. It was launched in 1985 by Patkar to protest a series of large dam projects across the river Narmada, which flows through three states (Gujarat, Madhya Pradesh, and Maharashtra), and demand just compensation for around 32,000 people who were displaced as a result of the project. The movement had managed to arm-twist the World Bank—one of the sponsors of the project—to withdraw funding in 1993. In 2017, India's top court had awarded 681 displaced people in Madhya Pradesh—a major beneficiary of the Narmada project—a compensation of $90,000 each.[6]

A few months after the court order, the women, led by Patkar, were standing neck-deep in the cold water of the Narmada on a chilly September morning, in what they called Jal Satyagraha (Water Protest), a unique and essential part of the Narmada movement. They were in a village in Madhya Pradesh demanding justice for 40,000 families whose homes were at risk from submergence of the Sardar Sarovar Dam, the centrepiece of the Narmada project. For five hours, they stood there, chanting slogans, singing, and listening to speeches.[7] And while their protests no longer make headlines, they are quietly continuing to do the work that matters.

'Women's involvement in any protest can make all the difference,' says S. P. Udaykumar, who organized the women of Idinthakarai fishing village in Tamil Nadu to lead the People's Movement Against Nuclear Energy. The women have been protesting against the Koodankulam Nuclear Power Plant in Tamil Nadu's Tirunelveli district since the 1980s, when the plant was first proposed. Construction of the plant began in 2001 and the plant has been operational since 2013. In 2011, after the Fukushima nuclear plant disaster in Japan, anti-nuclear protests gathered speed. The protests were renewed in 2019.[8]

'They were very convinced about the harmful effects of the nuclear plant,' Udaykumar told me. 'They were worried about their families, especially their children. As fisherwomen they also knew they would bear the brunt of the harmful effects. In difficult times, men have no compunction about abandoning their families. But a woman's first response is to stay and fight.'

The women protesters were from all different faiths. They were pious Christians, Hindus, and Muslims. They were staunch believers in non-violence. Fasting and praying were not alien concepts. They couldn't be bought with alcohol or money or intimidated through coercion because they were fighting for their children.

Udaykumar says, 'The women owned the struggle. They carried it on their shoulders. And it's not dead yet. Its embers are still burning under the ashes and it will erupt again, some day soon. That's the beauty of women-led movements. They never die.'

In the village of Badausa in Uttar Pradesh, a group of women led by Sampat Pal Devi, famously known as the Gulabi Gang because they wear pink clothes, have fronted fights for addressing many social evils such as domestic violence, hoarding, bribery, and caste discrimination.[9]

It all began when Devi came across a man in her village mercilessly beating his wife. She intervened but the man threatened and abused her too. That day Devi went away but the next day she returned with five other women armed with bamboo sticks and beat the man up. The news spread like wildfire and soon women started approaching Devi in droves requesting similar interventions. Many women came forward to join her team and in the year 2006, she decided that the sisterhood needed a uniform and a name. The pink sari was chosen to signify their womanhood and understated strength.

The Gulabi Gang is now an organized women's movement with tens of thousands of members spread over several districts in Uttar Pradesh. The members wear pink saris and arm themselves with bamboo sticks, which they use whenever they come up against violent resistance.

Their vision is to 'protect the powerless from abuse and fight corruption to ensure basic rights of the poor in rural areas and discourage traditions like child marriages'[10] and to 'support and train women to enhance their basic skills to become economically secure and develop confidence to protect themselves from abuse through sustainable livelihood options'.[11]

But in India, these women have remained uncelebrated. They are merely considered to be 'shields to the men's swords', Patkar says. 'When in fact, they are the swords.'

This is changing with the younger generation.

On the night of 15 December 2019, when gruesome images of the police crackdown on students in the Jamia Millia Islamia University started surfacing on social media, an image of three girls standing on a wall and encouraging a sea of protesters had instantly captured hearts.[12] This was followed by numerous images of young women protesting on the streets, challenging security forces, courting arrest, demanding answers from the government with attention-grabbing slogans and posters.

These young women are mainstreaming the idea of resistance in India, and successfully pushing the idea that anyone can protest, and everyone should resist. Their message is loud and clear: no more a victim.

And all these protests, though they burn out after a while, sparked a revolution in many hearts. The hearts they had managed to touch came together in one single expression at Shaheen Bagh. While many attempts were made to discredit the movement—by suggesting it had been funded by Islamic terror groups or that it was only a Muslim women's protest—it was, in actuality, every woman's protest. With the women at Shaheen Bagh, every woman in this country was staking her right to protest, her right to the public space, to speak, to be heard—to exist.

Protests like these also seep into familial structures and create intergenerational empowerment. The Bhopal protesters' daughters, many of whom accompanied their mothers to the protests in 1980s, later joined the protest themselves. They are now active members of the movement. Back in Shaheen Bagh, the women all agree that they now truly understand the importance of educating their daughters.

'We have never loitered on the roads. When we were students, we went out to go to school or college but after that we have forgotten how it is to be out on the streets without any household chore to run, sometimes not even that. Today we are not scared to walk out of our homes at 2–3 a.m. Before we wouldn't go out after 9 p.m. When all of this is over, we will go back to being housewives, but this spirit will never die. We never took the education of our daughters seriously. Now try and stop us from educating and empowering them. They have tried hard to keep women uneducated because an educated woman will not stay quiet, she will know her rights and demand those rights,' Ara told me, amid loud agreement from women who had gathered around us. 'Despite the fact that we sat here for days and weeks and months, the government didn't once initiate any negotiations with us. And it is because we are women. But this government apathy has made us really strong.'

'Women in our community mostly stay at home. Men go out to earn, while women will stay home and cook and that's how it has always been. But now things are changing,' Almas, a twenty-four-year-old protester told me.

After they began leading this protest against all odds, these women garnered greater appreciation at home and the men also started helping with household chores.

'They are cooking now—what can be more amazing than that?' a woman pipes up from behind Almas, amid peals of laughter.

Ara adds, laughing, 'Before this they didn't even know where the kitchen was or how to pour themselves a glass of water.'

∽

Empowerment is a two-way street. Daughters are also empowering their mothers.

'I have put up with all the abuse and indignities because I wanted to give my daughter a good start in life so that she wouldn't have to deal with what I had to deal with,' Suchi told me. Her daughter, in turn, empowers her too. 'She constantly asks me to leave [my husband]. But it's not time yet. Call it a sacrifice for my daughter or my struggle to find my self-worth, whatever you will, but I will set my daughter free before I set myself free.'

At the time of our interview, Suchi had recently been promoted to a leadership position at her college. Her husband's first reaction was to say, 'You won't be able to do it. Leave before you make a fool of yourself.' But Suchi says in the last one year, she has done a wonderful job. To identify and acknowledge this in itself is a huge achievement in a country where women play themselves down constantly. 'I am speaking up, I am standing up to authority at work. Maybe I will stand up to him too one day.'

Violence is about power—women are considered weak in this country and it is this perception that needs to change. Our daughters are ready to change this victim–protector equation between women and men.

When I had spoken to Ritu, one of the Madanpur Khadar girls, she told me about an incident on the metro train when she and her friend caught a man recording them on his cell phone. When they confronted him, the other passengers just looked away, not wanting to get involved. So, Ritu and her friend did what they thought was best at the moment. They snatched the man's phone, took off their sandals, and began hitting him. Before the Khadar women could report him to the police, the man jumped off at the next stop and ran away. 'You can't depend on other people to take action because you know they won't,' Ritu said. 'In this country, all you have is you.'

'When no one stands up for you, when you know that no one will stand up for you, you will have to learn to stand up for yourself,' she continued.

The girls had gone to the police station later, keen to report the incident. 'The policemen just confused us with jurisdiction talk and ultimately nothing came of the complaint. This is how we live here. But it is not necessary that we should continue to live like this.'

She is right. Women and girls are aware of this and of the need to script a new narrative. They are keen to redefine what being a woman means in this country—not a worker, a homemaker, or someone who is defined by her relationships to men, but someone who is enough in herself.

Epilogue

SCRIPTING A NEW NARRATIVE

Many moons ago, my maternal grandmother had walked out of her home towards a tragic end. She had walked, her shadow low and mournful, to the nearest railway tracks. She had laid down on the tracks and looked up at the stars above her.

My grandmother was widowed when she was twenty-five years old. My maternal grandfather worked in a jute mill and had contracted tuberculosis, a deadly disease in those times. He didn't survive it. He left behind a young widow with three young children in a society that hated her and mistrusted her because she was quiet and read, and insisted on educating her children. My grandmother hoped for a better life for her three daughters. My mother hoped for a better life for me.

I do not merely hope that our daughters' lives will be better. Rather, I am working consciously to make it better—as are thousands of other women.

'I am bringing up my daughter differently for sure than how I was brought up. My daughter recognizes and respects my struggles. Life has not been easy for me. If I had decided to stay in my marriage, life would have been more secure for me. My daughter knows she has to be strong and independent,' Anu had told me.

The tide is turning. Along with finding economic empowerment, young women today are becoming intellectually and socially empowered as well. The online space, with all its downsides, has encouraged women to speak up, share their experiences, and learn from others. There's a new generation out there that is ready to reclaim public spaces. They are also ready to reclaim their personhood at home.

Must We Marry?
The rejection of old, romantic notions of marriage is a part of disrupting the patriarchal expectations society has of women. For many women in our country, marriage was a means of escape from

the restrictions of their parental homes. But the restrictions of a marriage are even more inescapable. 'I was so eager to get married,' Divya, who had a semi-arranged marriage tells me. 'I thought I would finally have a say in my own life but I ended up with even more people controlling my life and choices.'

Vanaja had decided to call off her relationship with a man she dated for a few months when she felt he was trying to control her life.

'I am used to taking decisions on my own. I don't mind discussing [them] but I get irritated when people start asking me strange questions [and asking me] to justify my decisions. He would [ask] me about the time I spent with my field supervisor, how many times we met, how much time we spent together. During my fieldwork days, I would often come back home late and then we would have meetings where I was staying. My neighbours there asked me these questions. When he too started asking these questions, I got very irritated and I called off the relationship,' Vanaja, who has just finished her doctorate in economics from the prestigious Cornell University, told me.

'Not that I compare every man with my father, who strongly believed in gender equality, but when you grow up with certain equalities in your home, you expect to [be] treated with equality in your other relationships too,' she says.

'The inequalities I observe around me irritate me. I wouldn't like to be treated like that in my marriage. People keep telling me that you need to learn to make compromises, that if you meet the right person, you will make the compromises. I am not so sure.'

Vanaja is perfectly content to remain single if she doesn't find a man who would see her as his equal. (She has recently found such a man.)

'If I don't find someone, I am okay being on my own. I know what I want in my life, how I want to live my life. If there's someone out there for me, that's great, but I don't feel compelled to compromise just because society expects me to. I would rather stay single.'

The last Census in 2011 found never-married women comprised more than 47 per cent of the population.[1] This was a drop from Census 2001 when they were a little over 54 per cent of the population.[2]

Interestingly, while in 2001 only 0.2 per cent[3] of women were widowed, divorced, or single, that figure rose to 8.2 per cent in 2011.[4] This suggests that many educated young women from middle-class families are choosing to remain unmarried—it would be interesting to note the results of Census 2021[*] in this regard. According to the National Forum for Single Women's Rights, a national platform for single women leaders, the number of women over the age of thirty-five who have never married has seen a sharp increase of almost 66 per cent.[5] Ginny Srivastava, president of the group and one of India's top gender rights activists, told me during the writing of this book that the data regarding the numbers of separated women did not reflect reality as due to 'social stigma many women and their families would not admit of marriage breakdown to a data collector'.

But it is an unshakeable fact, she says, that a majority of young women today equate marriages with a destruction of self-worth. They are more observant—they are less inclined to let it go. Young women are taking notes from marriages around them. Vanaja, who is now a professor of economics at the Azim Premji University in Bangalore, was left fuming when she visited an acquaintance's home some years back. While she was there, she could see that the woman of the house was exhausted after a full day of caring for her toddler as well as taking care of other household chores.

'She asked the husband to get her a glass of juice. He pretended not to hear and just ambled over to the other side of the room,' Vanaja says, remembering how her friend looked embarrassed and then got up to pour the juice herself. 'Then he calls out to her and says "give me some, too". I could see that she was irritated but she didn't say anything and poured him a glass of juice, too.'

'Women are increasingly seeing marriage and husbands as a problem,' Srivastava told me. 'They also realize they don't need a marriage for a fulfilling and full life. They look around the harried lives of married women and decide they are better off single. It's not

---

*Census 2021 was delayed owing to the Covid-19 pandemic and preliminary results are now expected to be published in 2023–24.

always physical violence, you know? It's the daily indignities, the daily put-downs, the emotional and verbal violence.'

Yes, daily indignities form a part of most Indian marriages. Whether they happen consciously or unconsciously, their occurrence is guaranteed because of the power dynamics between breadwinners and homemakers that's embedded deep in our psyches. I have grown up witnessing this in my home. My mother had a very important job, she is an extremely intelligent and smart woman who could converse well, and whose writing skills were enviable. Yet, at the best of times, my father made her feel like a clueless idiot.

Even in the homes of younger women, this happens. Suchi's husband, for example, would tell her constantly, 'Tum rehne do, tumse nahin ho payega.' Leave it, you won't be able to do it. There are subtler ways, too, to rob women of their confidence, including not allowing a woman to handle her own finances, or dismissing her inputs for important family decisions. A journalist friend once told me that during a heated political debate at home with guests around, when she had tried to put her opinion forward, her husband, also a journalist, had derisively told her to keep quiet because 'this is not lifestyle or entertainment—this is politics. And what do you know about politics?' She had quietly let it pass because there were guests around.

'I don't think marriage is essential. It's a just social thing. I would marry only when I have lived with someone for a while because I don't want any nasty surprises; you can only really know a person when you live with them,' Suchi's seventeen-year-old daughter told me. Her conviction and confidence were a validation that feminist mothers like me have not failed. 'And I don't want to end up in a relationship where the gender roles I have grown up with will be repeated. It's much less messy to live with someone than be married to them. I can see how difficult it is for my mum to get out of her marriage.'

In 2016, the Ministry for Women and Child Development made quite a few recommendations for single women in its draft of national policy for women including a 'comprehensive social protection mechanism' for them.[6] It's remained a draft, underlining just how important women, especially single women, are to our policy makers.

Women choosing to remain single despite all odds is for sure the first open rebellion of middle-class women against patriarchy. When you say no to marriage you are saying no to the concept of housewives and reproductive and productive labour, and to overwork. Being single in India is not easy for women but the existence of single women is also an affirmation of a woman's choice to live alone, without the 'protection' of a man.

'I am not sure if it is conscious rebellion. I honestly think women are figuring out that it is easier and healthier to be single than to be married/partnered with men and India is perhaps at a place finally in its social configurations that women can escape the familial pressures of getting married. The 23 per cent of women who do work, I would think many of them do not live with their families and I think that has empowered them to remain single as a matter of choice,' the sociologist Pallavi Banerjee told me, adding that 'married men tend to lead longer and healthier lives, whereas marriage shortens women's lifespans and so I am happy that women in India are choosing to remain single. But I think women are staying single because they can and they are probably happier than way, rather than as an active act of resistance against the patriarchy. But the net effect could be seen as a form of unconscious resistance.'

Women have never been allowed to be alone in this country. They have always been told that they need someone to guide them and protect them. They have always been part of a family. They are not comfortable being seen in public spaces alone. And there's good reason for that. I have been watching movies alone or sitting at café tables alone since 2005 and I am tired of the numerous times the waiters would solicitously slide up asking me if I was waiting for somebody. No, I would tell them, only for them to respond with a pitying glance. But the thing is that I really like my own company. I have no problem being alone.

Many women I spoke to have told me that they stayed in bad marriages because they feared being alone. Thankfully, that is changing too, now. Women are opting to walk out of bad marriages and raise their children as single mothers. Divya did, too. Towards the end of

December 2021, she finally walked out of her marriage. Her sons supported her decision. 'I have been diminished so much in this relationship, I couldn't cope with it anymore,' she told me. 'Everything was always about him—our marriage, our life together. I slaved away in the kitchen, at work, I picked up tuitions after school so we would have enough money, and yet I was just the housewife. Even when I was not working, I raised the children, did all the housework—but no one considered that work.'

Ginny Srivastava told me that there is a need for more support groups for women so they do not feel alienated or isolated, and 'to allow them to discover their strengths'. She is right. When a woman stands in her strength, the world takes note. This should become the rule and not be celebrated as an exception.

Unlike Vanaja, the seventeen-year-old who wrote the report on open relationships grew up in a more patriarchal setting. But she, too, is determined not to walk blindly into a marriage. 'We live with patriarchy every day of our lives and while I hope things will change for our generation, I fear certain things will remain the same. Till everything about patriarchy changes, it is better to be in casual relationships,' she tells me.

Vanaja is completely comfortable living on her own. 'I am comfortable with who I am,' she told me in 2021. 'And with the current trajectory of my life.'

Pushing for Change

Change comes when the younger generation wants it, when they proactively look for it, and this is happening in India, too.

'What often pushes change is what the younger generation wants. And the fact that India has so many Millennials and Generation Z [who] are coming into the workplace with a different set of expectations. We know that younger generations value diversity more deeply than older generations. My hope is that it will act as an accelerant in India.' Lean In's Thomas said this in connection to workplace equality, but I feel it fits the concept of equality in general as well.

The youth of the country have learnt from the mistakes of

Gen X women, those who tried to do it all. Thankfully, perhaps, we are too disillusioned to hand down the lies our mothers told us—unlike them we have no stars in our eyes, only cautious optimism. The next generation of women are much more careful about their commitments and more aware of the traps of a patriarchal society like ours. 'I am about to get married and right now I am in negotiation with my future spouse about housework and who will do what,' a young publishing professional told me recently.

Decades of empowerment efforts by individual women, grassroots feminist activists, and non-profits are paying off too. I met Seema Lohar and Bhabani Munda in 2011 when I had gone on assignment to report on an all-girls football team in a remote tea garden in the north of Bengal. In this region, one of the most backward and remote regions of India, girls are often a burden. They are either sent to work in the tea estates as children, earning poor wages, or married off early. Munda dared to dream a different future for herself and other girls in the tea gardens after she caught the tail end of the Bengal women's football team playing in a local tournament in 1995.

Seven years old and forever being warned off by her family that football was not a game for girls, she was amazed to discover that women could play football professionally. 'My parents and brothers stopped me from playing football saying I would break a leg and then no one would marry me,' she said. 'So, I took to waking up at 3.30 in the morning to finish my morning chores and then sneak out to play football before anyone woke up.'

As the eldest sister, it fell to Munda to make sure the household chores got done on time. There was no question of following her passion by ignoring the housework. In fact, completing the housework on time was her passport to hours of practice. Her practice was, in fact, sandwiched between household chores.

For the next few years, Munda continued with this routine, all the while looking out for like-minded girls to form her own football team. It was only a few years down the line, in the late 1990s, when Munda finally got together with three friends and Dooars 11 was born. It took them a whole year to get permission from parents to send their girls to play with them.

Most parents would immediately refuse saying that it was against societal norms for girls to play football. Many feared that it would be difficult to find a groom for their daughters. The hardest part was convincing them to let their girls wear shorts.

'I wore shorts to convince them it was not that scandalous,' Munda said. 'I was called brazen and shameless.' Later on, she moved out of home. When I met her in 2011, she was living with four of her teammates in a two-room workers' quarter in the Kalchini tea estate.

Under Munda's guidance, Dooars 11, with its eleven fiery girls and just one set of jerseys and two footballs, has not just won trophies and accolades, but also the love and affection of the local community, who had once looked askance at them. When, between 2001 and 2005, the Kalchini tea estate had closed down leading to widespread poverty and starvation among its people, Munda and her girls had come to the rescue. They donated the little prize money they had won, a few thousand rupees, to the community.

I reconnected with Munda over a video call in June 2020. She has not changed much—only her face has filled out a little. She was still working at her little tea shop while trying to keep her dream alive. In 2015, she was forced to get married to a man she had hired to run her tea shop so she could better focus on her commitment to football. 'People started saying all sorts of things. My family and his family got into a fight. To stop all this, I decided to marry him,' she says, bringing her two children—a son and a daughter, both under four years of age—to the camera to say hello to me.

'Do you remember what you told me when I met you last?' I ask her. 'You said you never wanted to marry because what if your husband doesn't support your dream? Does he support your dream?'

She doesn't mince her words. 'So far, he has been supportive because I bring back trophies and money but I don't know what will happen in the future. I still worry about it because there is no doubt in my mind that if I have to choose between my family and my football, I will always choose football. Because football is not just a sport for me—it allows me to empower girls in this area, to give them hope and help them dream.' One of her former teammates, Kanika Burman, went on to become India's first woman referee. Burman, and many others, got jobs in the police force. 'Football changed my life,' Seema Lohar, a Dooars 11 teammate and the friend Munda stayed with, told me recently. 'Could I have dreamed of stepping out of home, having a job? No way.' She plans to marry soon, but is clear that if it ever comes to a choice between football and family and her job, 'I am not leaving football.'

Munda is still running from pillar to post to secure funding for her team and the girls. She still hasn't given up on her dream of building a coaching centre for girls in Kalchini with every facility.

'Are you happy in your marriage?' I ask. 'Do you still fear it will come in the way of your dreams?'

'I separated from him during my first pregnancy because I was so scared that after the baby was born, they will not allow me to do my work. So I thought if I have to separate then, I might as well do it now. But he convinced me to come back, promising to support me. As I said, so far it has been okay, but things can change any time. But I am prepared for that.

'Sometimes you do not have a choice but to be happy in the way your life is going. You have to work at happiness, keep smiling. Khush toh rehna padta hai!'

One woman—it really just takes one woman in one family or community to effect lasting change.

Recently, I received a message from Seema Lohar. When I opened the message, a smile spread across my face. Staring out at me was a young woman in a pair of shades and her police uniform. She called me that night and talked about how much she loved her work and football.

'I love my job, I am still playing football,' she said. I could hear her smile over the phone.

'And I am not going to spoil it all by getting married. I might if I find someone who will support my dreams but otherwise, I am happy alone.'

Agitating for Space

Reclaiming public space is an important aspect of a woman's empowerment. 'It is about the ability of women and girls to be safe in public spaces, it's about being able to wait for a bus...ride a subway... sell goods in a marketplace...walk to school, be in the school, a store or a voting booth...swim in a pool...visit a friend—safely and peacefully,' Michelle Bachelet, Executive Director of UN Women had said in a speech in 2013.[7]

In India, the demand for women's reclamation of public space started in earnest after the infamous Delhi gang rape, an incident that led to widespread global outrage. In India, it mobilized the youth, especially young women, who pushed back with unprecedented protests, forcing the government to update existing laws.

Social media was flooded with online campaigns that encouraged women to claim their right to public spaces. The book *Why Loiter?: Women and Risk on Mumbai Streets* (2011) by authors Shilpa Phadke, Sameera Khan, and Shilpa Ranade, became the basis of a very successful social media campaign that asked women to share pictures of them loitering in public spaces with the hashtag #WhyLoiter.[8]

Most of the social media campaigns that broke out during this period have been, however, simmering in the background for some time now. Another very successful campaign, Blank Noise, has been around since 2003. The project aimed at not just reclaiming public spaces but also unlearning societal biases and exploring discomfort and vulnerability. The campaign simply asked women to tell stories of harassment they faced in a public place and upload pictures of what they were wearing at that time, to drive home the point that sexual assault has nothing to do with how a woman dresses, and that she is never 'asking for it'.[9]

To fix women's relationship with the public space, as with every other inequality that has been discussed in this book, we have to walk back inside our homes. The changes made within our homes have the potential to reverberate outwards, onto our streets, our workplaces, and beyond.

A Final Word

While the cause of women's movement in India has progressed much since my uncle's paternalistic taunt to my mother, even after forty years, we are yet to acknowledge that our feminist movement has left behind a majority of women from the middle-classes, and that their lives and their struggles have remained largely invisible. Our feminism has benefited only 1 per cent of our country's women, who are mostly the elite and well-heeled. Activists and non-profits help to economically and socially empower the poor women of our country, but our middle-class homes have escaped reform. Feminism has stayed at the doorstep of our homes as we moved through the various stages of the feminist struggle. We must do the work to pull these women who have been left behind into the women's movement.

I want to end this book on some notes of hope. One day, when I was walking my dogs, someone suddenly stopped me, saying hello. I looked at her closely but couldn't quite place her. She saw the hesitation in my eyes and said with a smile, 'I am Seema. You took me to the police station, remember?' I did. She looked older, but happier. 'How are you?' I asked her.

'I have never been better,' she told me beaming. 'So, you are still with your husband...things have worked out?' I asked, tentatively. 'No, I kicked him out of the house,' she told me with a smile. 'I realized he will never change. I am getting remarried in a few months, to someone who supported me through this whole ordeal.'

I was not expecting this. This was good. This was hope.

Divya, too, is rebuilding her life. For the first time in twenty years, she has taken a vacation on her own. She has finally decided to put herself first. And her sons are standing by her staunchly. They tell her that she deserves to be happy, too.

We are raising compassionate sons. We are raising strong daughters. Our past and our present might lie in our mothers' lies but our future lies in the hope that our children inspire.

And finally—remember my neighbour with the two daughters? My last meeting with her was a few years back. I was walking to the ATM, when a car pulled up behind me and started honking. As I turned to look, I was surprised to see my neighbour, looking out of the window and smiling widely at me.

'I have never seen you drive before,' I said, returning her smile. She beamed at me.

'That was my husband's car—I never drove it. He didn't trust me with it. But this is my own car. I bought it with my own money.'

There was something different about her that day. A radiance, a confidence I hadn't seen before. 'It feels great to be in the driver's seat.'

Later, I heard she had split from her husband and moved abroad with her daughters.

She's now in the driver's seat.

ACKNOWLEDGEMENTS

Ma—you continue to inspire me with your strength, your resilience, and your determination to succeed against all odds. I am who I am because of you. It's my privilege to tell your story and through your story, the stories of so many other women.

I am deeply thankful to all the women who have believed I can, and to all the men who have said I can't.

To my late father-in-law Nabarun Bhattacharya, who reminded me almost every day 'Who's going to stop you?' He played a crucial role in my intellectual empowerment; we spent hours discussing books and spirituality. No topic was off limits with him.

To my grandmother-in-law Mahasweta Devi and her enduring friendship with my mother-in-law Pranati Bhattacharya—the love, the sisterhood they shared was beyond any I have seen. And the friendship my mother-in-law Pranati extended to me—standing by me through thick and thin, never letting me fall. My grandmother-in-law, whom we called Bui, played a very important role in helping me unlearn many biases that I grew up with—the doubts, the imposter syndrome, the compulsion to do it all. My mother-in-law was a physical manifestation of what the future can look like if women understood their power and brought up compassionate sons. She was a breadwinner at a time when women were just beginning to step out to work and allowed my father-in-law to focus on his writing, especially his magnum opus *Harbart*. She never doubted herself or her abilities even for a split second. Her confidence and compassion were unmatched. And the way they all rallied around me, to let me do my work, be the woman I wanted to be, I wish that solidarity and understanding on every woman in this country. The joy of seeing this book come to life is diminished much because the three people who would have been overjoyed and the proudest are no longer with us.

I cannot write an acknowledgement and not mention my partner, Tathagata, known to all and sundry as Bau. We have been married for seventeen years and he has remained my best friend, an intellectually stimulating companion, my most vocal critic, and my most ardent advocate. He read the first draft of this book, and the second, and the third—I think I know which book he is never going to pick up again! And my son, Che, of course, (who makes me feel adequate every day because I see him grow up into a person without any gender prejudices) and his amazing friends, who inspire me with so much hope for the future. He made me copious amounts of black coffee, helped with all the household chores, made me breakfast, and allowed me to take out the time I needed to work on this book. Oh! And then there are the two naughty beagles who kept me happy and entertained—Kuttush and Gypsy kept their favourite human on a tight leash. They have illuminated most of my darknesses since they came into my life. Also, between the two of them, they have deleted enough of my drafts (thank God for Google docs). If I was writing on paper, they would have chewed up the lot and yes, that's what some of my nightmares are made of.

In my book, I paint my father as the man he is—I love him, of course, I do. He is a loving and caring father but a cruel husband. It would have been a grave injustice to my mother and every other mother in middle-class homes, if I ask them to speak up while keeping what happens behind the closed doors of my home a secret. I haven't spoken much about my sister Debjani in the book, because she is a very private person, but I want to acknowledge here that she, along with my mother, gave me the wings to fly and the fearlessness to dream big. A shout-out to my brother-in-law Aloke Singh for always standing by my sister and being a co-spouse sharing in all her care and household responsibilities. Their home is truly gender neutral when it comes to paid and unpaid work.

I am also grateful to all the women who have shared their lives with me over the years, told me their deepest thoughts, let me into their lives, minds, and hearts, and allowed me to tell their stories. Many of them gave me the permission to use their names, but I took a call to keep them anonymous. These are not individual stories and this book is not about one woman's troubles or one woman's courage—it is about half a nation in distress. We need to press the panic button. Now.

Thanks also to Columbia J School professor Cynthia Gorney who introduced me to science author Mary Roach who, along with Cynthia, guided me indefatigably (despite her own writing deadlines) to write the proposal, then read through it, provided feedback, and stayed with me on the journey until I placed the book with Aleph. To my friends Indu Bhandari, Archana Chaudhury, and Kiran Pachoo—thank you for always having my back. Thank you for the unconditional love and solidarity and thank you for making me a part of your stories—you inspire me every day.

And how do I not pay my gratitude to my journalism course director Diane Kemp at the Birmingham City University? I adored her, idolized her, and it was while under her tutelage that I first began to break out of the cage that society had put me in. She didn't just teach me journalism but other key life lessons, too. Diane, I am your fangirl forever. And last but not least (at all), my editor Pujitha Krishnan, who was the only one who got the book as soon as I pitched it to her. For that—eternal gratitude! And Kanika Praharaj, who sent me such detailed edits that my back almost broke. But the two of them deserve all the credit for how the book ultimately turned out. I am blessed to be surrounded by such strong women, who embody the spirits of feminist solidarity and sisterhood. I have been fortunate to have gone through so far in life surrounded by women who held me up, stood by me like rock, empowered me. To all the women I have met in the last three and a half decades—I remember all of you, I remember all your stories. You are always in my heart.

In the end, the fact that I have managed to write this book speaks to the privilege I enjoy; the privilege that is not available to a large majority of women in this country—the privilege of time away from all our care and household duties, and the unconditional support of family. Here's to that day when this privilege will be available to all of us.

REFERENCES

Most of the data or projected data in terms of the middle classes in India, or social and economic development of women is pre-Covid. This pandemic is affecting women disproportionately, as every crisis does, and many of our advances in terms of social and economic parity will undoubtedly be lost. The pandemic has also exposed much of the middle-class malaise and the ways in which women are oppressed inside their homes and the inherent inequalities of our workplaces; a debate is already rearing its head among different groups of women. We are now talking about what we disregarded as of no interest to anybody but ourselves. I hope that more of us are able to open up our homes for scrutiny, that more of us are able to come out and own this problem, more of us call out the patriarchy in our homes.

Introduction

1   Ishaan Gera, 'Women are overworked, underpaid, and more stressed: Deloitte study', *Business Standard*, 19 May 2021.

2   Ministry of Statistics & Programme Implementation, 'NSS Report: Time Use in India- 2019 (January–December 2019)', PIB Delhi, 29 September 2020.

3   Ibid.

4   Christophe Z. Guilmoto, Nandita Saikia, Vandana Tamrakar, et al., 'Excess under-5 female mortality across India: a spatial analysis using 2011 census data', *Lancet Global Health*, Vol. 6, June 2018, pp. e650–58.

5   Geeta Pandey, 'What's behind suicides by thousands of Indian housewives?', *BBC*, 16 December 2021.

6   William Joe, Abhishek Kumar, Sunil Rajpal, et al., 'Equal risk, unequal burden? Gender differentials in COVID-19 mortality in India', *Journal of Global Health Science*, Vol. 2, No. 1, 2020.

7   Nilanjana Bhowmick, 'Why is there a gender gap in India's vaccination program?', *Devex*, 19 July 2021.

8   Nilanjana Bhowmick, 'How a Remote Himalayan District Achieved an Extraordinary COVID-19 Vaccination Rate', *TIME*, 12 February 2022.

9   'Global Gender Gap Report 2020', World Economic Forum, December 2019.

10   Shweta Sengar, 'For The First Time, India Has More Women Than Men, But Records Suggest It's Too Early To Cheer', *Indiatimes*, 1 December 2021.

11   'Crime in India: Statistics, Volume 1', National Crime Records Bureau, 2020, p. 2.

12   '1 in 3 women in India is likely to have been subjected to intimate partner

violence', *BMJ*, available at <www.bmj.com/company/newsroom/1-in-3-women-in-india-is-likely-to-have-been-subjected-to-intimate-partner-violence>.

13 Nilanjana Chakraborty, 'What is gender pay gap and why is it so wide in India?', *Mint*, 3 December 2019.

14 Tanushree Chandra, 'Literacy in India: The Gender and Age Dimension', *ORF Issue Brief No. 322*, Observer Research Foundation, October 2019.

15 National Statistical Office, *Annual Report: Periodic Labour Force Survey (PLFS), (July 2017–June 2018)*, Ministry of Statistics and Programme Implementation, May 2019.

16 'India Skills Report 2019', UNDP India, 29 May 2019.

17 Nikita Kwatra, 'The anatomy of India's middle class', *Mint*, 24 April 2019.

18 strawberry shortcake (badassflowerbby), Tweet, 16 August 2020, <https://twitter.com/badassflowerbby/status/1295052790549475328>.

19 Shoukai Yu, 'Uncovering the hidden impacts of inequality on mental health: a global study', *Translational Psychiatry*, Vol. 8, No. 1, 2018, p. 1.

20 Pallavi Koirala and Montakarn Chuemchit, 'Depression and Domestic Violence Experiences Among Asian Women: A Systematic Review', *International Journal of Women's Health*, Vol. 12, No. 21, 16 January 2020, pp. 21–33.

21 'What is Feminism?- Kamla Bhasin's Key note speech at the International Seminar Interpreting Feminism vis-à-vis Activism', *Sangat Blog*, 23 July 2019.

22 Ibid.

23 Abhijit Roy, 'The Middle Class in India: From 1947 to the Present and Beyond', *Education About Asia*, Vol. 23. No. 1, Spring 2018, p. 32.

24 Ibid., p. 33.

25 Jyothsna Latha Belliappa, 'The "New" Indian Middle Class Woman', *Gender, Class, and Reflexive Modernity in India*, London: Palgrave Macmillan, London, 2013, p. 46.

Chapter 1: Feminist Mothers and the Lie

1 Naina Lal Kidwai, 'The Sum and the Substance', *30 Women in Power: Their Voices, Their Stories*, Naina Lal Kidwai (ed.), New Delhi: Rupa Publications, 2015.

2 Surjit Bhalla and Ravinder Kaur, 'Labour force participation of women in India: some facts, some queries', Working Paper (40), Asia Research Centre, London School of Economics and Political Science, 2011.

3 Kiran Pandey, 'India lifted 271 mln people out of poverty in 10 yrs, claims govt report', *Down to Earth*, 14 July 2020.

4 'Vocational & Life Skills Training of Out-of-School Adolescent Girls in the age group 15–18 years', National Commission for Protection of Child Rights, p. 1.

Chapter 2: Her Domestic Burden

1 India Time Use Survey, 1998, available at <microdata.gov.in/nada43/index.php/catalog/140>.

2 Nilanjana Bhowmick, 'School is a Right, but Will Indian Girls Be Able to Go?', *TIME*, 29 April 2010.

3   Manoj Kumar Rai, '10-Addressing Gender Issues in Bundelkhand Region the Scenario, Status & Critical Issues', India Planning Commission, 2019.

4   McKinsey Global Institute, 'The Power of Parity: Advancing Women's Equality in the Asia Pacific, Focus India', McKinsey & Company, May 2018, p. 74.

5   'Vocational & Life Skills Training of Out-of-School Adolescent Girls in the age group 15–18 years', National Commission for Protection of Child Rights.

6   'Fate of Girl Child in India', Save the Children, 11 January 2018.

7   'Educating The Girl Child: Role of incentivisation and other enablers and disablers', New Delhi: Child Rights and You (CRY), March 2019, p. ix.

8   Annual Status of Education Report (Rural) 2018, January 2019.

9   'WINGS, The World of India's Girls: A Status Report', Save the Children, 2014.

10   'Educating The Girl Child', CRY, p. 28.

11   Libbet Loughnan, 'Lack of access to a toilet and handwashing materials hits women and girls hardest, especially when menstruating', *The Water Blog*, 14 April 2017.

12   '"Periods don't stop during pandemics"—WaterAid supports to find alternate MHM solution in view of sanitary pad shortage', WaterAid India, 28 May 2020.

13   Karan Babbar, 'Covid-19: Why Are Sanitary Products Not Deemed As "Essential"?', *Feminism in India*, 9 April 2020.

14   'Coronavirus sparks a sanitary pad crisis in India', *BBC*, 22 May 2020.

15   'Girls' education: A lifeline to development', *The State of the World's Children*, UNICEF, 1996, p. 71.

16   'Not Educating Girls Costs Countries Trillions of Dollars, Says New World Bank Report', The World Bank, 11 July 2018.

17   'Global Gender Gap Report 2021', World Economic Forum, March 2021, p. 40.

18   'A Statistical Analysis of Child Marriages in India: Based on Census 2011', Young Lives and National Commission for Protection of Child Rights, New Delhi, June 2017.

19   'Ending Child Marriage: A Profile of Progress in India', UNICEF, February 2019.

20   HT Correspondent, 'Govt may table bill to raise women's marriage age to 21', *Hindustan Times*, 17 December 2021.

21   Debbie Budlender, 'Domestic Work Policy Brief 3', ILO.

22   'Sweden, Norway, Iceland, Estonia and Portugal rank highest for family-friendly policies in OECD and EU countries', UNICEF, 13 June 2019.

23   Katelyn Mendez, 'How Proper Education Will Help End Poverty', *The Borgen Project*, 24 October 2020.

24   'Anganwadis: Services, Problems and Solutions', *Journals of India*, 13 March 2021.

25   PTI, 'Government plans to upgrade 2.5 lakh anganwadi centres in next 5 years: Women and Child Development Ministry official', *The Economic Times*, 17 December 2019.

26   Meg Towle, 'India is booming—so why are nearly half of its children malnourished? (Part 2)', *State of the Planet*, 24 March 2011.

27   Jagriti Chandra, 'Global Hunger Index ranks India at 101 out of 116 countries', *The Hindu*, 15 October 2021.

28   PTI, 'MPs for increase in salary of anganwadi workers and helpers', *The Print*, 11 February 2022.

Chapter 3: The Lie: Explained More

1 'Progress of the World's Women 2019–2020: Families in a Changing World', UN Women, 2019, p. 29.

2 Ritu Dewan, 'Invisible Work, Invisible Workers: The Sub-Economies of Unpaid Work and Paid Work, Action Research on Women's Unpaid Labour', New Delhi: ActionAid, 2017.

3 Nicholas D. Kristof and Sheryl WuDunn, *Half the Sky: Turning Oppression into Opportunity for Women Worldwide*, Vintage, 2010.

4 Judith Serrin, '"Superwoman" Complex: A Pain in the Ego', *Boca Raton News*, 28 July 1976.

5 Chetna Choudhry, 'Rich couples flying abroad for gender test & abortion, fear health officials', *Times of India*, 13 May 2017.

6 'Crime in India: Statistics, Volume 1'.

7 'How Nirbhaya case changed rape laws in India', *Times of India*, 19 December 2019.

8 Fayaz Wani, 'We got only half justice, says Kathua gang-rape victim's father', *New Indian Express*, 10 January 2021.

9 'The World's Most Dangerous Countries for Women', Thomson Reuters Foundation, 2018.

10 'Crime in India: Statistics, Volume 1', National Crime Records Bureau, 2018.

11 Neena Bohra, Shruti Srivastava, and M. S. Bhatia, 'Depression in women in Indian context', Vol. 57, Suppl. 2, *Indian Journal of Psychiatry*, 2015, pp. S239–45.

12 'Gender differentials and state variations in suicide deaths in India: the Global Burden of Disease Study 1990–2016', Vol. 3, *Lancet Public Health*, 2018, 12 September 2018, p. e478.

13 Ibid.

14 'Chapter-2: Suicides in India', *Accidental Deaths and Suicides in India*, National Crime Records Bureau, 2007.

15 'Gender differentials and state variations in suicide deaths in India', p. e486.

Chapter 4: The Grandmother I Never Met

1 'Indira Gandhi National Widow Pension Scheme', District Khargone, 1 April 2009, available at <khargone.nic.in/en/scheme/indira-gandhi-national-widow-pension-scheme>.

2 Bharvi Dasson, 'Lack of Professionals, Social Stigma: India Has Miles to Go in Establishing Mental Health Infrastructure', *News18*, 7 October 2021.

3 Rajesh Sagar et al., 'The burden of mental disorders across the states of India: the Global Burden of Disease Study 1990–2017', Vol. 7, Issue 2, *The Lancet Psychiatry*, 20 Dec 2019, pp. 148–161.

4 'The World's Most Dangerous Countries for Women', Thomson Reuters Foundation, 2018.

5 'Part-II: Suicides in India', *Accidental Deaths and Suicides in India - 1995*, National Crime Records Bureau, p. 65.

6 'Part-III: Suicides in India', *Accidental Deaths and Suicides in India - 1996*, National Crime Records Bureau, p. 51.

7   'Chapter-2: Suicides in India', *Accidental Deaths and Suicides in India 2020*, National Crime Records Bureau, p. 203.
8   Biswajit L. Jagtap, B. S. V. Prasad, and Suprakash Chaudhury, 'Psychiatric morbidity in perimenopausal women', *Industrial Psychiatry Journal*, Vol. 25, No. 1, 2016, p. 86.
9   Priya Shetty, 'India faces growing breast cancer epidemic', *The Lancet*, Vol. 379, Issue 9820, 2012, pp. 992–93.
10   Gayle Marcovitz, 'Why are women more depressed than men?', World Economic Forum, 6 March 2020.
11   Kounteya Sinha, 'Women more prone to depression than men, Indians worst hit: WHO', *Times of India*, 10 October 2012.
12   Choudhary Laxmi Narayan, Mridula Narayan, Deep Shikha, et al., 'Indian marriage laws and mental disorders: Is it necessary to amend the legal provisions?', *Indian Journal of Psychiatry*, Vol. 57, No. 4, 2015.

Chapter 5: The Father Who Forgot to Pick Up His Daughter from School

1   Arun Jaitley, 'Gender and Son Meta-Preference: Is Development Itself an Antidote?', *Economic Survey 2017: Volume I*, Working Papers id:12445, eSocialSciences, 2018, p. 116.
2   Ibid., p. 114.
3   Ibid., p. 111.
4   'School choice in low information environments: A study of perceptions and realities in four states', *Field Studies in Education*, Azim Premji University, November 2018.

Chapter 6: When the Kitchen Replaces the Classroom

1   'Ending child marriage and adolescent empowerment', UNICEF, available at <www.unicef.org/india/what-we-do/end-child-marriage>.
2   'A Statistical Analysis of Child Marriages in India: Based on Census 2011', NCPCR, June 2017.
3   Sravani Sarkar, Madhya Pradesh: Underage marriages reportedly held on Akshaya Tritiya, *The Week*, May 2019.
4   'National Plan of Action for Children 2005', Department of Women and Child Development, p. 18, available at <www.childlineindia.org/uploads/files/knowledge-center/National-Plan-of-Action-for-Children-2005.pdf>.
5   International Institute for Population Sciences (IIPS) and ICF, 'Women's Empowerment', *National Family Health Survey (NFHS-5), 2019–21*, Mumbai: IIPS, 2021, p. 2.
6   Saumya Khandelwal, 'Child Brides of Shravasti', 2015.
7   'Dependent, deprived: Child brides in India tell their stories', United Nations Population Fund, 10 June 2015, available at <www.unfpa.org/news/dependent-deprived-child-brides-india-tell-their-stories>.
8   'Goal 5: Child Marriage', *Sustainable Development Goals Report 2018*, United Nations, 20 June 2018.

9   Srinivas Goli, 'Elimination of Child Marriage in India: Progress and Prospects', ActionAid India, 2016, p. iii.

10   Ibid., p. vii.

11   Henrietta H. Fore, Natalia Kanem, and Mabel van Oranje, 'This is the economic cost of child marriage', World Economic Forum, 1 June 2018.

12   Quentin Wodon, Chata Male, Ada Nayihouba, et al., *Economic Impacts of Child Marriage: Global Synthesis Report*, Washington, DC: The World Bank and International Center for Research on Women, 2017, p. 42.

13   Ibid.

14   Vipul Vivek, 'Why are child marriages on the rise in India's cities?', *Hindustan Times*, June 2017.

15   'Status and Decadal Trends of Child Marriage in India', Child Rights and You (CRY): New Delhi, October 2020, p. ii.

16   Wodon, Male, Nayihouba, et al., *Economic Impacts of Child Marriage*, p. 24.

17   'ILO: Women do 4 times more unpaid care work than men in Asia and the Pacific', International Labour Organization, 27 June 2018.

18   'Progress of the World's Women 2019–2020: Families in a Changing World', UN Women, 2019, p. 53.

Chapter 7: Arranged and Approved

1   *Dr Mitu Khurana vs State Of Nct Of Delhi & Ors*, AIR (2016) SC 49729.

2   Ministry of Women and Child Development, 'Dowry System', 10 December 2021, available at <pib.gov.in/PressReleasePage.aspx?PRID=1780110>.

3   '1 in 3 women in India is likely to have been subjected to intimate partner violence', *BMJ*, 2 June 2020.

4   'Crime in India: Statistics, Volume 1', National Crime Records Bureau, 2020.

5   'Progress of the World's Women 2019–2020', UN Women, p. 83.

6   'Child Marriage and Domestic Violence', International Center for Research on Women, 2004.

7   Abhijit Banerjee, Esther Duflo, Maitreesh Ghatak, et al., 'Marry for what? Caste and mate selection in modern India', September 2009, p. 3.

8   Ibid.

9   Ibid., p. 2.

10   Ibid.

11   Ibid., p. 31.

12   Ibid., p. 32.

13   Sonalde Desai and Reeve Vanneman, 'India Human Development Survey-II (IHDS-II), 2011–12', Inter-university Consortium for Political and Social Research [distributor], 8 August 2018.

14   Tanya D'Lima, Jennifer L. Solotaroff, and Rohini Prabha Pande, 'For the Sake of Family and Tradition: Honour Killings in India and Pakistan', *ANTYAJAA: Indian Journal of Women and Social Change*, Vo. 5, No. 1, June 2020, pp. 22–39.

15   Ibid.

Chapter 8: Why Women Stay in Bad Marriages

1 Ditta M. Oliker, 'On Being a Burden', *Psychology Today*, 12 August 2014.
2 'Being a Wife Meant Handing Over My Salary and My Salary Slip to the In-Laws', *Akkar Bakkar*, December 2017.
3 IIPS and ICF, 'Women's Empowerment', *National Family Health Survey (NFHS-4), 2015-16*, Mumbai: IIPS, 2017, p. 509.
4 Ibid.
5 'Being a Wife Meant Handing Over My Salary and My Salary Slip to the In-Laws'.
6 'Introduction', *Domestic Violence in India: Exploring Strategies, Promoting Dialogue*, International Center for Research on Women, p. 3.
7 IIPS and ICF, 'Women's Empowerment', *National Family Health Survey (NFHS-4)*, p. 514.
8 Deepa Narayan et al., 'Chapter 5: Changing Gender Relations in the Household', *Voices of the Poor: Can Anyone Hear Us*, New York: Oxford University Press for the World Bank, 2000, p. 181.
9 'Introduction', *Domestic Violence in India*, p. 3.
10 Ibid., p. 59.
11 Ibid., p. 68.
12 Sumi Sukanya Dutta, 'About one-third shelter homes in India are not registered: WCD Ministry data', *New Indian Express*, 8 August 2018.
13 'Uttar Pradesh: After Deoria, 26 Women Found Missing from Two Shelter Homes in Pratapgarh during Inspection By District Magistrate', *Latestly*, 9 August 2018.

Chapter 9: Why Are Women Missing from Public Spaces?

1 'A third of India's girls fear assault or harassment in public places: WINGS 2018 report', Save the Children, 15 May 2018.
2 Ayona Datta, '"Khadar ki Ladkiyan"': A hip hop music video co-produced with young women in Delhi's urban peripheries', *Guftugu*, Issue 14, June 2019, p. 14.
3 'Report IAWRT Biennial Conference 15–18 September 2015, New Delhi, India', IAWRT, p. 40, available at <www.iawrt.org/sites/default/files/field/pdf/2016/02/biennial%20report%20-final-jan%2030.pdf>.
4 Ibid.
5 Nilanjana Bhowmick, 'Why Women Don't Loiter', *New Internationalist*, 20 October 2021.
6 Taslima Khan, 'Riddled with challenges, Smart City project is mostly "noise" for startups', 24 March 2017, *Economic Times*.
7 Bhowmick, 'Why Women Don't Loiter'.
8 Ibid.
9 Ibid.
10 Ibid.
11 Azman Usmani, 'Budget 2019: Will India's First Woman Finance Minister Renew Her Gender Budgeting Push', *Bloomberg Quint*, 4 July 2019.
12 Bhowmick, 'Why Women Don't Loiter'.

13   Anita Joshua, 'Clean India best tribute to Mahatma: PM', *The Hindu*, 26 September 2014.
14   'About SBM', Swachh Bharat Mission—Grameen, available at <https:// swachhbharatmission.gov.in/sbmcms/index.htm>.
15   'Public Toilets in Delhi: A Status Survey', ActionAid India, 2017.

Chapter 10: What's a Woman's Worth in a Capitalist–Patriarchal Society?

1   Cinzia Arruzza, Tithi Bhattacharya, and Nancy Fraser, *Feminism for the 99%: A Manifesto*, London: Verso Books, 2019, p. 20.
2   Nilanjana Bhowmick, '"I Cannot Be Intimidated. I Cannot Be Bought." The Women Leading India's Farmers' Protests', *TIME*, 4 March 2021.
3   'Global Gender Gap Report 2021', p. 10.
4   'Global Gender Gap Report 2020', World Economic Forum, December 2019, p. 11.
5   Ibid., p. 24.
6   Ibid., p. 31.
7   'Contribution of corporate sector towards women's economic empowerment in India', UNDP India, 26 September 2019.
8   Ibid.
9   Ibid.
10   Ibid.
11   Kathryn Moeller, *The Gender Effect: Capitalism, Feminism, and the Corporate Politics of Development*, Oakland: University of California Press, 2018, p. 37.
12   S. Rangwala, C. Jayawardhena, and G. Saxena, '"From caged birds to women with wings": A perspective on consumption practices of new middle-class Indian women', *European Journal of Marketing*, Vol. 54, No. 11, 2020, pp. 2803–24.
13   'India sees more women in leadership roles but boardroom diversity progressing at a snail's pace', Deloitte India, 8 February 2022 .
14   IIPS and ICF, 'Women's Empowerment', *NFHS-5*, p. 5.
15   Desai and Vanneman, 'IHDS-II, 2011–12'.
16   IIPS and ICF, 'Women's Empowerment', *National Family Health Survey (NFHS-4)*, p. 510.
17   Ibid., p. 511.
18   Ibid., p. 512.
19   Ibid.
20   Arruzza, Bhattacharya, and Fraser, *Feminism for the 99%*, p. 22.
21   Boike Rehbein, 'Capitalism and inequality', *Sociedade e Estado*, Vol. 35, 2020, p. 696.
22   Arruzza, Bhattacharya, and Fraser, *Feminism for the 99%*, p. 12.
23   Ibid.
24   'What do Marxists think…about housework?', *Morning Star*.
25   Alexandra Kollontai, 'Communism and the family', *Selected Writings of Alexandra Kollontai*, London: Alison and Busby, 1977.

26   Silvia Federici, *Wages Against Housework*, Bristol: Falling Wall Press, 1975.
27   Ibid.
28   Ibid.
29   PTI, 'Homemakers to get salaries according to new govt proposal', *India Today*, 9 September 2012.
30   Arruzza, Bhattacharya, and Fraser, *Feminism for the 99%*, p. 26.
31   'Global Gender Gap Report 2021', World Economic Forum, March 2021, p. 27.

Chapter 11: Why Are Women Not Working?

1   'Do not seek sympathy, it will stereotype you: Delhi HC judge to women lawyers', *Hindustan Times*, 15 December 2021.
2   'Progress of the World's Women 2019–2020: Families in a Changing World', UN Women, 2019, p. 120.
3   Ibid.
4   Ibid.
5   *Human Development Report 2015: Work for Human Development*, UNDP, 2015, p. 13.
6   'Global Gender Gap Report 2021', World Economic Forum, March 2021.
7   PIB Delhi, 'Global Gender Gap Report', Ministry of Women and Child Development, 17 December 2021.
8   PIB Delhi, '3703 Kasturba Gandhi Balika Vidyalayas (KGBVs) sanctioned & 3697 are operational in the country', Ministry of Human Resource Development, 9 August 2018.
9   Jonathan Evans, Neha Sahgal, Ariana Monique Salazar, et al., 'How Indians View Gender Roles in Families and Society', Pew Research Center, 2 March 2022.
10   Sheryl Sandberg, 'Introduction: Internalizing the Revolution', *Lean In: Women, Work, and the Will to Lead*, United Kingdom: Ebury Publishing, 2013, p. 8.
11   Karine Schomer, 'Work-Life Balance for Women in India and the United States', The India Practice: A Division of CMCT, 2011.
12   'Living Conditions in Europe: Childcare Arrangements', Eurostat: statistics explained, March 2021.

Chapter 12: The Housewife Conundrum

1   Indra Nooyi, '"Leave the crown in the garage": What I've learned from a decade of being PepsiCo's CEO', LinkedIn Pulse, 2017.
2   Howard Schultz, 'Builders & Titans: Indra Nooyi,' *TIME*, 12 May 2008.
3   'Top 10 most powerful women of 2015', *India Today*, 12 September 2015.
4   'Indra Nooyi- Pepsico.', *Profit*, No. 136, September 2020.

Chapter 13: Documenting the Housewife Experience

1   'My Village Life Tina', YouTube, available at <www.youtube.com/c/MyVillageLifeTina12>, accessed April 2022.
2   'Simply Living Wise Thinking', YouTube, available at <www.youtube.com/c/SimpleLivingWiseThinking>, accessed April 2022.
3   'Indian Vlogger Soumali', YouTube, available at <www.youtube.com/c/

IndianVloggerSoumali>, accessed April 2022.

4   'Hichk!', YouTube, available at <www.youtube.com/channel/UCmhCSh-2dkXbWhtgFtfyNtg>, accessed April 2022.

5   'Soumali Adhikary', YouTube, available at <www.youtube.com/c/SoumaliAdhikary>, accessed April 2022.

6   'indian youtuber ruchi', YouTube, available at <www.youtube.com/channel/UCKVxZG4vak-LSNtufFiebKw>, accessed April 2022.

7   'Ayan Mom and Beauty', YouTube, available at <www.youtube.com/channel/UCCZKS_WY6ZrGSxvwsKbhIYw>, accessed April 2022.

8   'Ayan Mom and Beauty: Description', YouTube, available at <www.youtube.com/channel/UCCZKS_WY6ZrGSxvwsKbhIYw/about>, accessed April 2022.

9   'Radhika Real Vlogs', YouTube, available at <www.youtube.com/channel/UCWzJV0Z8NsRPqFXinD45SUw>, accessed April 2022.

10   'Happy with MAMON', YouTube, available at <www.youtube.com/channel/UC-ZBR-4crHm5arYddoJkTQg>, accessed April 2022.

11   'Pakhi family vlogs', YouTube, available at <www.youtube.com/channel/UCxt8VEFPfKBACUvBi987juQ>, accessed April 2022.

Chapter 15: In the Name of Women

1   IANS, 'Improving sex ratio at birth visible in 104 districts: Government', 4 January 2019, *The Quint*.

2   '56% of "Beti Bachao, Beti Padhao" Funds Spent on Advertisements: Minister', *Outlook*.

3   'Setting the National Agenda of Women-led Development', Narendra Modi, 27 March 2019.

4   'Over 55% Jan Dhan Account Holders Are Women: Finance Ministry', 6 December 2021, *Business Standard*.

5   'Sukanya Samriddhi Yojana Interest Rate', policybazaar.com.

6   PIB Delhi, 'Pradhan Mantri Jan-Dhan Yojana (PMJDY) - National Mission for Financial Inclusion, completes seven years of successful implementation', Ministry of Finance, 28 August 2021.

7   IANS, '20% Jan Dhan accounts lying dormant: Minister', *Business Standard*, 22 March 2018.

8   PIB Delhi, 'Pradhan Mantri Jan-Dhan Yojana (PMJDY)', 28 August 2021.

9   ANI, 'At UNSC, India highlights govt initiatives like Mudra to empower women', *Business Standard*, 9 March 2022.

10   Aanchal Magazine, 'Just 1 in 5 Mudra beneficiaries started new business, half of extra jobs were self-employment: Govt survey', *Indian Express*, 4 September 2019.

11   PIB Delhi, 'More than 81% account holders are Women under Stand Up India Scheme', Ministry of Finance, 3 March 2020.

12   'Industry and Infrastructure', *Economic Survey 2019–20: Volume 2*, January 2020, p. 225.

13   'The Mastercard Index of Women Entrepreneurs: How targeted support for women-led business can unlock sustainable economic growth', Mastercard, March 2022, p. 14.

14 'Chapter VI: Women Entrepreneurs', *All India Report of Sixth Economic Census*, Ministry of Statistics & Programme Implementation, 2016, pp. 105–18.
15 'Key Highlights', *Early Stage Investment Insights Report-2019*, Innoven Capital, December 2019, p. 2.
16 'Powering the Economy with Her: Women Entrepreneurship in India', Bain & Company and Google, 2019, p. 1.
17 Ibid., p. 5.
18 Ibid., p. 1.
19 Ibid.
20 Ibid.
21 Ibid., p. 5.

Chapter 16: The First Husbands

1   Vimlesh Kumari, 'Issue Order Against "Pradhan Pati" System and Give Women Pradhans Their Due', Change.org, 2019.
2   Ibid.
3   Saubhdra Chatterji, 'Political will, patriarchy: Why the women's reservation bill has still not been passed', *Hindustan Times*, 8 March 2017.
4   'Women & Politics: Changing Trends and Emerging Patterns, Executive Summary', Lokniti-Centre for the Study of Developing Societies (CSDS) and German foundation Konrad Adenauer Stiftung (KAS), 2019.
5   Ibid.
6   Ibid.
7   Ibid.
8   Ibid.
9   'Lalu firm on opposing Women's Reservation Bill', *Indian Express*, 7 March 2010.
10 'Supreme Court Says Khap Panchayats Illegal, No Assembly Can Interfere in a Marriage Between Two Consenting Adults', *Outlook*, 27 March 2018.
11 Rohit Bhattacharya, '10 Regressive Khap Panchayat Rulings That Dragged India Back to the Stone Ages', *ScoopWhoop*, 25 April 2018.
12 IIPS and ICF, 'Women's Empowerment', *National Family Health Survey (NFHS-4)*, p. 516.
13 P. Pavan, 'Hyderabad: Veterinary doctor's rape and murder has left the entire nation shocked', *Mumbai Mirror*, 29 November 2019.
14 'Farhan Akhtar announced as UN Women's Goodwill Ambassador for South Asia', UN Women, 13 November 2014.
15 Farhan Akhtar, 'What Is a Real Man—A "Mard"?', *Huffington Post UK*, 30 November 2015.
16 'Farhan Akhtar announced as UN Women's Goodwill Ambassador for South Asia', UN Women.

Chapter 17: Is This All There Is?

1   Women @ work, Deloitte.
2   Koirala and Chuemchit, 'Depression and Domestic Violence Experiences Among

Asian Women: A Systematic Review', *International Journal of Women's Health*.

3   Didier L. Schrijvers, Jos Bollen, Bernard G. C. Sabbe, 'The gender paradox in suicidal behavior and its impact on the suicidal process', *Journal of Affective Disorders*, Vol. 138, Issues 1–2, April 2012, pp. 19–26.

4   Lakshmi Vijayakumar, 'Suicide in Women', *Indian Journal of Psychiatry*, Vol. 57, Suppl. 2, pp. S233–S238.

5   Sagar et al., 'The burden of mental disorders across the states of India', 2019.

6   Indira Sharma, Balram Pandit, Abhishek Pathak, et al., 'Hinduism, marriage and mental illness', *Indian Journal of Psychiatry*, Vol. 55, Suppl. 2, 2013, pp. S243–9.

7   Ibid.

8   Ibid.

9   Ibid.

10   K. Rajesh, A. A. Rao, D. Krishna, et al., 'Patients With Suicidal Patterns in the Emergency Room: A Clinical and Social Reflection', *Cureus*, Vol. 13, No. 10, 2021.

11   Meera Kay, 'Suicide is leading cause of death in young Indian women, finds international study', *BMJ*, 2013.

12   'Gender differentials and state variations in suicide deaths in India: the Global Burden of Disease Study 1990–2016', *Lancet Public Health*, Vol. 3, September 2018, pp. e478–89.

13   Peter Mayer (with Clare Bradley, Della Steen, and Tahereh Ziaian), *Suicide and Society in India*, London, New York: Routledge, 2011.

14   Kabir Garg, C. Naveen Kumar, and Prabha S., Chandra, 'Number of psychiatrists in India: Baby steps forward, but a long way to go', *Indian Journal of Psychiatry*, Vol. 61, Issue 1, 2019, pp. 104–105.

15   Utkarsha A Singh, 'Disentangling India's mental health distress: Does India have the resources to control the impending mental health crisis?', *Research Matters*, 30 October 2020.

16   Rajesh, Rao, Krishna, et al., 'Patients With Suicidal Patterns in the Emergency Room: A Clinical and Social Reflection'.

Chapter 18: Middle Class Morality and the Goddess Syndrome

1   'Gauhati High Court grants divorce to man after woman refuses to wear "sindoor", "shaka"', *The Economic Times*, 30 June 2020.

2   'Unbecoming of Indian woman to fall asleep after being ravished: Karnataka HC gives bail to rape accused', *India Today*, 25 June 2020.

3   Kalyanaraman Srinivasa, 'Noble virtues of a woman', *The Speaking Tree*.

4   'Indian women are "okay" with infidelity!', *Free Press Journal*, 26 February 2020.

5   'Gleeden—The extramarital dating app officially launches the first ever Infidelity survey in India!', *Retropop Lifestyle*.

6   'Gleeden—The Most Beloved Dating App for Women Reaches 1 Million Users in India', *The News Strike*, 11 May 2020.

7   Vicki Larson, 'A 'beta' marriage is a better marriage', *Whyy*, 9 July 2017.

8   Madhumita Chakraborty, 'Gen Z Ready To Take On World On Its Own Terms', *Business World*, 19 August 2019.

9   'In a truly liberating move, 8 out of 10 women in India come out in support of

live-in relationships!—Inshorts "Pulse of the Nation" poll', *Inshorts Blog*, 17 May 2018.

10 'SC brings live in relationships under Domestic Violence Act', *Firstpost*, 1 December 2013.

11 Aishwarya Ramesh, 'MTV Insights Studio presents new report—"Mera Bharat Amazeballs"', *afaqs!*, 28 Jan 2020.

Chapter 19: The Economics of Equality

1   Danish Siddiqui and Shilpa Jamkhandikar, 'Drought-hit Maharashtra village looks to "water wives" to quench thirst', *Reuters*, 4 June 2015.

2   Amrita Kohli, 'India's "Water Wives": A Hard Truth Told in a Short Film', NDTV, 30 November 2015, available at <www.youtu.be/bVNdsdQEfLI>.

3   Ibid.

4   'How many wives does it take to fetch water?', WaterAid India, 8 November 2015.

5   Research Foundation for Science: Technology and Ecology, *Report on Women and Water*, New Delhi: National Commission for Women, January 2005, p. 2.

6   'UNICEF: Collecting water is often a colossal waste of time for women and girls', UNICEF, 29 August 2016.

7   Ibid.

8   Ibid.

9   Ibid.

10 'The sweet taste of water and success', WaterAid India, July 2017.

11 Dewan, 'Invisible Work, Invisible Workers', 2017.

12 IndiaSpend Team, 'More Indian Women Could Opt For Paid Work, If They Found Reliable Caregivers', *IndiaSpend*, 7 August 2017.

13 'Contribution of corporate sector towards women's economic empowerment in India', UNDP India.

14 Maitreyi Bordia Das, Soumya Kapoor-Mehta, Emcet Oktay Taş, et al., 'Scaling the Heights: Social Inclusion and Sustainable Development in Himachal Pradesh', The World Bank, 2015, p. xvi.

15 Ibid., p. 41.

16 Ibid.

17 Lori Beaman, Esther Duflo, Rohini Pande, et al., 'Female leadership raises aspirations and educational attainment for girls: A policy experiment in India', *Science*, Vol. 335, No. 6068, 2012, pp. 582–86.

18 Anand Swamy, Stephen Knack, Young Lee, et al., 'Gender and corruption', *Journal of Development Economics*, Vol. 64, No. 1, 2001, pp. 25–55.

19 Mithila Biniwale, Stephan Klasen, Jan Priebe, et al., 'Can the female sarpanch deliver? Evidence from Maharashtra', *Ideas for India*, 23 October 2016.

20 Thushyanthan Baskaran, Sonia Bhalotra, Brian Min, et al., 'Women legislators and economic performance: S-35326-INC-1', International Growth Centre, May 2018.

21 'Are you ready for change?: Gender Equality Attitudes Study 2019', UN Women, 2020.

22 'New study from the Unstereotype Alliance finds that increased equality for women is essential to a country's success', UN Women, 17 June 2020.

23 Avivah Wittenberg-Cox, 'What Do Countries With The Best Coronavirus Responses Have In Common? Women Leaders', *Forbes*, 13 April 2020.

24 'Take Five: "Women leaders around the world have demonstrated successful management of the pandemic"', UN Women, 16 June 2020.

25 Ibid.

26 Karina Fuerte, 'The "Karoshi" phenomenon is now a worldwide problem', Institute for the Future of Education, 6 July 2021.

27 'Long working hours can increase deaths from heart disease and stroke, say ILO and WHO', International Labour Organization, 17 May 2021.

28 Fuerte, 'The "Karoshi" phenomenon is now a worldwide problem'.

29 Danielle Demetriou, 'How the Japanese are putting an end to extreme work weeks', *BBC*, 18 January 2020.

30 'Long working hours increasing deaths from heart disease and stroke: WHO, ILO', World Health Organization, 17 May 2021.

31 Ibid.

Chapter 20: Mobilizing Middle-class Women

1   Nilanjana Bhowmick, 'India's New Laws Hurt Women Most of All', *Foreign Policy*, 4 February 2020.

2   Supriti David, '"The world moves on, but we're stuck in the same evening": Remembering the Jamia violence of 2019', *Newslaundry*, 17 December 2021.

3   'India National Population Register: Database agreed amid protests', *BBC*, 24 December 2019.

4   Vyjayanti T. Desai, Anna Diofasi, and Jing Lu, 'The global identification challenge: Who are the 1 billion people without proof of identity?', *Voices*, 25 April 2018.

5   N. K. Singh, 'Bhopal gas victims adopt role of agitationists as MP govt fails to give jobs as promised', *India Today*, 15 July 1987.

6   Nilanjana Bhowmick, '"Women Don't Give Up." Why Female Protesters Are at the Forefront of India's Resistance', *TIME*, 15 January 2020.

7   Ibid.

8   Ibid.

9   'History', Gulabi Gang, available at <gulabigang.in/history.php>.

10 'Vision', Gulabi Gang, available at <gulabigang.in/vision.php>.

11 'Mission, Gulabi Gang, available at <gulabigang.in/mission.php>.

12 Prapti Sarkar, 'These Three Jamia Millia Girls Have Become the Face of CAA Protests', *shethepeople*, 5 January 2020.

Epilogue: Scripting a New Narrative

1   Office of the Registrar General and Census Commissioner, 'Chapter 2—Population Composition', *Census India 2011*, p. 22.

2   Office of the Registrar General and Census Commissioner, 'Age Structure And Marital Status', available at <censusindia.gov.in/census_and_you/age_structure_and_marital_status.aspx>.

3   Ibid.
4   Office of the Registrar General and Census Commissioner, 'Chapter 2—Population Composition', p. 22.
5   The National Forum for Single Women's Rights and the Centre for Equity Studies, 'Report: Overcoming Exclusion of Single Women in the Society', April 2015.
6   'National Policy for Women 2016: Articulating a Vision for Empowerment of Women—Draft', Ministry of Women and Child Development, May 2016, p. 17.
7   'Speech by Michelle Bachelet: Reclaiming Public Spaces for the Empowerment of Women and Girls', UN Women, 7 March 2013.
8   Rhitu Chatterjee, '#WhyLoiter reclaims public—and inner—space for Indian women', *The World*, 17 September 2015.
9   'About: Herstory', Blank Noise, available at <www.blanknoise.org/about/herstory>.

INDEX

www.ingramcontent.com/pod-product-compliance
Lightning Source LLC
Chambersburg PA
CBHW030907070526
44654CB00030B/395/J